Advance p

THE DECOLONI.
OF INDIGENOUS LITERATURES

A major contribution to research. The focus on craft, text, voice, and language is refreshing, important, and timely. Reading this book reminds me what the best of literary and cultural criticism can do: surprise and delight a reader with insightful commentary and convincing arguments whose implications are far-reaching and, potentially, paradigm-shifting.—SOPHIE McCALL, *First Person Plural: Aboriginal Storytelling and the Ethics of Collaborative Authorship*

Neuhaus is an astute theorist, a committed teacher, and a generous critic, and her provocative newest book offers much for readers and students of Indigenous literatures to ponder, debate, and embrace. You will find no simplistic boosterism or essentialized generalizations here: this is careful, challenging work that takes seriously the embraided strands of language, poetics, politics, and aesthetics in Indigenous writing. Of her many strengths as a scholar, Neuhaus is a brilliant close reader, with perceptive insight into the interpretive depths of these writers and their word-worlds. I always learn so much from her work.—DANIEL HEATH JUSTICE (CHEROKEE), CANADA RESEARCH CHAIR IN INDIGENOUS LITERATURE AND EXPRESSIVE CULTURE

Holophrasticism may be the way Indigenous mentality, intellect, and creativity survived residential and Indian boarding schools and lived to deal today with colonialism. Many, many thanks for *The Decolonizing Poetics of Indigenous Literatures*.—SIMON J. ORTIZ (ACOMA PUEBLO), REGENTS PROFESSOR OF AMERICAN INDIAN STUDIES AND ENGLISH, ARIZONA STATE UNIVERSITY AND AWARD-WINNING AUTHOR OF *Woven Stone; Out There Somewhere; From Sand Creek;* and *Beyond the Reach of Time and Change*

THE
DECOLONIZING
POETICS
OF INDIGENOUS
LITERATURES

MAREIKE NEUHAUS

University of Regina Press

Printed and bound in Canada at Marquis.
Cover and text design: Duncan Campbell, University of Regina Press
Copy editor: Alison Jacques
Index: Patricia Furdek
Cover Photo: "Open book with a single stone on it" by Elaine Kittleson / Snapwire.

Library and Archives Canada Cataloguing in Publication

Neuhaus, Mareike, 1978-, author
    The decolonizing poetics of indigenous literatures / Mareike Neuhaus.

Includes bibliographical references and index.
Issued in print and electronic formats.
ISBN 978-0-88977-390-5 (paperback).—ISBN 978-0-88977-392-9 (html).
— ISBN 978-0-88977-391-2 (pdf)

1. Canadian literature—Native authors—History and criticism.
2. Canadian literature—History and criticism. 3. Native peoples—Canada—
Languages—Compound words. I. Title.

PS8089.5.I6N47 2015   C810.9'897   C2015-904934-2   C2015-904935-0

10   9   8   7   6   5   4   3   2   1

University of Regina Press, University of Regina
Regina, Saskatchewan, Canada, S4S 0A2
TEL: (306) 585-4758 FAX: (306) 585-4699
U OF R PRESS   WEB: www.uofrpress.ca

We acknowledge the financial support of the Government of Canada. / Nous reconnaissons l'appui financier du gouvernement du Canada. We acknowledge the support of the Canada Council for the Arts for our publishing program. This publication was made possible through Creative Saskatchewan's Creative Industries Production Grant Program. This book has been published with the help of a grant from the Federation for the Humanities and Social Sciences, through the Awards to Scholarly Publications Program, using funds provided by the Social Sciences and Humanities Research Council of Canada.

for TER

TABLE OF CONTENTS

ILLUSTRATIONS

FIGURES

TABLES

ACKNOWLEDGEMENTS

This book was written during one long Saskatchewan winter, in a dome house in Shaunavon, Saskatchewan. My sincere thanks go to Ted Dyck and Penny Snelgrove, who gave my partner and me, and our cats, a home when we most needed one. This book would never have seen the light of day without your generosity and support.

In many ways, *The Decolonizing Poetics of Indigenous Literatures* is the product of numerous conversations I have had with fellow researchers over the past ten years, particularly during my time as Andrew W. Mellon postdoctoral fellow and Government of Canada postdoctoral fellow at the University of Toronto. I owe a big thank you to all of those who have listened patiently to my ramblings: Martin Kuester, Ted Dyck, Dorothy Thunder, Daniel Heath Justice, Susan Gingell, Nelson Gray, and Rüdiger Zimmermann; the 2008–2009 fellows at the Jackman Humanities Institute at the University of Toronto, particularly Neil ten Kortenaar, Shami Ghosh, Alma Mikulinsky, Maya Chacaby, and Jonathan Burgess; as well as the participants in the 2010 annual conference of the Canadian Society for the Study of Rhetoric, especially Bruce Dadey.

I am grateful to Ted Dyck for keeping me honest and to Bill Caton for being such a wonderful reader.

Dziękuję bardzo, Tereniu, for insisting I write this book. This one is for you alone.

Shaunavon, March 2015

INDIGENOUS POETICS AND HOLOPHRASTIC READING

Contemporary Indigenous literatures continue literary traditions whose origins are in oral performances, composed in ancestral languages. This may seem like a straightforward observation. However, once one considers that these ancestral languages are actually very different from the English, French, Spanish, and Portuguese in which many Indigenous storytellers and writers now work, things start to look a bit more complicated. Many languages indigenous to North America have a tendency to use holophrases. This may be an intimidating word, but holophrases are actually quite beautiful creatures; as their etymology suggests—*holos* derives from the Greek word for "whole"— holophrases are holistic expressions. More specially, a holophrase is a one-word sentence or clause, such as the Plains Cree word *ki-nohte-h-âcimo-stâ-tinâwâw*, which translates as "I want to tell you folks a story." A single word stands for a whole sentence; that is, it is a holophrase. If there is one thing that Indo-European languages agree on, despite all their differences, it is their dislike of such one-word sentences. Now why, you may wonder, would this stark difference between English and Indigenous languages matter to the study of Indigenous literatures? Anyone who has ever learned a language other than their mother tongue will know that grammar—the very structures of language—affects the ways in which speakers of that language produce discourse, how they build stories or even just everyday talk. Anyone who speaks two languages will also know that translation is fraught with loss—that some things just don't translate well. And yet, it would be presumptuous to assume that, moving from ancestral languages to English, Spanish, French, or Portuguese, Indigenous people have blindly adopted the languages of their colonizers. Indeed, residues of ancestral languages can be found in Indigenous uses of these languages, and these residues have profound consequences for Indigenous poetics. For if the English used by Indigenous poets, storytellers, biographers, novelists, and essayists is substantially influenced by ancestral language structures, then reading Indigenous literatures in English amounts to nothing less than an exercise in reading the English language by thinking outside that very language.

This book's main subject is Indigenous poetics. Poetics can mean different things in different contexts. For the purposes of this book, I use the term "Indigenous poetics" simply to mean the art of reading Indigenous discourse, or rather, I should say, the *arts* of reading Indigenous discourse; because just as there are as many Indigenous literatures as there are Indigenous nations, there are also as many Indigenous poetics as there are Indigenous literatures. I think of Indigenous poetics primarily as a way of making sense of Indigenous expressions, as a set of tools that readers may use when they read Indigenous texts—as a map, if you will, that can help guide their readings. Much important work has been done in the past two decades to emphasize the "Indigenous" in Indigenous literatures, by reading these literatures as extensions of political, historical, social, intellectual, and other realities. Indigenous literatures grow out of different realities than do Anglo-American literatures, and these other realities should be reflected in our readings of Indigenous texts. What about Indigenous *texts* as such, however? The *words* on the *page*? The *ways* in which stories are *built*? The *genres*? The *structures*? The *figures*? It is easy to assume that all those features that turn literature into literature are just the same whether used in Euro-Western or Indigenous writing. Well, are they really? Contemporary Indigenous literatures continue traditions that are rhetorically very different from Euro-Western traditions, yet most readers of Indigenous literatures are trained in reading Euro-Western literatures, so they aren't likely to be able to tell the difference. What is needed, then, is a reading strategy that allows us to ground our readings of Indigenous texts in Indigenous discourse traditions but without compromising the important political, historical, social, intellectual, and other contexts from which these texts emerge. In fact, it is the refocusing on some of the more technical features of Indigenous literatures that emphasizes the need for readers to consider these very contexts. This book aims to develop an Indigenous poetics that enables readers to approach Indigenous literatures for what they truly are: *Indigenous* and *literatures*.

HOLOPHRASTIC READING AS INDIGENOUS POETICS

How do you read Indigenous literatures as both Indigenous and literatures? The method I propose here is one that I call "holophrastic reading," a reading strategy that I first presented in *"That's Raven Talk": Holophrastic Readings of Contemporary Indigenous Literatures*.[1] As the name suggests, holophrastic reading has its basis in the single most dominant language structure of Indigenous languages in North America: the holophrase. While working on *"That's Raven Talk"* I thought of holophrastic reading primarily as a way of reading textualized orality from within Indigenous language and discourse traditions. However, as so often occurs in life, distance allows one to look at the same thing through entirely different eyes. Thus, over the years, what I had originally conceived as a very specific and narrow reading strategy for oral strategies in Indigenous writing morphed into a more general methodology that could be applied in very different interpretative scenarios.

This being said, I still think of holophrastic reading as an effective and ethical way of studying textualized orality in Indigenous writing. Holophrastic reading is invested in studying, from the perspective of Indigenous languages, the particular uses of language in Indigenous discourse, of which oral strategies are but one aspect. Oral strategies can be found in both speech and writing because they result from conceptual orality, a kind of orality that is associated not with the medium of a text (oral/written/visual) but with its use of a language of immediacy.[2] Literature and storytelling are prime examples of conceptual orality. Both strive for a high degree of contextualization and immediacy between storyteller/author and listener/reader, although the means by which this context and immediacy are achieved vary depending on the medium. Writing a novel, short story, play, poem, or essay usually involves more planning and results in a denser language than performing a story in front of an audience. And yet, literary critics have long pointed out that literature belongs to a

---

1   Mareike Neuhaus, *"That's Raven Talk": Holophrastic Readings of Contemporary Indigenous Literatures* (Regina: Canadian Plains Research Center Press, 2011).

2   The notion of conteptual orality was introduced by Peter Koch and Wulf Oesterreicher in "Sprache der Nahe—Sprache der Distanz: Mündlichkeit und Schriftlichkeit im Spannungsfeld von Sprachtheorie und Sprachgeschichte," *Romanistisches Jahrbuch* 36 (1985): 15–43.

body of writing deeply invested in an "oral sensibility."[3] Strategies such as author involvement, audience participation, and contextualization are not only oral strategies, then; they are also central components of literature. To put it differently, the discourse features I discuss as oral strategies in *"That's Raven Talk"* are, in fact, something more: They are figures of speech, intertextual references, formulae, instances of flashback and foreshadowing, variations in syntax and morphology, and so on—they are, in short, elements of language that readers invest with meaning. At its very core, holophrastic reading therefore contributes to Indigenous poetics because it pays attention to the specific tools and techniques of Indigenous literatures: "[their] kinds and forms, [their] particular resources of device and structure, the principles that govern [them], the functions that distinguish them from other [literatures], the conditions under which [they] can exist, and [their] effects on readers."[4] As such, holophrastic reading has a fairly broad spectrum of use in Indigenous literary studies. It is these broader contributions to Indigenous poetics that are the subject of this book, which is designed to serve as a comprehensive introduction to holophrastic reading and its application in reading Indigenous literary texts.

THE RELEVANCE OF ANCESTRAL LANGUAGES

Indigenous peoples have repeatedly stressed the importance of ancestral languages for their continuance as peoples (rather than cultures). Alongside land/territory, sacred history, and the ceremonial cycle, language is a key element whose interdependence with the others defines Indigenous notions of peoplehood.[5] If any one of these elements is destroyed or otherwise diminished, peoplehood is at stake. The interarticulation of language, history, ceremony, and land is complex but fragile; maintaining the balance

---

3   John Willinsky, "The Paradox of Text in the Culture of Literacy," in *After Literacy: Essays* (New York: Peter Lang, 2001), 61. See also Boris M. Éjchenbaum, "The Illusion of *Skaz*," *Russian Literature Triquarterly* 12 (1975): 233–36; Robert Kellogg, "Oral Narrative, Written Books," *Genre* 10 (1977): 655–65; Paul Goetsch, "Fingierte Mündlichkeit in der Erzählkunst entwickelter Schriftkulturen," *Poetica* 17.3–4 (1985): 202–18.

4   T. V. F. Brogan, "Poetics," in *The New Princeton Encyclopedia of Poetry and Poetics*, ed. Alex Preminger and T. V. F. Brogan (Princeton: Princeton University Press, 1993), 930b.

5   Tom Holm (Cherokee), Ben Chavis (Lumbee), and J. Diane Pearson propose the model of peoplehood as constituting four interrelated social concepts: land/territory, sacred history, language, and ceremonial cycle ("Peoplehood: A Model for the Extension of Sovereignty in American Indian Studies," *Wicazo Sa Review* 18.1 [2003]: 7–24).

requires constant care and nurturing. The colonization of North America entailed not only the theft of land and resources from Indigenous peoples, but also, as Andrea Bear Nicholas (Maliseet) observes, the destruction of their relations to the land. Since these relations were expressed in the oral traditions, Indigenous languages, too, had to be eradicated, through residential and boarding schools, through forced adoptions of Native children into non-Native families, and through further government policies designed to assimilate Indigenous people into mainstream society. The destruction and loss of land, Bear Nicholas argues, therefore correlates directly with the destruction of Indigenous languages.[6]

Indigenous mother tongues in North America have suffered immensely from colonialism; many of these languages have become extinct over the past five hundred years, while many others are in danger of becoming extinct in the very near future.[7] Thus, English, French, Spanish, and Portuguese have become the first languages of most Indigenous people living in North America today. The majority of contemporary North American Indigenous literatures are written in English—one of the "enemy's languages" that has to be *reinvented* to serve the purposes of healing and empowerment, as Gloria Bird (Spokane) and Joy Harjo (Muskogee Creek) famously argued in their 1997 anthology of Indigenous women's writing, *Reinventing the Enemy's Language*.[8] Almost twenty years prior to Bird and Harjo, Simon Ortiz (Acoma Pueblo) had posited in his seminal essay "Towards a National Indian Literature" that a people can survive and thrive using any given language—in other words, that English was an Indigenous language.[9] As a fluent speaker of Keres, Ortiz did not make this argument to undermine the significance of ancestral languages, but rather to claim English as a means for Indigenous people to heal from the wounds inflicted on them by hundreds of years of colonialism. Given the overwhelming presence of English in North America and the fact that it is

6   Andrea Bear Nicholas, "The Assault on Aboriginal Oral Traditions: Past and Present," in *Aboriginal Oral Traditions: Theory, Practice, Ethics*, ed. Renée Hulan and Renate Eigenbrod (Halifax: Fernwood, 2008), 19.

7   According to Frederick H. White, of the about two hundred Indigenous languages spoken in North America today, only 10 per cent will likely survive past the year 2020 ("Language Reflection and Lamentation in Native American Literature," *Studies in American Indian Literatures* 18.1 [2006]: 95).

8   Gloria Bird and Joy Harjo, "Introduction," in *Reinventing the Enemy's Language: Contemporary Native Women's Writings of North America*, ed. Gloria Bird and Joy Harjo (New York: W.W. Norton, 1997), 23–25.

9   Simon J. Ortiz, "Towards a National Indian Literature: Cultural Authenticity in Nationalism," *MELUS* 8.2 (1981): 10.

often the only language spoken by Indigenous people, the importance of the notion of English as suitable for Indigenous purposes cannot be overemphasized. Indeed, for Jace Weaver (Cherokee), Craig S. Womack (Muskogee Creek), and Robert Warrior (Osage), celebrating "the profound Indianness of English" is one of the prerequisites for ensuring the survival and continuance of Indigenous peoples in North America.[10]

But what exactly does the "Indianness of English" mean? How could English possibly be an Indigenous language? Obviously, Cree is not English and neither is Anishnaabemowin. At the same time, however, despite its overwhelming presence in today's globalized world, English is neither *lingua franca* nor *lingua nullius*, belonging to everyone and no one; it is a highly varied language whose national and regional nuances carry a large bundle of meaning.[11] Rather than becoming willing subjects of (neo)colonial linguistic practices, Indigenous peoples have claimed English in order to exercise rhetorical sovereignty, which Scott Richard Lyons (Anishnaabe/Mdewakanton Dakota) defines as "the inherent right and ability of *peoples* to determine their own communicative needs and desires in [their] pursuit [of sovereignty], to decide for themselves the goals, modes, styles, and languages of public discourse."[12] Rhetorical sovereignty, Lyons argues, "requires above all the presence of an Indian voice," a voice that ideally uses an ancestral language.[13] Wherever ancestral linguistic traditions have been destroyed or interrupted, Indigenous voices are often expressed in English; thus, English becomes a means of pursuing Indigenous purposes by mere habit of use. Equally, if not more important, in their use of this language, Indigenous people have reinvented English by indigenizing it. Most Indigenous languages are grammatically incompatible with the English language; yet, some discourse features and practices that have their origins in Indigenous languages are also present in Indigenous

---

10 Jace Weaver, Craig S. Womack, and Robert Warrior, *American Indian Literary Nationalism* (Albuquerque: University of New Mexico Press, 2006), xviii.

11 For a critique of the notion of English as a global language see Martin Kayman, who argues that "successive models of language underwriting the teaching of English have displaced and thereby masked the issue of culture that . . . necessarily persists under globalization" ("The State of English as a Global Language: Communicating Culture," *Textual Practice* 18.1 [2004]: 2).

12 Scott Richard Lyons, "Rhetorical Sovereignty: What Do American Indians Want from Writing?" *College Composition and Communication* 51.3 (2000): 449–50; emphasis in original.

13 Ibid., 462.

uses of English.[14] Reading English-language discourse from the point of view of Indigenous languages is a very valuable project, then, because it proves untenable a notion that is still quite pervasive in mainstream society, namely, that writing in the colonizer's language, using the colonizer's genres, implies hybridity by definition and thus a "giving in" to Euro-Western hegemony.[15] Once we shift how we read Indigenous literatures in English—namely by thinking outside the very language in which they are composed—we are able to realize how much the colonizer's language has become an essential factor in the project of *decolonization*, which permeates so much of contemporary Indigenous discourses.

PLACING READING AND TEXTS AT CENTRE STAGE

Over the past twenty years, the field of Indigenous literary studies has become increasingly polarized over the question of what constitutes an adequate approach to Indigenous literatures. On the one hand, there are critics who favour cosmopolitan approaches focused on hybridity and pan-Indigenous readings; on the other hand, there are critics who argue for nation-specific approaches that ground Indigenous literatures in their respective national histories, politics, and intellectual traditions. As some critics have observed, however, this cosmopolitan-nationalist binary is itself flawed and problematic. For one, the dichotomy between these two strands of criticism is too simplistic to adequately describe the field of Indigenous literary studies, because it covers up the nuances involved in individual approaches. Christopher Taylor, for example, points to the work of nationalist critic Robert Warrior as "provid[ing] a more complicated model than either [Arnold] Krupat's cosmopolitanism or [Craig] Womack's nationalism."[16] Similarly, while it is true that Indigenous literary nationalism emphasizes Indigenous worldviews, perspectives, and traditions through attention to nationhood, this focus "actually necessitates engagement with broader influences, as one cannot know the intimate without understanding the ways in which that intimacy has been shaped by exterior social and environmental forces," as Daniel Heath

---

14 For discussions of Indigenous English codes, see also William L. Leap, *American Indian English* (Salt Lake City: University of Utah Press, 1993) and Guillermo Bartelt, *Socio- and Stylolinguistic Perspectives on American Indian English Texts* (Lewiston, NY: Edwin Mellen, 2001).

15 Weaver, Womack, and Warrior, *American Indian Literary Nationalism*, xviii.

16 Christopher Taylor, "North America as Contact Zone: Native American Literary Nationalism and the Cross-Cultural Dilemma," *Studies in American Indian Literatures* 22.3 (2010): 29–30.

Justice (Cherokee) notes. "A literary nationalist is thus very well placed to study cosmopolitan concerns."[17] In fact, there exists more dialogue between cosmopolitan and nationalist strands of criticism than suggested by the binary that supposedly defines Indigenous literary studies today, one recent example being "Cosmopolitanism and Nationalism in Native American Literature," a 2011 panel discussion at Emory University that featured a conversation between both nationalist critics—Craig Womack and Lisa Brooks (Abenaki)—and cosmopolitan critics—Arnold Krupat and Elvira Pulitano.

The controversy over ethically sound approaches to Indigenous literatures has also done much good to the field of Indigenous studies, however, because it has brought more focused attention to Indigenous intellectual traditions and their value both to Indigenous peoples and, by implication, to Indigenous (literary) studies. What this book offers to this ongoing dialogue is the argument that Indigenous literatures can be read as grounded in Indigenous linguistic and discursive traditions regardless of the particular perspective from which readers may decide to approach the texts—a circumstance that should resonate particularly well for Indigenous works that do not fit into nationalist paradigms, such as the writing of pan-Native, multinational, and urban authors. If rhetorical sovereignty contributes to the decolonization of Indigenous peoples, so do Indigenous poetics that are grounded in Indigenous literary, critical, and intellectual traditions. Holophrastic reading contributes to such poetics.

In its attention to Indigenous languages as the basis of Indigenous writing in English, holophrastic reading provides a formal foundation to the study of Indigenous literatures. Holophrastic reading makes language use the focus of studying Indigenous literatures; it does so, however, not for the sake of form and structure per se but for the sake of gaining a deeper understanding of Indigenous texts and the issues they raise, the abuses they expose, the grievances they express, the oppression they critique, the survival and continuity they celebrate. Like reading itself, then, holophrastic reading is concerned with both questions of form and issues of content, with the texts *and* their larger contexts. What, then, makes reading Indigenous literatures *holophrastic*? It is the attempt to read the English written by Indigenous storytellers and writers so as to expose its Indigenousness. To read holophrastically means to let one's readings of

---

Indigenous literatures be informed by the uses of language and the construction of stories in Indigenous-language discourse, and to be guided by that knowledge in making sense of Indigenous texts. In other words, holophrastic reading attempts to empower Indigenous peoples within their own language and discourse traditions by helping us ground our readings of Indigenous writing within those very traditions, as they characterize and define the writing.

HOW TO USE THIS BOOK

The Decolonizing Poetics of Indigenous Literatures is, first and foremost, a handbook or manual designed to teach holophrastic reading so that readers may apply this method in their own approaches to Indigenous writing. The book is divided into two parts: one introduces the method of holophrastic reading, and one demonstrates how this method may be used to read and interpret contemporary Indigenous storytelling and writing.

Part 1, "A Primer on Holophrastic Reading," gives a theoretical survey of the method of holophrastic reading. Any kind of holophrastic heuristic is useful only for readers with some basic knowledge of Indigenous grammars. Before looking at any of the other chapters in the handbook, readers without any knowledge of Indigenous languages will therefore want to consult chapter 1, which gives a brief but succinct summary of Indigenous language and discourse traditions, paying close attention to the holophrase as the dominant structure of many of these languages. Based on this linguistic discussion, chapter 2 offers a comprehensive holophrastic heuristic. Holophrastic reading essentially means to read Indigenous texts for *holophrastic traces* and *relational word bundles,* the two main manifestations of the holophrase in Indigenous discourse in English. The heuristic provided in chapter 2 discusses the various technical aspects of holophrastic readings; readers may use the heuristic to follow the readings presented in the remainder of the book or as a reference for conducting their own holophrastic readings of Indigenous texts. Part 1 closes with an alphabetical list of critical terms relevant to holophrastic reading, including their definitions and, where applicable, examples.

Part 2, "Holophrastic Readings of Indigenous Writing," illustrates how the holophrastic heuristic introduced in part 1 may be applied in studying Indigenous texts. The chapters demonstrate the broad range of interpretative contexts in which holophrastic reading may serve as an ethical method for reading Indigenous literatures. The purpose of this part of the book, then, is not so much to teach readers how to discover holophrastic manifestations in the English used by Indigenous writers and storytellers;

rather, part 2 is meant to illustrate how diverse Indigenous texts may be invested with meaning using the method of holophrastic reading. Each of the analytical chapters in part 2 is centred on a particular question that readers may bring to the study of Indigenous writing. The interpretative contexts therein are not exhaustive but serve as representative examples of contemporary Indigenous writing as well as of the issues currently discussed in Indigenous literary studies.

Aside from their relevance, my choice of texts is rather idiosyncratic. I have selected works that I have enjoyed reading and teaching. Moreover, I have included four of the five texts that I originally discussed in *"That's Raven Talk,"* for two reasons: one, to give readers a reference point from which to consult more comprehensive holophrastic readings for at least some of the texts analyzed here; and two, to demonstrate that holophrastic reading may be applied to one and the same text for very different purposes. This book's preference for narrative genres is entirely the result of its central theme. Holophrastic reading concerns primarily narratology, the study of narrative structures and how they affect the production of meaning in texts; the method is therefore best illustrated by discussing literary works with some narrative quality. This is not to say that holophrastic reading applies only to narrative or literary texts. Since the holophrase is a key component of Indigenous expressions in English, holophrastic reading may be applied to non-narrative and non-literary texts as well, such as drama, speeches, and even political discourse. In short, just as my understanding of Indigenous poetics as referring to the study of Indigenous discourse more generally is quite broad, holophrastic reading as a reading method may be applied in far more discursive contexts than the ones I present in this book.

All chapters in this book are designed to stand as independent units, with the exception of chapters 1 to 3, which build on each other and form the theoretical basis of the readings that follow in the remainder of the book. The analysis chapters in part 2, on the other hand, may be read either independently or in chronological order. Holophrastic traces and relational word bundles concern different aspects of Indigenous poetics, namely language and style (holophrastic traces) and narrative structures (relational word bundles). The first two analysis chapters reflect these different focuses. In chapter 4, I examine ancestral language influences on Indigenous discourse in English, as evident in the use of holophrastic traces, whereas in chapter 5, I address narrative structures and the ways these structures affect our readings of Indigenous writing, by discussing the central role of relational word bundles in Indigenous discourse in English.

As such, chapters 4 and 5 discuss two areas that are given little attention in Indigenous literary studies: Indigenous languages and narrative structures. These two chapters address the more formal questions that are raised by Indigenous writing, but which critics of Indigenous literatures tend to avoid: How do Indigenous people achieve rhetorical sovereignty in language? How is peoplehood performed in narrative? The first two chapters in part 2 serve two ends, then: to introduce the two main components of holophrastic reading in regard to Indigenous writing, and to show how this reading method helps generate interpretations of Indigenous texts and thus goes beyond a mere study of form for form's sake. The remaining chapters in part 2 then move to other subject areas that have dominated discussions of Indigenous literary studies for quite some time; specifically, they are dedicated to studies of historical trauma and healing, of Indigenous literary nationalism, and of pan-Indigenous and urban Indigenous writing. In some of these chapters, the discussion concerns both components of holophrastic reading; ultimately, however, relational word bundles figure more prominently than holophrastic traces in chapters 6, 7, and 8 because they tend to be more relevant to holophrastic reading.

HOLOPHRASTIC READING AND THE ETHICS OF READING

The holophrase is the basis of holophrastic reading, but it is important to keep in mind that this reading strategy is not so much about holophrases per se than about an attempt to ground the reading of Indigenous texts within Indigenous language and discourse traditions. In other words, holophrases and holophrastic reading, though related, are two very different things. The holophrase is a linguistic concept and concerns questions of grammar, particularly morphology—that is, that part of linguistics that studies the ways in which words are formed in a given language. Holophrastic reading, on the other hand, is concerned with reading for holophrastic influences in English-language texts by Indigenous storytellers and writers in order to invest these texts with meaning. As such, holophrastic reading belongs to the realm of literary criticism. Granted, all holophrastic manifestations have their basis in language and therefore grammar. Yet the purpose of holophrastic reading is not to study the system language (that's the task of linguists) but to study Indigenous texts by reading for the particular *uses of language* in Indigenous discourse, and thus to grapple with the challenge that is at the heart of much Indigenous writing: to think outside the English language while simultaneously using that language.

It may seem ironic that, as a method of reading, holophrastic reading is based in linguistics, rhetoric, and strands of literary criticism that originate in Euro-Western discourses of science—discourses in which I was trained as a scholar whose roots, moreover, are in the Old World. Although I have studied two Algonquian languages, Nêhiyawêwin (Cree) and Anishnaabemowin (Ojibway), I have not become a fluent speaker of these languages. Still, as little as I may be able to converse in Nêhiyawêwin or Anishnaabemowin, I have developed a strong sense of the value and significance of ancestral languages for the continuance of Indigenous people as peoples. And just as holophrastic reading challenges me and others to read Indigenous works from inside Indigenous language and discourse traditions, I have also learned to respect and appreciate these languages in their own right. My work on holophrastic reading honours the crucial role ancestral languages play in Indigenous communities across North America. Indigenous languages deserve more attention than linguists, literary critics, and educators are already giving them; holophrastic reading, I hope, is a step in this direction. That this step may at times seem rather technical has everything to do with my attempt to remain critically honest to the literary traditions I read: the texts themselves will guide my readings, provided I pay close attention to the words on the page, to the clues found in the texts.

Finally, I must emphasize that I think of my model of holophrastic reading as descriptive rather than prescriptive. Since I started working on this reading method, some of its terminology has evolved, as have some of its relevant definitions. In many ways, holophrastic reading is still very much a method in progress—and one that other readers of Indigenous literatures are welcome to build on and modify. Equally important, holophrastic reading is a means, not an end. It helps readers make sense of Indigenous texts, but it doesn't adhere to any one school of interpretation; nor do I think of it as constituting Indigenous poetics per se, as I recognize that the notion of Indigenous poetics is rather generalized and calls for more specified studies into the poetics of specific Indigenous literatures. Ideally, the art of reading Indigenous literatures should be informed by the art of *making* Indigenous literatures, as suggested by my holophrastic reading of Cree poet Louise Bernice Halfe's writing (see chapter 7) as grounded in what Cree scholar Neal McLeod calls *mamâhtâwisiwin*, the "tapping into the Great Mystery" practiced by Cree poets and storytellers.[18] Yet even where holophrastic reading is not able to move beyond more gen-

---

18   Neal McLeod, "Cree Poetic Discourse," in *Across Cultures, Across Borders: Canadian Aboriginal and Native American Literatures*, ed. Paul DePasquale, Renate Eigenbrod, and Emma LaRocque (Toronto: Broadview, 2010), 109.

eric approaches to Indigenous writing, it still allows readers to move beyond merely scratching at the surface of Indigenous texts, thus laying the groundwork for more detailed studies in nation-specific poetics. At the same time, holophrastic reading may serve to complement studies of a more specified poetics, as, for example, those offered in *Indigenous Poetics in Canada*, a recent critical collection on Indigenous poetry edited by McLeod.[19] In one of the essays in the collection, Sam McKegney argues "that attentiveness to the cues to criticism emanating from poetry honours the participatory and reciprocal creative relationship between poet and audience in a manner that aspires toward generative alliance," which he contrasts with "passive allegiance to author intentionality."[20] The arguments I have made in this introduction are very much situated along McKegney's lines. It is high time that readers of Indigenous literatures began to do the obvious: to think outside the English language and its discursive and rhetorical traditions when working with Indigenous texts, and to finally approach these literatures for what they truly are.

---

19 Neal McLeod, ed., *Indigenous Poetics in Canada* (Waterloo: Wilfrid Laurier University Press, 2014).

20 Sam McKegney, "Writer-Reader Reciprocity and the Pursuit of Alliance through Indigenous Poetry," in Ibid., 44.

PART 1

A

PRIMER

ON

HOLOPHRASTIC

READING

INDIGENOUS LANGUAGE AND DISCOURSE
TRADITIONS: AN INTRODUCTION

From a linguistic perspective, North America is a very rich continent; in fact, it used to be even richer five hundred years ago—that is, before colonialism started to impact Indigenous languages, many of which are now extinct or at risk of disappearing in the very near future. Nevertheless, those Indigenous languages that are still alive today display a rich linguistic diversity. And yet, despite all this diversity, it is possible to make out at least one dominant feature that characterizes the North American continent linguistically: holophrasis. Not all but an astonishingly high number of North American Indigenous languages are holophrastic, which is to say, they have a tendency to use *holophrasis*.

The term holophrasis derives from the Greek word *holos* for "whole" and the Late Latin word *phrasis*, which in turn originates from the Greek verb *phrazein*, meaning "to declare, to tell." Once we put these two pieces together, we arrive at something like "to declare, or tell, whole." In a very general sense, then, holophrasis describes the process of expressing in a single word a whole phrase or complex idea. At least, this is how the *Oxford English Dictionary* defines the term. Following this definition, any single word that functions as a whole phrase or expresses a complex idea may count as a *holophrase*. We all go through a phase in life when we do just that: express a whole phrase or idea using one single word. Linguists call this phase the holophrastic stage of language acquisition. In this stage, toddlers use one-word utterances (usually nouns) to suggest a complete sentence, such as "Banana" for "I want a banana" or "Up" for "Take me into your arms." Holophrases also feature in theories on the evolution of human language. One such theory, for example, suggests that human protolanguage was holophrastic— in other words, that it consisted of single, grammarless units that were equivalent to sentences as they are used in human language today.[1]

Neither of these types of holophrases is the subject of this book, however. In fact, toddler and early humanoid holophrases are very different from the holophrases found in the languages indigenous to North America. Toddler holophrases depend fully on context: they suggest a complex idea by way of using a part for its whole, a figure of speech literary critics call "synecdoche," such as "wheels" to refer to "car" or "Banana" for "I want a banana." In other words, toddler holophrases *pretend* to be complete sentences when really they are not. Indigenous holophrases, on the other hand, do not function by way of synecdoche, at least not on the word level (see chapter 2); they actually *are* grammatically complete sentences or clauses because they include an expression of both the verb and the subject and, if applicable, its object(s). The province of Saskatchewan, for example, derives its name from the Saskatchewan River, which is called *kisiskâciwan'sîpiy* in Plains Cree. This word is a holophrase, whose constituent parts *kisiskâciwan* (it flows fast, swiftly) and *sîpiy* (river) explicitly include the information contained in this clause rather than suggesting this information through implication. The English language needs to render this holophrase using a noun phrase ("the river") that is modified by a relative clause ("that which flows swiftly"), arriving at the following: "the river that flows swiftly." This translation is actually very reminiscent of constructions sometimes found in personal names. In *Green Grass, Running Water*, for example, Cherokee novelist Thomas King uses the name "Young Man Walking On Water" to refer to Jesus.[2] This name expresses a complex idea but takes the form of an idiom-like lexical phrase, that is, a series of words that form a set expression of some sort and whose inter-

---

1   The theory that human protolanguage was holophrastic has been proposed by Alison Wray in "Holistic Utterances in Protolanguage: The Link from Primates to Humans," in *The Evolutionary Emergence of Language: Social Function and the Origins of Linguistic Form*, ed. Chris Knight, Michael Studdert-Kennedy, and James R. Hurford (Cambridge: Cambridge University Press, 2000), 285–302.

2   Thomas King, *Green Grass, Running Water* (1993; reprint, Toronto: HarperPerennial Canada, 1999), 349.

nal form cannot be changed, or only slightly so. Whether they are lexical phrases or noun phrases with modifying relative clauses, "the river that flows swiftly" and "Young Man Walking On Water" are rather clumsy attempts to find appropriate equivalents for Indigenous place and personal names—clumsy because English grammar does not leave much room for compounding (the process of joining words to create a new word), let alone for the construction of single words that express complete clauses or sentences. In a more narrow sense, then, the terms holophrasis and holophrase refer to a specific morphological phenomenon—a phenomenon that has long been identified as a dominant feature of many Indigenous languages in North America and that is testimony to the linguistic sophistication of these languages. At the same time, it would be wrong to reduce Indigenous languages to the holophrase. Some of these languages are, in fact, "only mildly synthetic" and therefore not holophrastic at all (see below).[3] And of course, all these languages are characterized by many other grammatical aspects and thus differ quite extensively from one language family to another, and sometimes even within a language family. Yet despite—or rather, because of—the linguistic diversity of the North American continent, the holophrase is a prominent feature. Indeed, it is so remarkably prominent that it may well serve as the centrepiece of a reading method that aims to ground Indigenous texts in the very language and discourse traditions from which they originate.

HOLOPHRASIS AND LANGUAGE TYPOLOGY

One of the first linguists to write about the holophrastic character of North American Indigenous languages was Peter Stephen Du Ponceau, an American linguist originally from France (1760–1844). In his 1819 report to the Historical and Literary Committee of the American Philosophical Society, about the structure and grammar of the languages indigenous to North America, Du Ponceau concluded as follows:

Three principal results have forcibly struck my mind. . . . They are the following:

1. That the American languages in general are rich in words and in grammatical forms, and that in their complicated construction, the greatest order, method and regularity prevail.

---

3 Marianne Mithun, *The Languages of Native North America* (Cambridge: Cambridge University Press, 1999), 38.

2. That these complicated forms, which I call *polysynthesis*, appear to exist in all those languages, from Greenland to Cape Horn.

3. That these forms appear to differ essentially from those of the ancient and modern languages of the old hemisphere.[4]

Contemporary linguists no longer share Du Ponceau's position that all North American languages, without exception, are holophrastic (the more technical but synonymous term is polysynthetic). There exists general agreement, however, that even though holophrasis (i.e., polysynthesis) is not universally found in North America, it is nonetheless particularly widespread in this part of the world, especially when compared to other regions that feature holophrastic languages, such as Meso-America, Siberia, Northern Australia, and Papua New Guinea. Holophrasis may hence be considered one of the defining features that distinguishes Indigenous languages from English and other Indo-European languages, which—from the mildly analytic (e.g., English) to the highly synthetic (e.g., German or Polish)—clearly do not qualify as holophrastic languages.[5]

As one-word sentences, holophrases concern morphology, that subfield of linguistics concerned with the internal structure of words. The central category in morphology is the morpheme, the smallest meaningful unit in the grammar of a given language. Any word consists of at least one morpheme, but while words are by definition able to stand on their own, not all morphemes are able to do so. The word "unnatural," for example, consists of two morphemes ("un" and "natural"), of which only "natural" can serve as an independent unit, that is, as a free-standing morpheme. How morphemes are combined to build words varies considerably among languages. Linguists have therefore developed morphological typology as one mode of classifying languages.

Morphological typology can be quite complex, and there exist different models of classification. One model that I have found quite useful in

---

4   Peter Stephen Du Ponceau, "Report of the Corresponding Secretary to the Committee, of his Progress in the Investigation Committed to him of the General Character and Forms of the Languages of the American Indians," in *Transactions of the Historical & Literary Committee of the American Philosophical Society, held at Philadelphia, for promoting Useful Knowledge*, vol. 1 (Philadelphia: American Philosophical Society, 1819), xxii–xxiii.

5   For contemporary perspectives on the dominance of holophrasis in North America, see, for example, Mithun (*Languages*, 38) and Nicholas Evans and Hans-Jürgen Sasse ("Introduction: Problems of Polysynthesis," in *Problems of Polysynthesis*, ed. Evans and Sasse [Berlin: Akademie, 2002], 1).

understanding holophrasis is the typology that distinguishes languages based on two parameters: an index of synthesis and an index of fusion. The index of synthesis measures the internal complexity of a word: if the number of morphemes equals one (such as in the cases of Chinese and Vietnamese), the language in question is analytic; if the number is higher than one (such as in French and Polish), it is synthetic. The index of fusion describes the transparency of morpheme boundaries in a given language: if the morphemes can be clearly distinguished from each other (as, for example, in Turkish), the language in question is agglutinating; if, on the other hand, the morphemes cannot be distinguished from each other (such as in Russian, which fuses the grammatical categories of number and case into one single morpheme), the language is fusional. According to this two-parameter typology, holophrastic languages perform synthesis to a very high degree, combining *many* morphemes into *very* large words; while some of these holophrastic languages may be agglutinating (such as Yupik Eskimo), others are fusional (such as Plains Cree).[6]

No single holophrastic language in the world actually consists only of holophrases, nor do holophrastic languages include rules according to which every word *must* necessarily correspond with one complete sentence or clause. What all holophrastic languages share, however, is a strong propensity for very complex synthesis that is centred around the verb. Indeed, a holophrase is not just any concatenation of morphemes. The German language, for example, is famous—even notorious, according to Mark Twain—for its ability to combine a seemingly endless number of nouns into a new, much more complex word (for example, "Repräsentaten-haustages-ordnung" for "agenda for the house of representatives"), but this ability makes German only highly synthetic.[7] For a complex word to become a holophrase it needs to have its basis in a verb and to express its subject and object(s) in the form of morphemes that are incorporated into this verb. In other words, the structure of holophrases is both complex and ordered.

---

6   The two-parameter typology of indexes of synthesis and fusion is discussed by Bernard Comrie, *Language Universals and Linguistic Typology: Syntax and Morphology* (Oxford: Basil Blackwell, 1981), 42–43.

7   Mark Twain dedicated one chapter of *A Tramp Abroad* to "The Awful German Language," which uses words that were so long that they couldn't even be found in dictionaries and could therefore hardly count as legitimate words (Twain, *A Tramp Abroad* [Hartford, CT: American Publishing Company; London: Chatto and Windus, 1880], 323–24).

THE STRUCTURE OF HOLOPHRASES

The central component of Indigenous languages is always the verb, which is the unit onto which Indigenous and other holophrastic languages tend to focus all the information contained in a sentence or clause, prompting one linguist, Wallace Chafe, to refer to verbs in holophrastic languages as "holistic verbs."[8] Holophrastic verbs express not just an event but also everyone involved in this event, as is illustrated in the following sentence taken from Plains Cree, an Algonquian language spoken in Alberta, Saskatchewan, Manitoba, and Montana.

(1) mîyweyimew.
     S/he likes him/her/them

The sentence in (1) is fairly unspecific as to who (male vs. female) likes whom (male vs. female, singular vs. plural), and yet the conjugated verb *"mîyweyimew"* is an independent utterance, because the suffix "-ew" indicates both the subject and object of the verb (who does something to whom?), that is, the latter is incorporated *into the verb*, thus turning *"mîyweyimew"* into a perfectly grammatical sentence. What would happen if one were to further specify the subject and object of this sentence?

(2) Paul mîyweyimew ohtâwiya otemiyiwa.
     Paul–he likes it–his father's–dog
     Paul likes his father's dog.

Unlike the holophrase in (1), the sentence in (2) includes independent noun phrases for both its subject (Paul) and its object (*ohtâwiya otemiyiwa,* his father's dog), gathering them *around the verb* instead of incorporating them into the verb. In fact, as a rule, once a subject or object is further specified in Plains Cree, it tends to appear as a separate word in the sentence.[9] On the other hand, in Mohawk, a Haudenosaunee language spoken in New York State, Ontario, and Quebec, noun phrases may or may not stand alone.

---

8   Wallace L. Chafe, "Discourse Effects on Polysynthesis," in *Discourse across Languages and Cultures,* ed. Carol Lynn Moder and Aida Martinovic-Zic (Amsterdam: John Benjamins, 2004), 44.

9   Exceptions to the tendency in Plains Cree to specify subjects and objects as separate words include *nôcihiskwewew* ("s/he is sexually involved with women") or *wanihastimwêw* ("s/he loses his/her horse, or dog").

(3)   (a) Sak shako-nuhwe's ne owira'a.
        Sak–he/her-likes–the–baby
        Sak likes the baby.
        (b) *Sak ra-wir-a-nuhwe's.*
        Sak–he–baby–likes
        Sak likes the baby.[10]

The independent noun phrase in (3a), *"owira'a"* (Mohawk for "baby"), is incorporated into the verb to form the holophrase in (3b), *"ra-wir-a-nuhwe's."* Yet both sentences express the same idea, namely, that Sak likes the baby. Mohawk may therefore be considered more holophrastic than Plains Cree. What these two Indigenous languages have in common, however, is their ability to produce fully grammatical sentences without having to rely on independent noun phrases. English, on the other hand, is not able to express a sentence's subject or object as part of its verb; it requires all its verbs to be accompanied by either independent noun phrases or pronouns.

Compared to most Indo-European languages, holophrastic languages, then, have a very high degree of expressivity, at least when measured in terms of information expressed per word.

(4)   washakotya'tawitsherahetkvhta'se' (Mohawk)
        He made the thing that one puts on one's body [i.e., the dress] ugly for her.[11]

(5)   kikînohtenitawikociwîcinehiyaw'kiskinohamâkosiminâwâw
        (Plains Cree)
        You folks wanted to come and try to learn Cree with me.

(6)   tauqhirniatchiarvingmuqatiginianngitchangnarniripkin
        (Inuvialuktun)
        I do not think I will go to the new store with you.[12]

---

10   The Mohawk holophrase and its translation are taken from Mark C. Baker, *The Atoms of Language: The Mind's Hidden Rules of Grammar* (New York: Basic, 2001), 112.

11   The Mohawk holophrase and its translation are taken from Baker, *Atoms*, 87.

12   The Inuvialuit holophrase and its translation were given to me by Ted Dyck, who received them from Inuvialuk elder Rosie Albert in Inuvik.

Words such as those in sentences (4) through (6) are breathtaking for speakers of analytic or synthetic languages. For native speakers of Cree, Mohawk, or Inuvialuktun, however, they are very natural. In fact, speakers of holophrastic languages constantly invent new holophrases and their listeners readily understand them—provided that the various morphemes within the newly invented holophrases are combined according to the order outlined in the grammar of the language used.

THE DISCOURSE CONSEQUENCES OF HOLOPHRASES

Now, why would it matter whether or not the information contained in a sentence or clause is expressed in a single word? This question triggers yet other questions. How is the structure of words related to the structure of sentences and to that of discourse more generally? Why would the internal structure of words matter to people concerned with the readings of texts? Linguistics and literary studies are distinct and independent disciplines, although they share a common interest in language and how it is used by humans. While one discipline studies the microcosm of language—the structure, formation, and meaning of words and their arrangement in sentences—the other discusses the function and meaning of words and sentences as they are used in discourse. Discourse is made of sentences, which, in turn, are formed by words. So, the short answer to all the questions raised above is that holophrases matter to readers of Indigenous literatures because the holistic nature of this particular language structure has significant discourse effects. Holophrases influence the construction of discourse; they shape the ways in which stories are told. First, there seems to be a strong relation between the holophrastic nature of many Indigenous languages and their tendency towards evidentiality, the process of identifying or qualifying one's (source of) knowledge. Second, holophrasis seems to be correlated to the tendency of Indigenous languages toward figurative uses of language. And third, Indigenous storytellers working in their ancestral languages have the option to use either a holophrase or a series of words, giving them interesting stylistic alternatives, including the ability to tell a story using a minimalism of text.[13] It is these discourse consequences that make the holophrase such a significant category for the study of Indigenous literatures, including those literary works not composed in Indigenous languages.

---

13   On the role of stylistic alternatives in holophrastic discourse, see Mithun, *Languages*, 39. See Chafe, "Discourse Effects," 45–51, for a detailed linguistic discussion of the discourse patterns resulting from holistic verbs in Seneca, another Haudenosaunee language.

As discussed above, Indigenous storytellers working in their ancestral languages may express an event and its participants using a single word. As interesting as holophrases are in themselves, equally fascinating is what happens around holophrases in storytelling. As it happens, the languages indigenous to North America have been strongly associated not only with holophrasis but also with what linguists call "evidentiality," the "citing" of one's (sources of) knowledge. Cree narrative genres, for example, can be distinguished from one another by way of discourse markers that specify the storyteller's knowledge. *Âtayohkewina*, the sacred stories, begin with *pêyak êsa*, which can be translated as "once upon a time." *Kayâs-âcimow-ina*, the historical narratives, always include a source, which is not needed in *âcimowina*, personal stories. [14] Similarly, Cree speakers consistently begin or end reported speech with either *"ê-itêyihtahk"* ("[this is] what he thought") or *"itêyihtam"* ("so he thought"),[15] as evident in the following story narrated by Cree storyteller Xavier Sutherland in Swampy Cree.[16]

"šââ!" *mamâ itwêw* ana iskwêw. "'kwâni kwayask kâ-kî-pêci-kîwêyin," *manâ itwêw*. "mistâpêskwêwak oš' ân' ê-kêkišêpâ-manihtêcik, anima kâ-pêhtaman," *manâ itwêw*, "ê-matwê-kahikêcik oš' âni animêniw kâ-itihtâkwaninik," *manâ itwêw*. "'kâwina mîna wîskâc antê ohc'-îtohtê, kâ-k'-îsi-pêhta-man anima kêkwân," *itwêw*.

"O-oh dear!" *said that woman*. "Then it was right that you came back home," *she said*. "It was the giant women, you realize, gathering wood early in the morning, that is what you heard," *she said*. "As they were noisily cutting it, indeed that is what made the sound," *she said*. "Don't ever go there again where you heard that thing," *she said*.

Some Indigenous languages even mark evidentials—those narrative units that identify a speaker's (source of) knowledge—by way of a grammatical

---

14 Regna Darnell, "The Primacy of Writing and the Persistence of the Primitive," in *Papers of the Thirty-First Algonquian Conference*, ed. John D. Nichols (Winnipeg: University of Manitoba, 2000), 61.

15 H. Christoph Wolfart and Janet F. Carroll, *Meet Cree: A Guide to the Cree Language*, 2nd ed. (Edmonton: University of Alberta Press, 1981), 91.

16 The excerpt of Xavier Sutherland's story is taken from "cahkâpêš nêsta mâka mistâ-pêskwêwak / Chahkabesh and the Giant Women," in *âtolôhkâna nêsta tipâcimôwina / Cree Legends and Narratives from the West Coast of James Bay*, ed. and trans. C. Douglas Ellis (Winnipeg: University of Manitoba Press, 1995), 104; emphases added.

category (usually in the form of a syllable attached to the verb).[17] Whatever the form of evidentials, evidentiality is an important structural device in Indigenous-language discourse.[18] In fact, it is an integral part of an ancient Indigenous "copyright system based on trust," according to which one can tell a story only with permission of its owner(s) and, if one does, always providing the story's source.[19] There is, of course, nothing holophrastic per se about the use of evidentials in Indigenous languages. At the same time, the widespread use of evidentiality in Indigenous languages appears to be invited by the holistic nature of holophrastic verbs. The ability to express a grammatically complete sentence or clause in a single word allows Indigenous storytellers working in their ancestral languages to focus their attention on other aspects of storytelling, such as (the source of) their knowledge.

The high expressivity of Indigenous languages is usually also accompanied by a high degree of figurativity. Athabaskan languages, for example, generally recycle their lexicon not through borrowing—the process of incorporating new words by borrowing them directly from another language—but rather through recombining or reinterpreting words already existing in their lexicon.[20] In Dene Sųłiné, an Athabaskan language spoken in northwestern Canada, for example, the word for "They are married" literally means "They are sitting together"; "She's pregnant" is expressed as "Her child sits in (her) womb"; and "S/he's delaying a decision" is literally rendered as "S/he's butt-sitting on it."[21] That is to say, the meaning of these holophrases is not readily accessible by merely "un-chunking" them into their individual parts. Rather, their constituent parts form a complex whole that is more than its pieces added together.

---

17 Anyone interested in grammaticalized forms of evidentials will find useful the survey provided by Thomas Willett, "A Cross-Linguistic Survey of the Grammaticization of Evidentiality," *Studies in Language* 12.1 (1988): 51–97.

18 M. Dale Kinkade and Anthony Mattina, "Discourse," in *Languages*, ed. Ives Goddard, vol. 17 of *Handbook of North American Indians*, ed. William C. Sturtevant (Washington, DC: Smithsonian Institution Press, 1996), 262.

19 Alexander Wolfe, *Earth Elder Stories: The Pinayzitt Path* (Saskatoon: Fifth House, 1989), xiv.

20 Sally Rice, "'Our Language Is Very Literal': Figurative Expression in Dene Sųłiné," in *Endangered Metaphors*, ed. Anna Idström and Elisabeth Piirainen (Amsterdam: John Benjamins, 2012), 21.

21 Sally Rice, "Posture and Existence Predicates in Dene Sųłiné (Chipewyan): Lexical and Semantic Density as a Function of the 'Stand'/'Sit'/'Lie' Continuum," in *The Linguistics of Sitting, Standing, and Lying*, ed. John Newman (Amsterdam: John Benjamins, 2002), 74.

These holophrases are *figures of speech* (metonymy and metaphor, respectively)—just like the Cree word for iceberg, *papaamahokowii maskwamii*, which translates as "around-and-around-bobbing-up-and-down-floating-downriver ice,"[22] is a figure of speech, namely, a metaphor. Similarly, the Cree word for "northern lights," *kânîmihitocik*, translates into "when they are dancing." The actual meaning of this noun (or rather, verb, for in Cree this word is a verb and not a noun) only becomes apparent if one knows the cultural context of the language in which this word is used. (Cree people think of the northern lights as their ancestors dancing in the sky.) We can therefore say that holophrases in Indigenous languages regularly, albeit not always, take the form of figures of speech, even if speakers of these languages are often not aware of this.

The high degree of expressivity of holophrases gives storytellers numerous stylistic possibilities for the telling of their tales. They may decide to use a series of words instead of a holophrase for the sake of emphasizing a particular word that has particular significance to the story. Or, they may choose not to specify the information expressed in a given holophrase, but to elaborate only in the next sentence, if required by the audience. Because of the holistic nature of their verbs, Indigenous grammars thus contain what we might call built-in silences that allow speakers to produce fully grammatical sentences with a minimalism of text. In practice, Indigenous-language discourse consists of more than a series of holophrases. Yet the ability to invent a story consisting of nothing more than a concatenation of holophrases is remarkable because it points to what I think is a major function of holophrases on the level of discourse: holophrases lend themselves to summary. One may delete all non-holophrases in Indigenous-language discourse and still keep the gist of the story; however, if one drops all its holophrases, the story is lost.

Included in table 1.1 is the beginning of a story narrated in Plains Cree by the late Glecia Bear. It is accompanied here by two translations, one an interlinear translation provided by myself, the other provided by the late Freda Ahenakew (Cree) and H. Christoph Wolfart, as published in the children's book *Two Little Girls Lost in the Bush*. Holophrases are marked in boldface in both the original story (left column) and the interlinear translation (middle column).[23]

---

22 George Fulford, "What Cree Children's Drawings Reveal about Words and Imagery in the Cree Language," in *Papers of the Twenty-Eighth Algonquian Conference*, ed. David H. Pentland (Winnipeg: University of Manitoba, 1997), 175.

23 Glecia Bear, *wanisinwak iskwesisak: awasisasinahikanis / Two Little Girls Lost in the Bush: A Cree Story for Children*, ed. and trans. Freda Ahenakew and H. Christoph

TABLE 1.1 THE NARRATIVE FUNCTION OF HOLOPHRASES

CREE ORIGINAL (BEAR)	INTERLINEAR TRANSLATION (NEUHAUS)	PUBLISHED TRANSLATION (AHENAKEW/ WOLFART)
ê-pê-kîwêyâhk êkwa,	[**we are coming to go home**] [and]	On our way home,
nipâpâ êkwa—	[my father] [and]	my dad—
nikî-wîhtamâkonân sâsay,	[**he told us**] [already, yet]	he had told us,
otâskosihk isi **ê-wîhtamâkoyâhk,**	[yesterday] [like this] [**he is telling us**]	telling us the previous evening already,
mostos awa **ê-wî-otawâsimisit** nânitaw ôtê sakâhk;	[cow] [this one] [**she is going to be having a child**] [approximately, about; simply] [here] [in the woods]	that one cow would be calving somewhere in the bush over here;
êkwa, "**aswahohk!**"	[and] [**be on her guard**]	so he had said,
itwêw,	[**he says**]	"Watch out for her
"atisamânihk;"	[at the smudge]	at the smudge!"
(kayâs mâna **kî-atisamânihkêwak**	[a long time ago] [habitually] [**they made smudges**]	(they used to make smudges long ago,
êkota mostoswak **ê-asikâpawicik**),	[there] [the cows] [**they stand up as a crowd**]	with the cows standing out there),
"**asawâpamihk** êwako ana onîcâniw!"	[**guard someone/something**] [that one] [that one] [cow (that never had a calf)]	"Look out for that female!"
itwêw,	[**he says**]	he had said,
"**sêskisici,**	[**she leaves the prairie to enter the forest**]	"When she goes into the bush,
pimitisahwâhkêk!"	[**follow her**]	then you all follow her!"
nititik awa nipâpâ;	[**he says to me**] [this one] [my father]	my dad had said to me;
"**ka-pimitisahwâwâw,**	[**you will follow her**]	"you follow her,
mâka êkâya cîki ohci **ka-pimitisahwâyêk,**	[but] [not] [near] [from, for] [**when you are following her**]	but you should not follow her too closely,
nâh-nakîci,	[**she stops now and then**]	for when she stops now and then,

Wolfart (Saskatoon: Fifth House, 1991), 2. The table comparing the original story with Ahenakew and Wolfart's published translation as well as my interlinear translation is taken from the appendix in Neuhaus, "That's Raven Talk," 226–27.

CREE ORIGINAL (BEAR)	INTERLINEAR TRANSLATION (NEUHAUS)	PUBLISHED TRANSLATION (AHENAKEW/ WOLFART)
ka-kiskêyihtam ê-pimitisahwâyêk,	[she will know] [you are following her]	she will know that you are following her,
piko wâhyawês ohci piko ka-pimitisahwâyêk,	[only] [far, far away] [from, for] [only] [you are following her]	you have to follow her from a little distance,
êkâ ka-wâpamikoyêk,"	[not] [that she will see you]	so that she will not see you,"
itwêw.	[he says]	he had said.

The words and phrases marked in boldface in table 1.1 summarize Bear's story; they hold it together, providing its narrative grid. All the other words grouped around those holophrases are important, too, because they give the story further shape, but their meaning and function depends on the holophrases around which they are grouped and without whom they lose all reference. In other words, holophrases are synecdochic after all— not in and of themselves but once they are seen in relation to one another and the discourse in which they are used. A given text's holophrases have the ability to summarize that very text; they are parts standing for the whole, *synecdoche writ large*. As such, holophrases fully mirror Indigenous notions of kinship and community, which Cherokee scholar Jace Weaver has described as synecdochic (part to whole), in contrast to Euro-Western understandings of community, which are essentially metonymic (part to part). As Weaver further notes, with reference to Donald Fixico (Shawnee/Sac and Fox/Muscogee Creek/Seminole), Indigenous people "tend to see themselves in terms of 'self in society' rather than 'self and society.'"[24]

Given the connection between holophrasis, on the one hand, and evidentiality, figurativity, and a tendency for a minimalism of text, on the other, holophrasis is obviously a morphological phenomenon that produces significant discourse effects—a phenomenon that leaves a noticeable fingerprint on the ways Indigenous-language discourse and storytelling unfold. The interlinear translation in table 1.1 highlights the omnipresence of holophrases in Cree discourse, but it also shows something else, especially when compared to the published translation, which renders Bear's story into plain, grammatical English while remaining as close as possible to the original text: Cree discourse is very different from English

---

24 Jace Weaver, *That the People Might Live: Native American Literatures and Native American Community* (New York: Oxford University Press, 1997), 39.

discourse; it weaves story by building it around its holophrases, which function as the story's backbone. A translation of Bear's story into English, no matter how literal, has to work with the rules and idiosyncrasies of English, and in the process loses the unique form of Cree discourse. This is a natural course insofar as translation is always fraught with loss. Residues of the peculiar form of Indigenous-language discourse may yet remain in the English used by Indigenous people, however, because language is never as rigid as some grammarians would like to have it. It is these residues of Indigenous-language discourse that are worth studying, because they point to the inventive use of English practiced by Indigenous people. Indeed, the discourse effects of holophrases are not restricted to Indigenous-language discourse alone but also figure in the English used by Indigenous storytellers and storywriters. What is more, these "holophrastic influences" in Indigenous discourse in English may be used as part of Indigenous poetics, an art of reading Indigenous literatures that, informed by the very language and discourse traditions from which these literatures derive, aims at reading Indigenous texts in English by thinking outside that very language. We will take a look at these holophrastic influences in more detail in chapter 2.

FURTHER READING

Readers interested in Indigenous languages in North America will find a helpful survey in Marianne Mithun's *The Languages of Native North America* (Cambridge: Cambridge University Press, 1999). Wallace Chafe's "Discourse Effects on Polysynthesis" (in *Discourse across Languages and Cultures*, ed. Moder and Martinovic-Zic, Amsterdam: John Benjamins, 2004) provides an insightful discussion of the discourse consequences of holophrasis, using the example of Seneca, a Haudenosaunee language.

HOLOPHRASTIC READING: A HEURISTIC

T he holophrase is a dominant structure in many Indigenous languages that clearly distinguishes these languages from Indo-
European tongues, which range from the mildly analytic (e.g.,
English) to the highly synthetic (e.g., German or Polish) and
are not holophrastic. At the same time, the holophrase is also a language
structure with significant discourse effects that bear a striking resem-
blance to certain features found in contemporary Indigenous writing in
English. Therefore, despite the stark differences between Indigenous and
English grammars, it makes sense to ponder the question of "holophrastic
influences" in Indigenous discourse composed in English. First, however,
a clarification is required. When I speak of holophrastic influences, I do
not posit that there exists a *causal* relationship between the holophrases
used in many Indigenous languages and certain features of Indigenous
discourse in English. When I look at contemporary Indigenous storytelling and writing in English, I notice elements that may be related to holophrasis in one way or another; whether these elements exist *because* of this
language structure is an entirely different question that is for others to
answer. Rather, what I am interested in doing as a reader of contemporary Indigenous literatures in English is to approach these literatures from
within the language and discourse traditions from which these literatures
originate. This is the central aim of holophrastic reading: to practice an

Indigenous poetics by thinking outside the English language while simultaneously using that language.

The main assumptions of holophrastic reading are, then, (a) that the holophrase, a dominant Indigenous language structure, may be translated into English-language discourse and (b) that the results of this translation constitute a reading method for Indigenous literatures that is derived from Indigenous linguistic and discursive traditions. Translation is an art fraught with loss. A translation of a text or concept can only reproduce its source in a different medium, language, or context, but it can never conserve the original. Something is always lost in translation, which is why it can only ever aim at equivalence rather than replication. But equivalence is a broad category; it may be based on form, such as a concept's particular structure, or it may be based on function, such as the concept's role and purpose in a specific setting.[1]

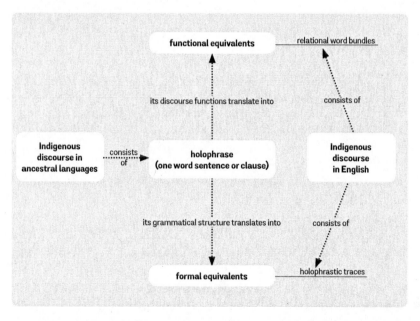

FIG. 2.1 THE HOLOPHRASE AND ITS EQUIVALENTS IN ENGLISH–LANGUAGE DISCOURSE

---

1   This distinction between formal and functional equivalence is borrowed from *The Theory and Practice of Translation* (Leiden, The Netherlands: E.J. Brill, 1969), in which Eugene A. Nida and Charles A. Taber argue for a move away from formal correspondence and toward dynamic equivalence (the effects a text has on its readers) as the aim of translation. Dynamic equivalence is modified here to encompass primarily function, which has certain, if non-specifiable, effects.

The holophrase has a unique morphological structure—it is able to express both an event and all its participants—but it also serves specific narrative functions in discourse, primarily to hold together the text in question. Similarly, holophrastic manifestations in the English used by Indigenous storytellers and writers can be seen on both formal and functional levels, as suggested by the fish skeleton structure in figure 2.1. We may hence distinguish between two types of holophrastic manifestations in English-language discourse, one formal and the other functional:

(1) Formal equivalents of the holophrase, so-called *holophrastic traces*, are elements that resemble holophrases formally, either in their structure (*direct holophrastic traces*) or because they evoke discourse features that are invited by holophrasis (*indirect holophrastic traces*).

(2) Functional equivalents of the holophrase, so-called *relational word bundles*, are structures that serve similar discourse functions in English as do actual holophrases in ancestral-language discourse.

Of course, neither of these equivalents actually constitutes a holophrase. That they may nevertheless be associated with the holophrase has to do with the fact that they are able to evoke this language structure in a different, non-holophrastic language, either in terms of their form (holophrastic traces) or in terms of their function (relational word bundles).

The holophrastic heuristic offered in table 2.1 allows readers to approach Indigenous literatures in English from the point of view of Indigenous language and discourse traditions by focusing their attention on the formal and functional manifestations of holophrases in English-language discourse. Reading is much like navigating an unknown territory using a map: readers pay attention to particular clues—signs, if you will—as they navigate a text in order to invest that text with meaning. In the case of holophrastic reading, these clues are provided by holophrastic traces and relational word bundles. Both are rather complex categories, however, and require further explanation, which will be offered in the remainder of this chapter.

TABLE 2.1 HOLOPHRASTIC MANIFESTATIONS IN ENGLISH–LANGUAGE DISCOURSE

	FORMAL EQUIVALENTS OF THE HOLOPHRASE		FUNCTIONAL EQUIVALENTS OF THE HOLOPHRASE
Category	direct holophrastic traces	indirect holophrastic traces	relational word bundles
Definition	words, compound words, or phrases that mimic the structure of the holophrase	discourse features that, in one way or another, are invited by holophrasis	any kind of figure of speech that has a significant narrative function and together with other such figures forms a given text's narrative grid
Examples	quotation compounds; idiom-like lexical phrases; synthetic compounds; compound nouns with verbal modifier; deverbal noun-noun compounds	evidentials; echoes of Indigenous verb complexity; textual silences; highly descriptive or figurative language	series of figures of speech (metaphor, metonymy, symbol, irony, synecdoche, etc.) that help establish specific narrative structures, such as narrative frames or cyclical structures; weaving together of scattered or seemingly unrelated stories/ poems

HOLOPHRASTIC HEURISTIC: DIRECT HOLOPHRASTIC TRACES

Direct holophrastic traces mimic the morphological structure of holophrases and, as a rule, constitute more complex words or phrases; these, however, vary in terms of the degree with which they are able to evoke the structure of actual holophrases in Indigenous-language discourse (see table 2.2). Particularly evocative of the complex and holistic structure of holophrases are *idiom-like lexical phrases* and *quotation compounds*. The lexical phrase "Young Man Walking On Water"[2] expresses a complex idea by using a series of words as a set expression of some sort (in this case, a personal name) whose internal form cannot be changed, or only slightly so, and which takes on an idiom-like character. Idiom-like lexical phrases are, then, not actually holophrases—by definition, they consist of more than one word—but they express an intricate idea and are therefore *holophrase-like*. Quotation compounds are equally holophrase-like. Constructions such as "Eli Stands Alone," "Count My Blessings Grandmother," and "dontwasteit grip" contain a phrase, clause, or sentence that read as if they

---

2   Example taken from King, *Green Grass.*

were quoted from elsewhere (hence the term quotation compounds).[3] What makes quotation compounds resemble the structure of the holophrase is that they are usually processed or understood as a single unit—in these examples, as a personal name in the cases of "Eli Stands Alone" and "Count My Blessings Grandmother" and as a newly invented adjective in the case of "dontwasteit."

Other direct holophrastic traces include various kinds of compounds, all of which contain a verb (the central component of the holophrase), in some form or another (as head or modifier, sometimes in deverbalized form; see below).

TABLE 2.2 DEFINITIONS AND EXAMPLES OF DIRECT HOLOPHRASTIC TRACES

DIRECT HOLOPHRASTIC TRACES		
TYPE	**DEFINITION**	**EXAMPLE**
idiom-like lexical phrase	a series of words that form a set expression of some sort whose internal form cannot be changed (or only slightly so) and that takes on an idiom-like character	Young Man Walking On Water
quotation compound	a phrase or sentence that can be analyzed as a single word; a compound that looks like quoted speech	Eli Stands Alone; Count My Blessings Grandmother; dontwasteit grip
synthetic compound	a compound whose head is formed by affixation of a verb	taxi driver; night swimmer
compound noun with verbal modifier	a verb-noun compound whose head is formed by the noun	drawbridge; pickpocket
deverbal noun-noun compound	a noun-noun compound whose modifier is a deverbalized noun	breathing holes

Compounds are composites of two or more words—a noun, verb, adjective, or preposition—one of which serves as the compound's head,

---

3   Examples taken from, respectively, King, *Green Grass*; Louise Bernice Halfe, *Blue Marrow* (Regina: Coteau, 2004), 57; Richard Van Camp, *The Lesser Blessed* (1996; reprint, Vancouver: Douglas and McIntyre, 2004), 37.

determining its semantic category; all other elements are mere modifiers of the head. Or, to use a different image, if a compound is a train, then its head is the engine, and its modifiers the cars pulled by the engine. In the noun phrase "songbird," for example, the head (or engine) is "bird" because a songbird is a kind of bird rather than a particular type of song.

FIG. 2.2 INTERNAL STRUCTURE OF NOUN COMPOUNDS

In "birdsong," on the other hand, "song" is the head (or engine) and "bird" its modifier (or car; see fig. 2.2).

Compound verbs (i.e., compounds functioning as verbs, such as "highlight" or "panfry") are rare in English, but English-language discourse frequently features compound nouns (i.e., compounds functioning as nouns) that include some form of a verbal element. Particularly noteworthy are synthetic compounds, because they use as their head (or engine) a noun that is formed by affixation of a verb, that is, by adding a syllable to the verb. For example, in the case of "blues shouter," a synthetic compound used by the Inuk writer Alootook Ipellie in *Arctic Dreams and Nightmares*, the verb "shout" is turned into the noun "shouter" by adding the suffix "-er" (see fig. 2.3).

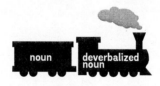

FIG. 2.3 SYNTHETIC COMPOUND

There are two more classes of compound nouns in English that evoke the central role of verbs in the structure of holophrases, though in slightly less evocative ways than synthetic compounds, because the verbal element of these compounds is restricted to the modifier (or car), which, in the English language, is always given less attention than a compound's head:

(1) *compound nouns with a verbal modifier,* such as "cutthroat," which may be analyzed as follows: $[cut] + [throat] = [verb]_{mod} + [noun]_{head}$

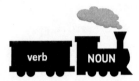

FIG. 2.4 COMPOUND NOUN WITH VERBAL MODIFIER

(2) *deverbal noun-noun compounds,* such as "breathing hole" in Ipellie's *Arctic Dreams and Nightmares,* which may be analyzed as follows: $[[breathe] [ing]] + [hole] = [deverbalized noun]_{mod} + [noun]_{head}$

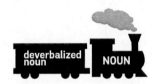

FIG. 2.5 DEVERBAL NOUN–NOUN COMPOUND

It is important to keep in mind that the last three types of compound nouns discussed above are unable to evoke the holistic nature of the holophrase. And yet they all contain a verbal element of some sort, thereby pointing to the holophrase's most central component, the verb. Idiom-like lexical phrases (e.g., "Young Man Walking On Water") and quotation compounds (e.g., "Eli Stands Alone"), on the other hand, are able to do both, suggesting the holistic nature of the holophrase *and* its central component. In fact, idiom-like lexical phrases and quotation compounds achieve a descriptiveness that, more often than not, enables them to suggest stories in their own right, for example, the story in the New Testament of Jesus walking on water (Matt. 14:22–33) or that of Eli protesting the operation of the Grand Baleen Dam in Cherokee writer Thomas King's *Green Grass, Running Water.* This ability to evoke stories distinguishes idiom-like lexical phrases and quotation compounds from other kinds of direct holophrastic traces. Further, both quotation compounds and idiom-like lexical phrases create the illusion of loan translations; that is, used in an English-language text, they look as though they were borrowed directly from an Indigenous language.

What makes direct holophrastic traces relevant to the reading of Indigenous literatures? For one, it is their structure, which is more or less reminiscent of the structure of holophrases, and second, it is the context of their use in Indigenous discourse. It is particularly noteworthy that place names and personal names in Indigenous writing often take the form of direct holophrastic traces, given the significance of names in Indigenous contexts. As Cree poet and scholar Neal McLeod stresses, "Indigenous names are absolutely essential for the description of Indigenous realities."[4] Interestingly, it is through Indigenous names that direct holophrastic traces have some presence even in mainstream North America: first, through prominent place names, such as Saskatchewan (from Plains Cree *kisiskâciwan'sîpiy* for "the river that flows swiftly"; see chapter 1) and Toronto (which is sometimes traced to the Huron word for "where there are trees standing in the water"[5]); and two, through prominent personal names, such as Sitting Bull and the infamous Dances with Wolves (infamous because of the romanticization of Indigenous people in the movie with the same title).

HOLOPHRASTIC HEURISTIC: INDIRECT HOLOPHRASTIC TRACES

Direct holophrastic traces are grammatical structures that are more or less suggestive of the morphological structure of the holophrase. Indirect holophrastic traces, on the other hand, echo discourse features *associated with* the particular structure of verbs in Indigenous languages or of, in the case of descriptive and figurative uses of language, the complexity of Indigenous words more generally (see table 2.3).

Particularly strong indirect holophrastic traces are found in evidentials as well as echoes of Indigenous verb complexity. Evidentiality—the identifying or qualifying of one's (sources of) knowledge—is strongly associated with Indigenous languages in North America (see chapter 1). Holistic verbs—that is, verbs that express both an event and its participant(s)— leave speakers room to include other kinds of information in their speech, including their source(s) or the degree of their knowledge. In the following example, the late Cree elder Minnie Fraser tells in Cree the story of her late husband catching his first moose. In her performance, Fraser repeatedly

---

4 McLeod, "Cree Poetic Discourse," 111.
5 Alan Rayburn, "The Real Story of How Toronto Got Its Name," *Canadian Geographic* 114.5 (1994): 68–70.

shifts the narrative perspective between her husband's telling of the story and her own retelling, as signalled by quotatives (marked in italics).[6]

[4] "And then my late mom knelt down there and prayed," *he said*; "'You kneel down, too!' she said to me," *he said*. "She asked this for me," *he said*, "that, in the life ahead of me, I should be a good trapper and a good hunter," *he said*, "that is was she asked for me—I had almost made her break into tears with all my crying. And so, when we had prayed, now we got up and left."

—he was thirteen, I think *he had said*, when he killed a moose for the first time.[7]

TABLE 2.3 DEFINITIONS AND EXAMPLES OF INDIRECT HOLOPHRASTIC TRACES

INDIRECT HOLOPHRASTIC TRACES		
TYPE	**DEFINITION**	**EXAMPLE**
evidentials	discourse markers that identify or qualify a speaker's (source of) knowledge	"I think"; "she supposes"; "they say"; "according to"
echoes of Indigenous verb complexity	remnants of the complex structure of verbs in Indigenous languages; reflected in English-language discourse by "pronoun copying" and "subject dropping"	"I saw him, the dog"; "my wife, she just hates cooking"; "Got a new laptop yesterday. Great design. Sleek and dynamic. Love it."
figurative / descriptive language	particularly high degree of figurative or descriptive uses of language, especially in relation to context and/ or genre	Eli Stands Alone (synecdoche)
textual silences	a text's deliberate keeping away of information; intended to further draw the audience into the text	

---

6 The following excerpt is the literal translation of Minnie Fraser's original perform-ance of the story in Cree.

7 Minnie Fraser, "His First Moose," in *Kôhkominawak otâcimowiniwâwa / Our Grand-mothers' Lives, as Told in Their Own Words*, ed. Freda Ahenakew and H. Christoph Wolfart (Regina: Canadian Plains Research Center, University of Regina, 1998), 107, 109.

To indicate that the story she tells is not her own, that it was given to her by someone else, Fraser repeatedly inserts the quotative "he said," even in sentences within her husband's story that already include reported speech. The frequent repetition of the husband's quotative is as natural in Cree as it seems odd in the English translation. Similarly, in the following passage taken from "Coyote Tricks Owl"—a story the late Okanagan storyteller Harry Robinson told in English rather than in his native Okanagan—the repetition of the quotative (again marked in italics) seems unnecessary in standard English discourse.

> And he [Coyote] bring 'em [the young people]
> and he come to Owl Woman
>   and *he says* to Owl Woman,
>   "I found these young people over there
>   and I see them and tell them to come.
>   Come along with me and then we going to be here."
> And *he says*
>   "Build a bigger fire,"
>   *he says* to these young people.
> "Gather some wood from long ways,
>   and get 'em,
>   and make a big fire,
>   so we'll have a good light."
> It's getting to be dark, you know, at night.
> And *he said*,
>   "We'll cook something.
>   Roast 'em on the stick
>   and eat that."[8]

Robinson's published stories are composed in Okanagan English, using Okanagan discourse features (see chapter 4), but there exist also examples of Indigenous writing in English that use a more standard form of English than Robinson's and still feature an equally prominent use of quotatives.

> Where did all the water come from? says that God.
> "I'll bet you'd like a little dry land," says Coyote.

---

8   Harry Robinson, *Write It on Your Heart: The Epic World of an Okanagan Storyteller*, comp. and ed. Wendy Wickwire (Vancouver: Talonbooks, 1989), 69.

What happened to my earth without form? says that God.

"I know I sure would," says Coyote.

What happened to my void? says that God. Where's my darkness?

"Hmmmm," says Coyote. "Maybe I better apologize now."

"You can apologize later," I says. "Pay attention."[9]

In this excerpt from *Green Grass, Running Water*, the tags "says that GOD," "says Coyote," and "I says" allow King to invent a scene that uses an amount of dialogue usually found only in scripts. Evidently, in some Indigenous discourse in English, evidentials are almost as pronounced as they are in Indigenous-language discourse.

Another significant set of indirect holophrastic traces are echoes of Indigenous verb complexity. In Indigenous languages that are holophrastic, subjects and objects are already always embedded in the verb and are defined with a higher degree of detail (i.e., in the form of independent noun phrases) only when required by context. To use yet another example from Plains Cree:

(3) (a) kîwâpamew.
S/he saw him/her.
(b) *iskwew kîwâpamew maskwa.*
the woman–she saw him/her–the bear
The woman saw the bear.

Because of the ability of the verb *"wâpam"* to express both subject and object, an interlinear translation of the sentence *"iskwew kîwâpamew maskwa"* would be "the woman, she saw him/her, the bear." This repetitive structure—that is, repetitive from the point of view of English grammar—is an echo of transitive animate *verb complexity* in the case of Plains Cree. A structure in English that mimics this verb complexity—or rather the structure of its interlinear translation into English—is referred to as *pronoun copying*, the process of repeating a subject or object (pro)noun, a phenomenon usually encountered only in colloquial discourse. Although structurally different from holophrastic verbs, pronoun copying marks one means by which English grammar is able to echo Indigenous verb complexity, if only indirectly. This indirect holophrastic trace can be found in texts as significant as Métis storyteller Maria Campbell's *Stories*

---

9   King, *Green Grass*, 38.

of the Road Allowance People, as evident in the following excerpt (marked in italics).

> Ole Arcand he says *him and dah Jesus*
> *dey* finish dah wine an *dah Jesus*
> *he* make mouth music an teach him dis song.[10]

Similarly, the passage below from *Keeper'n Me,* the debut novel of Anishnaabe novelist Richard Wagamese, includes two very different kinds of echoes of Indigenous complexity: pronoun copying as well as *subject dropping,* the dropping of a sentence's grammatical subject (both marked in boldface).

> **Always got** a storyteller to pass those old teachin's down. **Works** good long as there's old guys like me. And **we** got it good **us.** Young ones bringin' us fresh fish, fresh meat, driving us here and there, doin' all kinda work around the place, hanging around all the time. Not just rich Americans got hired help, eh? Heh, heh, heh. Nope. **Us old guys** had 'em beat years ago. Anishanabe got a good word no one ever argues with, Indyun or not, **makes** everything right and okay. We say—TRA-DISH-UNN. Heh, heh, heh. **Wanna** make white people believe what you tell 'em? **Say** it's TRA-DISH-UNN. **Same thing** with the young ones round here. You gotta do it, we say, it's TRA-DISH-UNN. **Good word that.** **Makes** life easy.[11]

In many ways, subject dropping is the mirror image of pronoun copying. Pronoun copying uses repetition for the sake of emphasis or flow of language; subject dropping, on the other hand, avoids the use of a grammatical subject because, it is assumed, the grammatical subject of the sentence may be gathered from the context. Neither of these discourse phenomena is able to replicate what actually happens in holophrastic verbs, yet both pronoun copying and subject dropping are highly suggestive of Indigenous verb complexity and therefore qualify as indirect holophrastic traces.

Evoking the often figurative uses of language and the tendency for a minimalism of text in Indigenous-language discourse (both triggered by

---

10   Maria Campbell, trans., *Stories of the Road Allowance People,* rev. ed. (Saskatoon: Gabriel Dumont Institute, 2010), 62; emphases mine.
11   Richard Wagamese, *Keeper'n Me* (Toronto: Doubleday Canada, 1994), 2.

the use of holophrases), highly figurative or descriptive uses of language as well as textual silences also count as indirect holophrastic traces. More so than evidentiality and echoes of Indigenous verb complexity, however, the deliberate keeping away of information from the reader as well as a heightened use of figurative language are also common in some Euro-Western and other literatures around the world.[12] These particular kinds of indirect holophrastic traces are therefore somewhat weaker than the other kinds of indirect holophrastic traces discussed above (that is, evidentials and echoes of Indigenous verb complexity). At the same time, figurative uses of language and textual silences allow readers of Indigenous literary texts to approach more universal features of language use in these texts from a perspective informed by Indigenous rather than Euro-Western traditions.

To summarize, then, we may say that holophrastic traces are formal manifestations of the holophrase in Indigenous discourse in English; reading Indigenous texts for these traces therefore implies some linguistic analysis, but always for the sake of interpreting the text at hand. The presence of holophrastic traces in Indigenous writing in English is based on negation: holophrastic traces evoke (the use of) a language structure that does *not* exist in English grammar. And yet, holophrastic traces remain significant elements of discourse. Depending on the context of use, they may serve important discourse functions, for example, the establishing of linguistic, cultural, and/or other contexts that may be relevant for understanding some of the deeper meanings and connotations of Indigenous discourse. The pronoun copying in the excerpt quoted from *Stories of the Road Allowance*, for example, marks Campbell's attempt to tell her people's stories in the way these stories are told in her community, thus exercising her people's right to rhetorical sovereignty (see chapter 4). Holophrastic traces are testament to the value of close reading—provided readers are able to move beyond the mere pinpointing and listing of such traces.

HOLOPHRASTIC HEURISTIC: RELATIONAL WORD BUNDLES
As with their formal counterparts, the functional equivalents of holophrases do not actually constitute holophrases. What defines them, instead, is their discourse function, which is equivalent to that of holophrases in

---

12   In fact, figures of speech are an essential part of rhetoric, which is itself sometimes regarded as one of the most, if not the most Euro-Western discipline. German critic Wolfgang Iser developed his notion of *Leerstellen*—textual gaps (literally, "empty spaces") that readers need to fill during the process of reading—largely from reading Euro-Western texts.

Indigenous-language discourse. Due to their holistic structure, holophrases have significant discourse consequences (see chapter 1): one, a tendency for evidentiality, reflected in English-language discourse in the use of evidentials as indirect holophrastic traces; two, a propensity for figurative uses of language; and three, a minimalism of text. As the interlinear translation of Glecia Bear's story discussed in chapter 1 illustrates, holophrases lend themselves to summary. The various holophrases in Bear's story produce its narrative grid; they alone are able to suggest Bear's story. This ability of a part (*a story's holophrases*) to stand for the whole (*the story*) is called synecdoche, which is a particularly prominent figure of speech—though, in the case of holophrases, it exists not on the word but on the discourse level. In the English used by Indigenous storytellers and storywriters, we can find structures that serve similarly significant narrative functions and that are just as synecdochic as holophrases in Indigenous-language discourse.

In *"That's Raven Talk,"* I called the functional equivalent of the holophrase a paraholophrase—something that is "analogous or parallel to, but separate from or going beyond" the holophrase.[13] The term "paraholophrase" highlights the relationship between the holophrase and its functional equivalent in English: while the holophrase is a linguistic category, the paraholophrase is a rhetorical category, and yet the two structures are analogous. This connection is crucial because it is what allows us to read Indigenous literatures in English from within Indigenous languages and thus to ground our reading in Indigenous linguistic and narrative traditions. Names are important, and since writing *"That's Raven Talk,"* I have come to adopt a different term for the functional equivalent of the holophrase, one that is more fully grounded in Indigenous traditions: *relational word bundle*. Relational word bundle is a straightforward term because it is self-explanatory. What is more, the term evokes Maria Campbell's notion of the "word bundle": "I always tell my students don't just settle for the word, but imagine that the word is carrying this big huge bundle," Campbell observed in an interview with Susan Gingell. "What's inside? What are the roots of that word? What is the story? Is there a song in the bundle, a ceremony, a protocol? Where did it come from? The word bundle is full of treasure."[14] Evoking Cree sacred bundles, Campbell's notion of the word bundle need not be restricted to literary contexts but also has

---

13   *Oxford English Dictionary Online*, draft rev. March 2009, s.v. "para" (def. A1).
14   Maria Campbell, "'One Small Medicine': An Interview with Maria Campbell," by Susan Gingell, *Essays on Canadian Writing* 83 (2004): 200.

spiritual connotations. Similarly, the relational word bundle is not merely a particular figure of speech; in its embodiment of Indigenous notions of community, it also has much larger implications, as we shall see in the discussion below of "The Republic of Tricksterism," a short story by Cree writer Paul Seesequasis.

The connection between Campbell's notion of word bundles and the functional equivalent of the holophrase will become apparent once we study this equivalent more closely. Like holophrases in Indigenous-language discourse, relational word bundles express complex ideas, perform significant narrative functions, and form the narrative grid of a given text. One central language structure that has a high degree of expressivity is figures of speech, specifically all those figures that involve a change in the meaning of a word. A figure of speech is essentially a word bundle, as it carries a surplus of meaning—that is, a large bundle of meaning, a complex idea. The full significance of any figure of speech always depends on context, however, and depending on how they are used, rhetorical figures may also serve narrative functions: they may help turn a large concatenation of words into a text. But just as a single thread doesn't make a spiderweb, no figure of speech alone can form a text's narrative grid. Multiple threads, or figures, are needed to hold everything together; in the end, it is the connections between threads, or figures, that produce the whole. Figures of speech that have significant narrative function are therefore always related to other such figures: they are not just word bundles but *relational* word bundles.

Because of the interdependence of relational word bundles, the question of how this rhetorical structure actually works is best illustrated by discussing examples in a specific text. I have chosen Paul Seesequasis's "The Republic of Tricksterism" for this purpose.[15] "The Republic of Tricksterism" tells the story of Uncle Morris, a fictional character modelled on two Métis leaders, Louis Riel (1844–1885) and the lesser known Malcolm Norris (1900–1967), cofounder of l'Association des Métis de l'Alberta and the Métis Association of Saskatchewan. In Seesequasis's story, Uncle Morris leads a revolution of mixed-blood, non-status Indians roaming the streets of Prince Albert, Saskatchewan. This revolution uses the power of collective memory rather than violence and is directed not so much against the Canadian government as against Native politicians who gov-

---

15 For the purpose of analysing Paul Seesequasis's "The Republic of Tricksterism," I am using the version published in the third edition of *An Anthology of Canadian Native Literature in English*, ed. Daniel David Moses and Terry Goldie (Toronto: Oxford University Press, 2005), 68–74.

ern the reserves based on colonial definitions of authenticity and purity, as dictated in the Indian Act, not noticing that these definitions are, in fact, aimed at the elimination of Aboriginal people as legal and social facts. First passed in 1876 and amended several times since, the Indian Act is a Canadian statute that, among other things, defines the requirements for "qualifying as Indian." Between 1951 and 1985, the Indian Act included a subsection that introduced compulsory enfranchisement (the loss of Indian status) for every Indian woman who married a man without status, forcing her and all her children to move off-reserve, with no entitlement to treaty benefits. Thus it happens that, in Seesequasis's story, the narrator and Chief Tobe are both mixed-blood but only the latter has status, because he has a Cree father, while Uncle Morris never had status, because his Cree mother married a white man. Completely missing the irony of the situation, Chief Tobe imagines himself as a "mixed-race pure-blood" (469) and fears the hybrid shape-shifting of Uncle Morris, who embraces traditional notions of kinship and community when he proclaims what he calls "the Republic of Tricksterism." This republic is "a place where humour rules and hatred is banished, where love's freedom to go anywhere is proclaimed"; it is a republic that doesn't "seek permanence . . . but a moment of time that lasts forever" (472). The Republic of Tricksterism lives on even beyond the words of Seesequasis's story, because this republic is essentially a story that is born in the people's imagination and continues to exist as long as the people fulfill their responsibility to share and to remember. Uncle Morris's tricksterism brings the people together through story and, in effect, through kinship: urban orphans are not orphans anymore, their "tribal links" no longer remain "obscure" (468), because in the Republic of Tricksterism the people are defined not according to laws of purity targeted at their elimination but through the practicing of kinship, the relationships people share with one another and with the world around them. Uncle Morris creates community, understood not according to the simplistic binary of purity vs. assimilation but as based deeply in relationships. Seesequasis's story tells a story of kinship, then, and evokes kinship even on a formal level: the story's form is also its content.

"The Republic of Tricksterism" is divided into eight paragraphs, with paragraphs two through seven serving as an explanation, elaboration, or flashback to the opening paragraph, and the closing paragraph providing further commentary on the story's opening. Each of these eight paragraphs centres on the issue that is at the heart of the story: the conflict between "Indiancracy" and the Republic of Tricksterism, between self-*government* (as Chief Tobe proclaims, "we are heading toward self-government"

[468]) and self-*determination* ("Let's define ourselves," Uncle Morris counters [470]), between purity politics and kinship. Uncle Morris leads a revolution of urban mixed-blood people to expose Chief Tobe's politics of self-government as internalized colonialism that needs to be overcome by tending to one's roots. Tobe is described as an embodiment of the "main cannibal spirit" of the "wetigoes and the hairy hearts" (471, 469) who populate the city in Seesequasis's story as well as Cree oral tradition, where they feed on and kill humans. Uncle Morris, on the other hand, is "a *rigoureau*; [the] mixed-blood shape-shifter" of Métis tradition (470), a hybrid figure much closer to the Cree culture hero *wîsahkêcâhk* than to the French loup-garou from which the Métis word *rigoureau* is derived.[16]

The allusions to Cree and Métis oral traditions—*wîhtikow*, hairy hearts, *wîsahkêcâhk*, *rigoureau*—provide Seesequasis's story with much of its interpretative context. Not only do these allusions evoke a multitude of outside texts; they are also part of a series of yet other phrases that, in their entirety, "embody" the story's main conflict between purity politics and kinship and help establish the central binary structure of Seesequasis's narrative, thus providing it with its narrative grid. These other phrases include, for example, the "urban animals" (472) or "urban orphans" (470, 471, 473) who, "without pedigree" (469) or "colonial pedigree papers" (470), have "fallen between the seams" (468) of ethnic purity, inhabiting that "no-man's land between Indian and white" (469). They are exiled by Chief Tobe and his fellow politicians, administrators of "bureaucratic apartheid" (468), "pure-bred breeders" (469) who exercise coercive forms of power characteristic of Euro-Western nation-states and thus become "Indian-crats" (473). Rulers at the colonizer's mercy, they don't seem to realize that their work is part of the "Wild Jean's Indian Affairs Bandwagon and Wild West Show" (470), from which only the colonizers will profit. The story's satiric climax is reached when Tobe becomes chief of what the narrator calls the "Fermentation of Saskatchewan Indian Nations" (468–69). This parody—a play on the Federation of Saskatchewan Indian Nations—exposes the consumptive desires of the cannibal spirits as much as it points to the breaking down of traditional notions of peoplehood through government intervention and internalized colonialism.

Let me come back to the question of how relational word bundles actually function in Indigenous discourse. The phrases I have discussed

---

16   Warren Cariou, "Dances with Rigoureau," in *Troubling Tricksters: Revisioning Critical Conversations*, ed. Deanna Reder and Linda M. Morra (Waterloo: Wilfrid Laurier University Press, 2010), 160–61.

above are essentially relational word bundles and share the following characteristics:

(a) they are figures of speech of some kind or another (metaphor, paradox, etc.),

(b) they perform a significant narrative function by creating the story's central binary structure (the conflict between purity politics and kingship), and

(c) they hold the story together, thus forming its narrative grid.

What is more, the series of relational word bundles in "The Republic of Tricksterism" is also *synecdoche writ large*: in their interdependence, the story's relational word bundles (*part*) are able to suggest the story (*whole*). In so doing, they not only serve functions similar to those of holophrases in Indigenous-language discourse, but they also embody Indigenous notions of community as synecdochic.[17] The central theme of Seesequasis's story—kinship—is then reflected also on a formal level. Based on the discussion above, we may thus define relational word bundles as figures of speech that perform a significant narrative function and, combined with other such figures, constitute the narrative grid of a given story (see table 2.4).

Take, for example, Seesequasis's phrase "a moment of time that lasts forever." The phrase is a paradox, a seemingly self-contradictory observation: no moment of time lasts forever—if it did, it wouldn't be a moment—and yet this moment will carry on, in other forms or ways, even after it has ended, just like the Republic of Tricksterism lives on beyond the eventual death of Uncle Morris, provided the people remember to remember. As a paradox (that is, a rhetorical figure), the phrase "a moment of time that lasts forever" carries an additional bundle of meaning: it is a circumlocution for the Republic of Tricksterism that is introduced in Seesequasis's story as a direct contrast to the permanence that the self-government toward which Chief Tobe is heading purports to bring. This self-government, on the other hand, is repeatedly associated with the "cannibal spirits," a metaphor and intertextual reference to Cree oral tradition (and thus, by definition, a rhetorical figure). These two phrases, then— "a moment of time that lasts forever" and "cannibal spirits"—express the story's main conflict, between purity politics and kinship. What is more,

---

17   Weaver, *That the People Might Live*, 39.

that same conflict is expressed in other binary pairs found throughout the story—such as "pure-bred breeders" and "no-man's land between Indian and white"—which in turn also function as rhetorical figures, such as (in the case of the example above) metaphor. Because that conflict between purity politics and kinship is evoked in a *whole series of phrases*, Seesequasis's story is literally held together by a set of interrelated phrases. Relational word bundles, then, establish relationships between themselves and other such figures and, in so doing, create an ever bigger figure of speech, *synecdoche writ large*, the narrative grid standing for the narrative. Simply put, the relational word bundle achieves in Indigenous discourse in English what the holophrase achieves in ancestral-language discourse; namely, it invents narrative. Relational word bundles are the driving force of Indigenous storytelling and writing in English.

TABLE 2.4 DEFINITIONS AND EXAMPLES OF RELATIONAL WORD BUNDLES

RELATIONAL WORD BUNDLE

any kind of figure of speech that has a significant narrative function and, together with other such figures, forms a given text's narrative grid

ELEMENT	DEFINITION	EXAMPLES/EXPLANATION
figure of speech	any enhanced use of language that involves a change in the meaning of a word	*metaphor* "fallen between the seams" *synecdoche* using "wheels" to mean "car" *backshadowing* (figure of recovery/recollection) *foreshadowing* (figure of anticipation)
significant narrative function	to help produce a given text's narrative structure	opening and closing frames; binary narrative structures; cyclical narrative structures; weaving together of scattered stories/poems
a text's narrative grid	a series of narrative units that can hold the text together	synecdoche writ large: a series of relational word bundles standing for the narrative

Relational word bundles are, arguably, significant discourse structures. Part of their significance lies in the fact that they concern both the content and the form of discourse: they are both figures of speech and significant narrative units and therefore influence the *arrangement* of discourse as well as its *style* and *arguments*. To understand the full scope of relational word bundles, one must understand this rhetorical structure in relation to the main canons of rhetoric that are relevant to the study of written texts: invention (*what is said*), style (*how it is said*), and arrangement (*how what is said is structured*), which I will discuss below in the reverse order.[18]

Arrangement (Dispositio)

Of course, every narrative unit has meaning and so performs some kind of a function, but narrative units can be distinguished based on their relevance within a given narrative: some units are simply more important than others.[19] A figure that functions as a significant narrative unit exists only insofar as there are in any given text always also figures or other narrative units that are less significant simply because they do not contribute to the narrative's grid. Giving discourse its specific shape—for example, by creating the pattern of binary structures in Seesequasis's story, which embodies the story's central conflict between kinship and purity politics—relational word bundles perform significant narrative functions. In their ability to structure narrative in one way or another, relational word bundles thus also speak directly to the question of arrangement, or how narrative is structured.

Style

Figures of speech are enhanced uses of language. As figures that involve a change in the meaning of a word, relational word bundles contain a "big huge bundle" of meaning that is never explicitly stated; whatever additional meaning is wrapped up in this word bundle has to be inferred by the audience. Relational word bundles thus determine a text's style. As a series of figures that in their interdependence turn into an even larger figure (*synecdoche writ large*), relational word bundles create discourse that tends to be inexplicit and indirect, therefore depending heavily on the participation of the audience. In Seesequasis's story, readers need to unravel the hidden meaning of phrases such as "cannibal spirits" and "no-man's land between Indian and white," but ultimately they also need to discern the

---

18 The other two canons, memory and delivery, concern primarily oral text. The following discussion of the rhetoric of relational word bundles is based on the assumption that narrative has the ability to argue and persuade. For a discussion of the rhetoric of narrative, see John Rodden, "How Do Stories Convince Us?: Notes towards a Rhetoric of Narrative," *College Literature* 35.1 (2008): 148–73.

19 Roland Barthes discussed the relative significance of narrative units within narrative, in "An Introduction to the Structural Analysis of Narrative," *New Literary History* 6.2 (1975): 246–48.

connection between these two metaphors and the other relational word bundles in the story to fully grasp the issue Seesequasis criticizes in "The Republic of Tricksterism." Further, some relational word bundles take the form of intertextual or intratextual references; that is, they evoke an outside text or a different passage in the same text. In these cases, their bundle of meaning lies in establishing narrative relations, either inside or outside the text, and this is also reflected in the rhetorical figures on which they are based (see table 2.5). Relational word bundles that take the form of intratextual references include *backshadowing* (to an earlier point in the narrative) and *foreshadowing* (to a later point in the narrative), which are based on the figure of recovery/recollection and the figure of anticipation, respectively.

TABLE 2.5 RELATIONAL WORD BUNDLES THAT ESTABLISH NARRATIVE RELATIONS

	RELATIONAL WORD BUNDLES	
TYPE	**NARRATIVE PROCESSES INVOLVED**	**FIGURES INVOLVED**
intratextual reference	*backshadowing* referring to an earlier moment / phrase / passage in the narrative	figure of recollection / recovery
	foreshadowing referring to a later moment / phrase / passage in the narrative	figure of anticipation
intertextual reference	*intertextuality* referring to an outside text	synecdoche

Relational word bundles that take the form of intertextual references, on the other hand, involve synecdoche because they evoke an outside text (e.g., Cree story of Creation) by referring to one of its parts (e.g., *wîsah-kêcâhk* in Seesequasis's "The Republic of Tricksterism").

Invention

Figures of speech also constitute small arguments and thus point to the interdependence of invention and style, that is, between *what* is said and *how* it is said. In classic rhetoric, common categories of thought—so-called topoi—are used to generate, or invent, arguments. More specifically, E. F. Dyck argues that figures of speech are enthymemes (shortened syllogisms) that are derived from a particular topos.[20] The topos of analogy, for example, is the basis of metaphor, a figure in which two elements are linked by analogy. Seesequasis's metaphor "no-man's land between Indian and white," for example, contains a hidden argument, which unfolds like this:

> If the space between two nations that belongs to neither one of them is a no-man's land, and if, moreover, the "space" between Indian and white is analogous to that "empty" space between nations, then those people who are neither purely Indian nor purely white live in the no-man's land between Indian and white: they are neither Indian nor white and have but themselves.

Seesequasis's "no-man's land between Indian and white," however, needs to be seen in connection with the story's other relational word bundles, including "pure-bred breeders," in order to realize its full potential within the story. In "The Republic of Tricksterism," it is the pure-bred breeders' politics of purity that creates "urban orphans," individuals of Native ancestry who are relegated to the "no-man's land between Indian and white." Once these two relational word bundles are connected, a more substantial argument arises, namely, a critique of the politics of purity. As complex figures of speech—relational word bundles combine with other relational word bundles to form the narrative grid of a given text, hence functioning as synecdoche writ large—relational word bundles contribute substantially to a given narrative's underlying argument: they create a *series* of interdependent smaller arguments that allows narrative to persuade.

HOLOPHRASTIC READING AS MAPPING

Evoking three of the five canons of rhetoric—arrangement, style, and invention—relational word bundles are a more or less "holistic embodiment" of rhetoric. This in turn makes relational word bundles such salient structures of Indigenous discourse in English. Why, you may wonder, would this observation matter to a reader of Indigenous literatures? Well, reading is much like *writing backwards*: that is, as readers we may attempt

---

20   E. F. Dyck, "Topos in Rhetorical Argumentation: From Enthymeme to Figure," in *Proceedings of the Fifth International Conference of the International Society for the Study of Argumentation*, ed. Frans H. van Eemeren, Rob Grootendorst, J. Anthony Blair, and Charles A. Willard (Amsterdam: SIC SAT, 2003), 261.

to trace the writer's thought processes as they made it onto the printed page. For this purpose, we can use structures as reading tools. Earlier in this chapter, I used the metaphor of reading as navigating an unknown territory with the help of a map. As readers, we all look for textual clues that may help us gather an understanding of what we are reading—just as travellers use the information provided in a map to get from A to B. In the case of holophrastic reading, these clues are provided by holophrastic traces and relational word bundles, the two main manifestations of holophrases in English-language discourse. To perform a holophrastic reading of an Indigenous text, therefore, means to let one's understanding of the text be guided by reading for holophrastic traces and relational word bundles. Above all, then, holophrastic reading is a reading strategy that readers can use to "navigate" Indigenous discourse. How readers end up interpreting the text in question is an entirely different matter, of course—just as there exist different possible ways of getting from A to B, which in turn may be influenced by the kind of map one is using (a road atlas, a geographical map, or a political map). In this sense, holophrastic reading is always only a means to an end, never the end itself; it facilitates interpretation but it is not interpretation itself. It is, in other words, not part of a particular literary theory; rather, it forms part of Indigenous poetics, the art of reading Indigenous discourse from within its own language and discourse traditions.

Before closing this chapter, let us look in more detail at this notion of reading as mapping. The Cree people, for example, map *nêhiyânâhk* (Cree country) by way of place names that evoke certain stories and knowledge of the land that is important for the survival of *nêhiyawak*, the Cree people. In their interdependence, these place names form the geographical frame of *nêhiyânâhk* as well as the cultural, historical, and spiritual frames of Cree peoplehood—frames that may shift over time as traditional stories and knowledge are reinterpreted and new stories and knowledges emerge. If mapping a text by studying its narrative structure is like mapping the land (e.g., by studying its various forms), then relational word bundles are the land markers—the place names, if you will—that help readers move through the stories, investing them with meaning. In their interdependence, these story markers become a story's narrative grid, holding the text together. Relational word bundles thus connect an individual figure of speech with the text's structure; they link the special with the general, the part with the whole. Where do holophrastic traces fit into this metaphor of reading as moving within an unknown territory? Holophrastic traces tend to be less prominent in Indigenous writing than do relational word bundles, although they may be more easily spotted by readers with an eye for unconventional uses of English. And yet, reading for holophrastic traces is as much a part of holophrastic reading as reading for relational word bundles. Rather than pointing readers to a text's narrative structure, as in the case of relational word bundles, holophrastic traces help readers of Indigenous stories to navigate these texts by providing important contexts, whether they be linguistic, spiritual, or cultural. Holophrastic traces are at their most potent, however, when they also function as relational word bundles; this does not happen very often, but when it does, the effect is all the more powerful.

As I have repeatedly stressed, holophrastic reading is not the only available (let alone meaningful) method for reading Indigenous literatures, but it is arguably a significant contribution to Indigenous poetics, because it generates readings of Indigenous literatures that are grounded in Indigenous language and discourse traditions (see fig. 2.6).

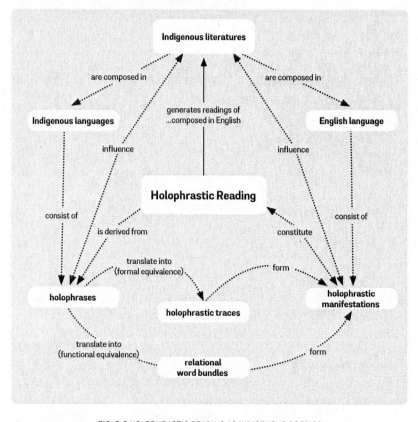

FIG. 2.6 HOLOPHRASTIC READING AS INDIGENOUS POETICS

Finding a balance between form and content, between text and context(s), holophrastic reading provides a formal foundation for the study of Indigenous literatures, all the while contributing to the discussion of the issues raised and critiqued by Indigenous texts, old and new. As a reading method rather than a literary approach, holophrastic reading can be applied in a broad range of interpretative settings, as the holophrastic readings presented in part 2 will demonstrate.

FURTHER READING

A comprehensive, though also more theoretical, discussion of the formal and functional equivalents of the holophrase is found in the introductory chapter of *"That's Raven Talk": Holophrastic Readings of Contemporary Indigenous Literatures* (Regina: CPRC Press, 2011). I have discussed issues of terminology and ethics in holophrastic reading, in the dialogue "'Holo What?' or, The Exceptional Business of Naming: A Dialogue" (*ESC: English Studies in Canada* 37.1 [2012]). A more detailed discussion of Paul Seesequasis's story is found in my article "Indigenous Rhetorics and Kinship: Towards a Rhetoric of Relational Word Bundles" (*Canadian Journal of Native Studies* 33.1 [2013]).

ALPHABETICAL LIST OF CRITICAL TERMS

ADJECTIVE-NOUN COMPOUND

A **compound** that is derived from combining an adjective with a noun, the latter serving as the **head** (*a train's engine*). In these examples, heads are marked in boldface:

high **school**; black**board**

AFFIX (in linguistics)

A syllable added to the base or stem of a word, either to modify its meaning or to form a new word. Affixes attached at the beginning of a word are called **prefixes**, while those attached to the end of a word are called **suffixes**.

AFFIXATION (in linguistics)

The process of attaching an **affix** to a word, either to modify its meaning or to invent an entirely new word.

"go" + "s" (third person singular) = goes

"drive" + "er" = driver

AGGLUTINATING (of a language)

Referring to a language in which **morphemes** usually represent a single unit of meaning (e.g., past tense, number, gender), such as Turkish. *See also* **Fusional**.

ANALYTIC (of a language)

Referring to a language that uses only a single **morpheme** per word and expresses grammatical relations in the form of separate words, such as Chinese or Vietnamese. *See also* **Synthetic**.

BACKSHADOWING (in narratology)

The process of making an intratextual reference to a moment earlier in the narrative; also called analepsis, retroversion, or flashback; based on the figure of recollection/recovery.

CODE SWITCHING

The switching back and forth between two languages in the course of speaking or writing.

COMPOUND

A composite of two words or more—noun, verb, adjective, or preposition—one of which serves as the **head**, determining the compound's semantic category; all other elements are mere **modifiers** of the **head**—or, to use the imagery of a compound as a train, the head is the train's engine, and the modifiers are the cars pulled by the engine. In these examples, the heads are marked in boldface:

song**bird**; draw**bridge**; cat **house**

COMPOUND NOUN

A **compound** that acts as a noun.

drawbridge; cat house; basketball

COMPOUND VERB

A **compound** that acts as a verb.

highlight; panfry

CONCEPTUAL ORALITY

A term introduced by Koch and Oesterreicher (1985) to describe a type of orality that is independent of the medium; it is characterized by a **language of immediacy**.

DEVERBAL (in linguistics)

Referring to a word, such as noun or adjective, that is derived from a verb.

"swim" + "er" = swimmer

"natural" + "ize" = naturalize

DIRECT HOLOPHRASTIC TRACES

Traces of the morphological structure of the **holophrase**; one of two classes of holophrastic traces, the formal equivalents of the **holophrase** in English-language discourse. May take the form of idiom-like **lexical phrases**; **quotation compounds**; **synthetic compounds**; **compound nouns** with verbal **modifier**; and **deverbal noun-noun compounds**. *See also* **Indirect holophrastic traces**.

ECHO OF INDIGENOUS VERB COMPLEXITY

A discourse feature that mirrors the complex structure of Indigenous verbs; reflected in Indigenous discourse in English by **pronoun copying** and **subject dropping**. *See also* **Holistic verbs**.

EVIDENTIALITY (in linguistics)

The process of identifying or qualifying one's (source of) knowledge.

EVIDENTIALS (in linguistics)

Those grammatical or narrative units that identify or qualify one's (source of) knowledge. *See also* **Quotative**.

FIGURES OF SPEECH

Any enhanced use of language. Rhetoricians usually distinguish between two categories of figures of speech: tropes, which involve a change in the meaning of a word (e.g., metaphor, synecdoche, metonymy); and schemes, which involve a change in the arrangement of words (e.g., alliteration, anaphora).

FORESHADOWING (in narratology)

The process of making an intratextual reference to a moment later in the narrative; also called prolepsis or flashforward. Based on the figure of anticipation.

FORMAL EQUIVALENCE

An approach to translation that strives for an equivalence of form, that is, the particular structure of a word/phrase/text/concept. *See also* **Functional equivalence**.

FUNCTIONAL EQUIVALENCE
An approach to translation that strives for an equivalence of function, that is, the specific role and purpose performed by a word/phrase/text/ concept in a specific context. *See also* **Formal equivalence.**

FUSIONAL (of a language)
Referring to a language in which the **morphemes** cannot be distinguished from each other, such as Russian, which fuses the grammatical categories of number and case into one **morpheme**. *See also* **Agglutinating.**

HEAD (in linguistics)
That component of a **compound** that defines its semantic category; to use the imagery of the compound as a train, the train's engine. In these examples, heads are marked in boldface:
truck **driver**; night **swimmer**; bird**song**

HOLISTIC VERB (in linguistics)
A term used by Chafe (2004) to describe the ability of verbs in holophrastic languages to express both the event (verb) and all its participants (subject, object). *See also* **Echoes of Indigenous verb complexity.**

HOLOPHRASE (in North American Indigenous languages)
A single word that expresses a complete sentence or clause.
kinohtehâcimostâtinâwâw (Plains Cree for "I want to tell you folks a story")

HOLOPHRASIS (in linguistic morphology); ALSO **POLYSYNTHESIS**
The process of joining both lexical and grammatical **morpheme**s into one word to form what in Indo-European languages corresponds to a complete sentence.

HOLOPHRASTIC TRACES
Traces of the **holophrase** on the level of form (i.e., grammar); **direct holophrastic traces** are traces of the morphological structure of the holophrase, whereas **indirect holophrastic traces** are traces of discourse features invited by **holophrasis.**

INDIRECT HOLOPHRASTIC TRACES

Traces of discourse features invited by the use of **holophrases**; one of two classes of holophrastic traces, the formal equivalents of the **holophrase** in English-language discourse. May take the form of **evidentials, echoes of Indigenous verb complexity**, descriptive or figurative uses of language, or **textual silences**. *See also* **Direct holophrastic traces**.

INTERTEXTUALITY

A term used to describe the interaction and relations between texts; every text is thought to refer and relate to earlier texts, either through participatory or transformatory processes.

LANGUAGE OF IMMEDIACY

A term introduced by Koch and Oesterreicher (1985) to describe a language that is characterized by a high degree of immediacy between speaker/author and listener/reader; it is characterized by low degrees of information density, compactness of language, integration, complexity, elaborateness, and planning.

LANGUE (French, meaning "language")

The abstract system of language; the term is used by Ferdinand de Saussure in his *Course in General Linguistics* (1960) to distinguish the system of language (*langue*) from the actual utterances that are produced based on this system (*parole*). *See also* **Parole**.

LEXICAL PHRASE (in linguistics)

A series of words that form a set expression of some sort and whose internal form cannot be changed (or only slightly so).

so be it; rock the boat

META-FICTION

A text's self-reflexive tendencies; more specifically, fiction that addresses the conventions of fiction, often in a playful and self-conscious manner.

METAPHOR

A **figure of speech** that is based on the **topos** of analogy and describes the process of referring to one thing or person as if it were another.

"Life is a highway"; he was a lion in the battle

METONYMY

A **figure of speech** that is based on the **topos** of contiguity (subject/adjuncts) and describes the process of referring to a thing or person by naming one of its attributes.

"Parliament Hill" for the Canadian government

"the Crown" for the British monarchy

"tongue" for language

"china" for Chinese (and other) porcelain and ceramic

MODIFIER (in linguistics)

That element of a **compound** that modifies its **head**; to use the imagery of the compound as a train, one of the train's cars pulled by the train's engine. In these examples, modifiers are marked in boldface:

night swimmer; **song**bird

MORPHEME (in linguistics)

The smallest meaningful unit in the grammar of a given language. A word consists of at least one morpheme, but not all morphemes can stand on their own. In these examples, free-standing morphemes are marked in boldface:

dis**belief** ("dis" + "belief"); un**natural** ("un" + "natural")

NARRATOLOGY

The study of narrative structures and the ways they affect meaning in narrative.

NOUN–NOUN COMPOUND

A **compound** that is derived from a concatenation of nouns.

cat house; football; housewife; lawsuit; basketball

ORAL STRATEGIES

Strategies associated with a **language of immediacy**; markers of **conceptual orality**.

ORATURE

Orally communicated and received texts, including a people's or culture's oral tradition. Introduced as an alternative term for the still more commonly used "oral literature," orature grants oral texts their own validity because it does not mark them as inferior or as merely a transitional phase in a people's or culture's development to a literate society.

OXYMORON

A **figure of speech** that describes a condensed **paradox**; placing two contradictory words aside each other; a strong contradiction.

"pretty ugly"; Simon and Garfunkel's song title "The Sound of Silence"

PARADOX

A **figure of speech** that describes an observation or statement that is self-contradictory but may yet contain some truth.

"a moment of time that lasts forever"

PARAHOLOPHRASE (from para, Greek for "analoguous to, yetn different from"); ALSO **RELATIONAL WORD BUNDLE**

The term used in *"That's Raven Talk"* to describe the functional equivalent of the **holophrase**.

PAROLE (French, meaning "speech")

The actual utterances produced by an individual; the term is used by Ferdinand de Saussure in his *Course in General Linguistics* (1960) to distinguish actual speech acts (*parole*) from the system of language from which they are derived (*langue*). *See also* **Langue**.

POETICS (from *poesis*, Greek for "making")

In a very narrow sense, the art of making poetry; in a broader sense, the art of making discourse more generally; a general theory of discourse, here understood to imply specifically the art of *reading* discourse.

POLYSYNTHESIS (in linguistic morphology); ALSO **HOLOPHRASIS**

The process of joining both lexical and grammatical **morpheme**s into one word to form what in Indo-European languages corresponds to a complete sentence.

PREFIX (in linguistics)

An **affix** attached to the beginning of a word, either to modify its meaning or to form an entirely new word. In these examples, prefixes are marked in boldface:

review; **re**do; **pre**view; **un**comfortable; **dis**qualify

PRONOUN COPYING (in linguistics)

The repetition of a subject or object noun or pronoun; in English, restricted to colloquial language. Used in Indigenous discourse in

English, pronoun copying functions as an **echo of Indigenous verb complexity.**

My wife, she hates to cook.

Me, I've never liked soccer.

QUOTATION COMPOUND

A phrase, clause, or sentence that may be analyzed as a single unit; hence not necessarily a **compound** but an utterance that often reads like a little snippet of speech quoted from elsewhere.

Eli Stands Alone; Count My Blessings Grandmother

QUOTATIVE

A grammatical unit that marks reported speech; an indicator of **evidentiality.**

be like; he said; I says

RELATIONAL WORD BUNDLE; ALSO PARAHOLOPHRASE

The functional equivalent of the **holophrase**; a **figure of speech** that has significant narrative function and, together with other such figures, forms a given text's narrative grid; **synecdoche writ large.**

SUBJECT DROPPING

The process of dropping the grammatical subject in a sentence or clause; often found in colloquial speech; the assumption is that the subject may be gathered from the context. Used in Indigenous discourse in English, subject dropping functions as an **echo of Indigenous verb complexity.**

SUFFIX (in linguistics)

An affix attached to the end of a word, either to modify its meaning or to form an entirely new word. In these examples, suffixes are marked in boldface:

house**s**; show**ed**; sing**er**

SYNECDOCHE

A **figure of speech** that is based on the **topos** of division and involves the substitution of a part for its whole.

wheels used to mean "car"

banana used to mean "I want a banana"

SYNECDOCHE WRIT LARGE

Synecdoche not on the word level but on the discourse level. *See also* **Holophrase; Relational word bundle.**

SYNTHETIC (of a language)

Referring to a language with a high number of **morpheme**s per word, such as Greek, Spanish, French, Polish, and German. *See also* **Analytic.**

SYNTHETIC COMPOUND

A **compound** that uses a **deverbalized head** (*a train's engine*; marked in boldface in the examples below).

truck **driver**; night **traveller**

TEXTUALIZED ORALITY

The use of **oral strategies** in written discourse; a particular form of **conceptual orality**.

TEXTUALIZED ORATURE

An oral discourse that has been put into writing or print; the transcription of an example of **orature**. The published stories of the late Okanagan storyteller Harry Robinson are examples of textualized orature: they were recorded, transcribed, and eventually published in print.

TEXTUAL SILENCES

A text's deliberate keeping away of information, intended to draw the audience further into the text. Wolfgang Iser (1976) has described textual silences as *Leerstellen* (German for "empty spaces"), gaps in the text that readers need to fill with meaning in the process of reading.

TOPOS

In classic rhetoric, a category of thought that is used to generate or invent an argument. Thus, the topos of analogy is used to generate a metaphor, a figure in which one thing or person is referred to or spoken of as though it were another.

VERB–NOUN COMPOUND

A **compound noun** with a verbal **modifier**; that is, a **compound** that is derived from combining a verb stem with a noun, with the latter serving as **head** (*a train's engine*; marked in boldface in the examples below).

pickpocket; **draw**bridge

PART 2

HOLOPHRASTIC READINGS OF INDIGENOUS WRITING

CHAPTER 4

ANCESTRAL LANGUAGE INFLUENCES

B efore contact, about three hundred different languages were spoken in North America. After more than five hundred years of colonialism and forced assimilation, many of these languages are now extinct, including, for example, Beothuk, a language isolate spoken in Newfoundland; the Iroquoian languages Huron-Wendat and Laurentian; Ts'ets'aut, an Athabaskan language spoken in British Columbia; and the Salish language Pentlatch, also native to British Columbia.[1] In North America today, 184 Indigenous languages remain alive; however, only around twenty of these languages "are still being learned at home by children."[2] With the number of fluent speakers rapidly declining, many Indigenous languages are endangered or near-extinct. In fact, although a few languages remain comparatively strong (including Nêhiyawêwin, Anishnaabemowin, and Inuktitut[3]), and although

---

1   Darin Flynn, "Decline of Aboriginal languages," University of Calgary website, accessed January 27, 2013, http://www.ucalgary.ca/dflynn/aboriginal/aboriginal-languages-of-canada/decline-of-aboriginal-languages.

2   Leanne Hinton, "Language Revitalization," *Annual Review of Applied Linguistics* 23 (2003): 44.

3   Nêhiyawêwin (Cree) is an Algonquian language spoken in Aboriginal communities from the Northwest Territories and Alberta to Labrador in the east and parts of Montana in the south. Variants and dialects of Anishnaabemowin, also in the Algonquian language family, are spoken in southwestern Quebec, Ontario, Manitoba,

Indigenous communities in both Canada and the United States have worked to revitalize ancestral languages, some scholars predict that of the extant Indigenous languages "only 10 percent have a chance of enduring beyond the second decade in the new millennium."[4] Whether or not this prediction indeed holds true, the first language of many Indigenous people in North America today is one of the colonizer's languages. Wherever ancestral linguistic traditions have been destroyed or interrupted and Indigenous voices are expressed in English, English is used as a language of choice by Indigenous people for Indigenous purposes and is, in the process, indigenized: that is, some of the linguistic and discursive features of the respective ancestral language are incorporated into the English used by Indigenous people. The result is sometimes referred to as Red or Rez English, an Indigenous English code that coexists with standard uses of English all across Indigenous North America. Strictly speaking, however, Indigenous English per se does not exist, because the base for indigenized variants of English is always formed by a given ancestral language.[5] There are, in other words, as many different Indigenous English codes as there are languages indigenous to North America.[6]

Indigenous English may be encountered in a variety of discourse settings, ranging from informal and communal to educational and literary. Regardless of its context of use, however, Indigenous English always marks an expression of Indigenous rhetorical sovereignty. Wherever Indigenous people decide to use an Indigenous English code rather than standard English, they excise their rhetorical sovereignty, that is, their "inherent right and ability . . . to determine their own communicative needs and desires in [their pursuit of sovereignty], to decide for themselves the goals, modes, styles, and languages of public discourse."[7] In the published stories by the late Okanagan storyteller Harry Robinson, for example, we can make out a use of English that is clearly inflected by his ancestral Okanagan, a Southern Salish language native to British Columbia and Washington State. In the following passage taken from one of

---

and parts of Saskatchewan as well as in Michigan, Wisconsin, Minnesota, and parts of North Dakota and Montana. Inuktitut, belonging to the Eskimo-Aleut language family, is spoken in Alaska, the Yukon, the Northwest Territories, Nunavut, Nunavik (northern Quebec), Nunatsiavut (northern Labrador), and Greenland.

4   White, "Language Reflection and Lamentation," 95.

5   Leap, *American Indian English*, 91.

6   Guillermo Bartelt, "American Indian English in Momaday's *House Made of Dawn*," *Language and Literature* 19 (1994): 38.

7   Lyons, "Rhetorical Sovereignty," 449–50.

Robinson's stories, "Puss in Boots," Okanagan influences are marked in italics.

> He force *'em.*
> He beat *'em.*
> Otherwise, *if they don't do that, he kill him.*
> So he really beat *'em* anyway.[8]
> Well, old man, he thought,
> Supposing if *I [am] against him.*
> *He [is] going* to kill me
> and I'm going to die right now.[9]

Robinson's use of the English language is sometimes stereotyped as evidence of a lack of education, when in fact it is a result of his translating his stories directly from Okanagan into English. Marked by an Okanagan English code, Robinson's stories are able to communicate Okanagan knowledge in ways that are reflective of Okanagan language, discourse practices, and worldviews. A reading for ancestral language influences in Robinson's works, and in that of other elders and storytellers, therefore allows us to illustrate the rhetorical ingenuity of Indigenous discourse composed in an Indigenous English code, thereby combatting persistent stereotypes in mainstream society about Indigenous uses of English as inferior to standard English. To put it differently, paying close attention to the language, forms, and structures of contemporary Indigenous discourse actually helps readers gain a deeper understanding of the texts they are reading.

How can readers of Indigenous literatures possibly detect ancestral language influences in Indigenous discourse that is composed in English? It is true that advanced studies of ancestral language influences in Indigenous writing and storytelling require some knowledge of the respective ancestral language. For example, to notice the Okanagan influences in Harry Robinson's stories, one would need to know two things about Robinson's mother tongue: First, Okanagan does not differentiate between third person singular and plural ("he," "she," "it," "they"). Second, Okanagan makes extensive use of equative constructions that lack any form of the verb "to be" (i.e., a copula). These two grammatical features are mirrored

---

8   Robinson, *Write It on Your Heart,* 286; emphases mine.
9   Ibid., 285–86; emphasis mine.

in Robinson's "random" use of third person pronouns ("if *they* don't do that, he kill *him*") and his occasional deletion of forms of the verb "to be" (*"He going* to kill me"). For anyone who does not speak Okanagan, Robinson's unorthodox pronoun uses and verb constructions will read merely as a violation of the rules of standard English. Advanced studies of ancestral language influences in Indigenous writing in English therefore require an intimate study of the respective ancestral language. At the same time, however, some ancestral language influences may yet be detected by even the lay reader, simply by reading Indigenous texts for holophrastic traces. After all, holophrastic traces are essentially ancestral language influences. Whether they take the form of words or phrases that mimic the holistic structure of holophrases in Indigenous-language discourse (direct holophrastic traces) or mark discourse features that, in one way or another, are invited by the use of holophrases (indirect holophrastic traces), holophrastic traces are the formal manifestations of the holophrase in English-language discourse. The holophrase, in turn, is a dominant language feature of many of the languages indigenous to North America. Accordingly, holophrastic traces may be regarded as ancestral language influences, if of a more general nature and only with regard to Indigenous texts whose ancestral language traditions are indeed holophrastic. In other words, reading for holophrastic traces often serves as the foundation of more specialized studies on ancestral language influences in Indigenous writing and storytelling in English. What is more, as a reading method it is a very powerful tool because it allows readers without any knowledge of an ancestral language to develop a sensibility for Indigenous uses of English; it is this sensibility that invites readers to look at the English used by Indigenous storytellers and writers, thinking outside that very language, and thus to understand Indigenous texts on their terms.

It is not so difficult, then, for readers of Indigenous literatures to become more attuned, to listen more deeply to Indigenous uses of English and some of the deeper layers of meaning that these uses may indicate in Indigenous writing and storytelling. All it requires is attentive reading: readers must pay attention to the more formal features of literary discourse. This task may be facilitated by the holophrastic heuristic offered in chapter 2 (see tables 2.2 and 2.3). Holophrastic traces are formal language features that have important discourse functions and affect how a text produces meaning; as such, holophrastic traces are part of an Indigenous poetics that aims at approaching Indigenous texts from within the very language and discourse traditions from which these texts derive. The specific functions of holophrastic traces, of course, always depend on the text in question, and holophrastic traces may be put to a variety of uses by readers of Indigenous literatures. Above all, however, reading for holophrastic traces proves to be a particularly useful method of tracing expressions of rhetorical sovereignty in Indigenous writing and storytelling, as will become apparent in the following discussion of *Keeper'n Me* (1994), the debut novel of Anishnaabe writer Richard Wagamese; *Stories of the Road Allowance People* (1993/2010), a story collection translated by Métis writer Maria Campbell; and "Puss in Boots," the retelling of a European folktale by Okanagan storyteller Harry Robinson.

RICHARD WAGAMESE'S *KEEPER'N ME*

The central theme of Richard Wagamese's *Keeper'n Me* is homecoming. The novel's protagonist, Garnet Raven, is a twenty-five-year-old Anishnaabe who was separated from his family at the age of three, falling victim to the infamous "sixties scoop-up"—the practice of the Children's Aid Society of forcefully adopting Native children out into non-Native families, in an attempt to further assimilate Indigenous people into mainstream Canadian society. Garnet grows up in foster homes but eventually runs away and starts living on the streets. In Toronto, an Afro-Canadian family takes him in as one of their own, but when Garnet gets caught dealing drugs he is put in jail, which is where one of his brothers eventually tracks him down. The main focus of *Keeper'n Me* is the story of Garnet's return to his family's reserve, White Dog, in Northern Ontario—some twenty years after he was forcefully separated from his roots and family—and his subsequent quest to find his place in the world of White Dog and beyond.

Most of *Keeper'n Me* is narrated by Garnet himself. His narration is interrupted occasionally by his teacher and friend Keeper, an Anishnaabe elder and friend of Garnet's grandfather, Harold Raven. Much of the novel is indeed Keeper's "story too" (4). Keeper had been picked by Harold to be the next keeper of the drum, which "holds the heartbeat of the people"; however, instead of staying with Harold and learning Anishnaabe teachings, Keeper disappeared into a world of alcoholism (71–72). When Garnet returns to White Dog, Keeper decides to be Garnet's guide and thus pay off his debt to Harold. The novel's title, then, evokes Anishnaabe notions of community and tradition or, given the main characters' history, a re-embracing of such notions. The elders teach the younger generation; as a result, traditional knowledges are passed down from one generation to the next, ensuring continuance of the community.

Keeper'n Me is divided into four "books," which trace the various stages of Garnet's homecoming: his return to White Dog (book 1); his introduction to Keeper (book 2); his learning the lessons of balance (book 3); and his spiritual journey (book 4).[10] These four stages correspond roughly with Garnet's spatial, linguistic, emotional, and spiritual homecoming. The different dimensions of Garnet's homecoming, in turn, reflect the four central elements that define peoplehood in Indigenous contexts:

- *land/territory* (spatial homecoming; book 1)
- *language* (linguistic homecoming; book 2)
- *sacred history* (emotional homecoming; book 3)
- *ceremonial cycle* (spiritual homecoming; book 4)

The interdependence of these four elements determines the social, cultural, political, and economic realities within a particular people or community, such as the Anishnaabe community of White Dog in *Keeper'n Me*.[11] As someone who has never known his people, Garnet needs to learn how to live among them, how to participate in the "relational reality" that characterizes this community, which implies that he must develop an understanding of "the tribal web of kinship rights and responsibilities that link the People, the land, and the cosmos together in an ongoing and dynamic system of mutually affecting relationships."[12] When, in the closing words of the novel, Garnet speaks of "that bumpy as hell gravel road" (214) that he had taken in a cab five years earlier, when he first came back to White Dog, this road can also be taken as a metaphor for Garnet's quest to find and stay "on that good red road" that teaches him to be a good human being, a good man, and a good Anishnaabe (189–90). For Garnet, then, to come home ultimately means to become a good Anishnaabe, to find both his own self and that self's position within the web of relationships that defines the community to which he belongs.

Walking "that good red road" is, of course, a process, not a state; the real challenge for Garnet isn't so much his gradual reintroduction to his family and White Dog—specifically, getting used to life on the reserve with all its peculiarities—but to live well among his people. According to

---

10   Geraldine Balzer, "'Bring[ing] Them Back from the Inside Out': Coming Home through Story in Richard Wagemese's *Keeper'n Me*," in "Textualizing Orature and Orality," ed. Susan Gingell, special issue, *Essays on Canadian Writing* 83 (2005): 234–36.

11   Holm, Chavis, and Pearson, "Peoplehood: A Model," 12 (see Introduction, note 5).

12   Daniel Heath Justice, *Our Fire Survives the Storm: A Cherokee Literary History* (Minneapolis: University of Minnesota Press, 2006), 24–25.

Neal McLeod (Cree), "the alienation from one's stories" amounts to "*ideological diaspora*: this alienation, the removal from the voices and echoes of the ancestors, is the attempt to destroy the collective consciousness." On the other hand, "'to be home' . . . [is] to dwell within the landscape of the familiar, a landscape of collective memories."[13] This landscape of collective memories is expressed in storytelling. Keeper's stories provide Garnet with guidance in his quest for belonging, giving him access to the collective imagination of his people. By telling his own personal story of homecoming in the space of the novel, Garnet in turn steps into Keeper's footsteps and assumes the role of a modern storyteller—as much a teacher as he is himself a student, and one who assumes responsibility for his community by giving back, thus continuing the cycle initiated by his grandfather when he had embraced Keeper as his student. In the end, then, *Keeper'n Me* tells the story of Garnet's "gravitating towards bein' a storyteller" (16). Indeed, this is exactly what Keeper, in his opening speech, envisions Garnet to be: "*But he learned and that's why I told him to write things down. Be a storyteller. Any damn fool can get people's attention but it takes a storyteller to get their attention and hold it. Lots of people out there gotta know what happened, how you found your way and what it takes to be an Indyun these days. Real Indyun, not that Hollywood kind. That's what I told him*" (3–4). Thus, it is when Garnet embraces the role of storyteller at the end of the novel that he has truly come home. He has received the gift of story and keeps it alive and strong to ensure his people's continuance.

In reading Garnet's story in *Keeper'n Me* as a continuation of Anishnaabe collective memories, the role of story in performances of peoplehood is emphasized. In fact, with Garnet Raven, Wagamese has invented not just any storyteller but one whose very use of language reflects his people's self-determination: Garnet communicates his people's stories by carrying Anishnaabe language and worldviews into English. As Wagamese explained in an interview with Paula E. Kirman, his own life served as the skeleton for *Keeper'n Me*, but his homecoming was different from Garnet's.[14] Wagamese is not Garnet, of course; yet, by writing a novel in English that borrows from Anishnaabemowin, the language of his people, Wagamese has achieved his own rhetorical homecoming. Readers may become witnesses to this homecoming by reading the novel for holophras-

13   Neal McLeod, "Coming Home through Stories," in *(Ad)dressing Our Words: Aboriginal Perspectives on Aboriginal Literatures*, ed. Armand Garnet Ruffo (Penticton, BC: Theytus Books, 2001), 19, 17.

14   Richard Wagamese, "Cultural Selves: An Interview with Richard Wagamese," by Paula E. Kirman, *Paragraph: The Canadian Fiction Review* 20.1 (Summer 1998): 4.

tic traces. Holophrastic reading alone is unable to capture the nuanced portrayal of Anishnaabe voices in *Keeper'n Me*; therefore, we have to pay attention to the novel's use both of holophrastic traces and of language more generally.

Once one analyzes the novel's nuanced uses of language in both dialogue and narration, it becomes evident that Wagamese employs different speech patterns for the different main characters in *Keeper'n Me*. As Geraldine Balzer points out, these speech patterns vary in their relative reliance on features of Anishnaabemowin, the Anishnaabe language.[15] By the time Garnet reconnects with his family, English has already become the main language used in the community, although generational differences in the ways it is used are clear. The English of Keeper and of Garnet's mother, for example, is clearly inflected by Anishnaabemowin; they speak a very strong Anishnaabe English code, which Wagamese signals to his readers through spelling, code switching, syntax, and inventive uses of language. As a rule, he renders the words on the page as they are actually pronounced by Keeper and by Garnet's mother. The Anishnaabemowin "sound" of their speech is suggested by using informal contractions (e.g., "lotta," "lotsa," "kindsa," "gotta," "useta"), deleting the final "-g" in present participle constructions, and exchanging consonants. Thus "Indian" becomes "Indyun," "tradition" turns into "TRA-DISH-UNN" (2), and "natural" is rendered "natchrel" (78). Wagamese further indigenizes the speech of Keeper and of Garnet's mother by incorporating the occasional Anishnaabemowin word, as exemplified in the following scenes (and marked in italics):

> He got up slowly and went into the cabin. I could hear things being moved around and finally the first faint glow of the fire flickered through the door as he opened it and gestured to me.
> "*Peen-dig-en. Peen-dig-en.* Come in. Got something to show you." (69; emphasis mine)

> "*Ahnee,*" he called from the top of the steps leading down to the dock behind Ma's. "*Minno gezheegut.* It's a good day. How's things?" (159)

> "*Ahnee,* my boy," she said and smiled. "*Nuhmutabin.* Sit here. Tea?"
> "Sure," I said, settling into the chair and looking around. "Nice view up here."

---

15 Balzer, "'Bring[ing] Them Back,'" 228–30.

"Hey-yuh," she said," Me, I come out here lots. Winter even too sometimes."

[. . .]

"Don't speak Indyun, eh?" she asked.

"No. Never learned."

"Ah, s'easy. What I said to you there, *nuhmutabin*, means sit. Try it."

"Me? Nah. I'll never learn."

"Never know 'less you try. *G'wan.*"

"Well. Okay." (54–55)

Keeper and the mother's switching back and forth between English and Anishnaabemowin further highlights the influence of the Anishnaabe language on their use of English. It also marks them as Anishnaabe who are still strong in the language of their people.

Wagamese uses yet another strategy besides "eye vernacular"[16] (rendering the words on the page as they are pronounced) and code switching to signal to readers the Anishnaabe English code on which Keeper and Garnet's mother rely. Moreover, this other strategy is clearly grounded in Indigenous language and discourse practices; in fact, it may be traced by reading the speech of these characters for holophrastic traces. Keeper and Garnet's mother's syntax disrupts the flow of "standard" English discourse, as Wagamese weaves into their use of English echoes of Anishnaabemowin verb complexity—one very dominant indirect holophrastic trace—as evident in the following two passages. (The first passage gives Keeper's words, the second Garnet's mother's; echoes are marked in boldface.)

> **Got used** to dealin' with time diff'rent even though they were just like us once. **They them** lost touch with the rhythm of the earth, left their drums behind a long time ago, forgot their old songs, their old teachings and got lost in the speed of things. (3)

> **Us we** were drinkin' it up all over. **Lucky** she found us. **Tol' me** 'bout the other two boys bein' okay an' then she tol' me you were gone, she di'n' know where. **We** cried together in that bush that day **me'n Jane.** (56)

---

16   Susan Gingell, "Lips' Inking: Cree and Cree-Metis Authors' Writings of the Oral and What They Might Tell Educators," *Canadian Journal of Native Education* 32 (2010): 49.

Two things are happening in these excerpts. In some cases, Keeper and Garnet's mother duplicate the subject of a sentence or clause by adding an additional pronoun ("us we," "they them") or a noun phrase ("We . . . me'n Jane"). In other cases, they delete the subject entirely ("Got used," "Tol' me"). Different though they are, pronoun copying and subject dropping mimic features of Anishnaabemowin discourse that are clearly invited by that language's use of holophrases. Like any holophrastic language, Anishnaabemowin is able to express subjects and objects within its verbs; it may therefore produce grammatically complete sentences without using independent noun phrases—a feature suggested in English discourse through the use of subject dropping. If, however, context requires that the subject or object of a sentence is clarified with a higher degree of certainty, Anishnaabemowin simply adds an independent noun phrase, thus creating a structure that seems rather redundant from the point of view of the English language. For example, the interlinear translation of *nikiiwaapamaa makwa* is "I saw him/her, a bear." In English, this particular structure of Anishnaabemowin discourse is mimicked by duplicating the subject (or object) through pronoun copying, such as Keeper's line, "They them lost touch." Clearly, Keeper and Garnet's mother speak an English code inflected with features of Anishnaabemowin that result from the latter's holophrastic nature.

In the case of Garnet's mother's use of English, holophrastic traces are restricted to echoes of Anishnaabemowin verb complexity. Keeper's speech, moreover, showcases holophrastic traces that result from his use of words and phrases in discourse. In general, Keeper displays a very inventive use of language. His figures of speech mimic the figurative uses of language commonly found in Indigenous languages, which in turn are correlated with holophrasis (see chapter 2). When figures of speech occur in Indigenous texts in English and are notable features of the text—as in Keeper's inventive constructions, such as the metaphor "havin' the old slidey foot" (15; his circumlocution for the inability to settle down)—these figures contain traces of holophrastic discourse from ancestral languages and are thus important markers of rhetorical sovereignty. Even more often than figures of speech, Keeper uses quotation compounds, as exemplified in phrases and clauses such as "the movin'-between kinda Indyuns" (138) and "that brother of yours that's got a lotta the bear in him" (102). In the case of the last example, the relative clause "that's got a lotta the bear in him" is derived from an idiom-like lexical phrase that Keeper repeatedly uses earlier in the conversation to refer to Garnet's brother Jackie: "Gotta lotta the bear in him" (98, 99, 101). Because Keeper's quotation compounds ultimately function as a single unit, they evoke the holistic structure of the holophrase and thus qualify as strong direct holophrastic traces (see chapter 2) that, together with all the other holophrastic traces discussed above, assign a very distinct voice to Keeper in the novel—a voice that is deeply grounded in his ancestral language.

Garnet's siblings also speak Anishnaabe English, but a variant that is less pronounced than that spoken by Keeper (and by their mother). It lacks the code switching between English and Anishnaabemowin and the Anishnaabemowin-inflected pronunciation, and it generally tends to be less inventive, using fewer quotation compounds and figures of speech. At the same time, the English spoken by Stanley, Jane, and Jackie includes echoes of Anishnaabemowin verb complexity that are as strong as those in the Anishnaabe English used by Keeper and their mother, as evident in the following excerpts (pronoun copying and subject dropping are indicated by italics).

"And besides, you haven't really lived till you get some a Ma's hamburger soup and bannock into your belly. *Me, I* like it a little too much!" (45)

"Anyways, he didn't have no Indian status, lost his treaty rights, and all and he wanted Ma to marry him. *Wanted* it real bad. *Us we* liked him. *Wasn't* nothin' like our father but we liked him okay." (46)

"I remember when you were small. Little guy just learnin' to run around. *Had* my gumboots on one day, runnin' around in them. No clothes on an' *them gumboots* were way too big for you, *kept* runnin' right outta them." (106)

Because Keeper is one of the novel's two main narrators, his voice is ultimately given more space than those of Garnet's siblings, which may explain their sparse use of direct holophrastic traces in comparison to Keeper or even their mother.[17] What is more noteworthy about the English used by

---

17   One noteworthy exception is when Stanley introduces Garnet: "This is my ... my ... my brother. ... The one that disappeared. He's home" (35). The additive clause "The one that disappeared" reads like a personal name, a name that summarizes Garnet's personal history up to that moment in just a few words, turning it into an idiom-like lexical phrase, that is, into a phrase that in its ability to function as a single unit based on a verb evokes the holistic structure of the holophrase and therefore qualifies as a direct holophrastic trace.

Stanley, Jane, and Jackie is their lack of code switching. As Balzer points out, by varying the speech patterns of individual characters featured in *Keeper'n Me*, "Wagamese illustrates the changes that have taken place in one generation."[18] Keeper and the Ravens' mother belong to a generation of White Dog Anishnaabe who have held onto the language despite being sent to residential schools. Their children, however, taken away from their families when they were still little and placed in non-Native foster homes, have largely lost the ability to use Anishnaabemowin for their daily needs—a circumstance reflected in the particular variant of Anishnaabe English they speak throughout the novel.

When the Raven children were taken away from their parents by the Children's Aid Society, Garnet was separated from his siblings. While Stanley, Jane, and Jackie stayed together all those years and were occasionally visited by their mother, eventually even moving back home, Garnet spent his entire childhood and teenage years away from his community. Studying his particular use of language is therefore especially interesting. Garnet's speech patterns only eventually develop into an Anishnaabe English code. In the first few pages of the novel, before he arrives in White Dog, Garnet uses one of two linguistic and "ethnic caricatures" (Black English and "white" English).[19] It is only when the narration shifts to his eventual return to White Dog that his English starts to morph into an Anishnaabe English code that, in its echoes of Anishnaabemowin verb complexity, is quite similar to that of his siblings, as exemplified in the following passage taken from the beginning of book 2 (echoes are marked in italics):

> *Us we* appreciate that. Looking after our own's a big source of pride with us and it's good they understand that. Our Indian leaders are all calling it self-government these days and making big noise about how they're gonna bring it to the people. *Us we* always had it. (83)

Although Garnet picks up enough of his mother tongue to listen in on conversations (90–91), he doesn't use the language himself; nor does he switch codes and pronounce English Anishnaabemowin-style as do his mother and Keeper. Indeed, the only difference between Garnet's speech and that of his siblings is his linguistic inventiveness and playfulness, which, in its reliance on quotation compounds (direct holophrastic trace) and figures

---

18   Balzer, "'Bring[ing] Them Back,'" 229.
19   Ibid., 230.

of speech (indirect holophrastic trace), resembles that of Keeper. Examples of these two kinds of holophrastic traces, as found in Garnet's speech and narration, are listed below.

Quotation Compounds
- "'bait the tourist' game" (83)
- "that first real staying-on the ground snow" (102)
- "the pullin' rabbits outta hats kinda magic" (8)
- "the top-rated prime-time kinda Indians" (16)

Figurative Language
- "teepee-creepin'" (139; metaphor)
- "washboard road" (4; metaphor)
- "the hook to hang my life on" (170; metaphor)
- (referring to one of Mabel's aunts) "has a face like a fresh-scraped deer hide once the wet's all squeezed out" (61; simile)
- (upon seeing Keeper for the first time) "an old man with so many wrinkles he looked like he was folded up wet and left overnight" (41; simile)

Stanley, Jane, and Jackie are minor characters in the novel and given voice only in dialogue, which may account for why, of all the children, Garnet displays the more imaginative use of language. He also relies extensively on evidentiality, the process of acknowledging or qualifying his (source of) knowledge in both speech and narration. As the two main narrators in a novel that frequently uses direct speech, Garnet and Keeper ultimately rely on the use of quotatives. In fact, their narration is generally very clearly marked with the indirect holophrastic trace of evidentiality, as evident in table 4.1 (quotatives are indicated by italics).

The only noteworthy difference in the way they identify their sources of knowledge is that Keeper relies more heavily than Garnet on "double quotatives," that is, the use of two consecutive quotatives, such as "he told me he said." This structure is quite reminiscent of the seemingly redundant use (from the point of view of English, at least) of quotatives and evidentials in much Indigenous-language discourse (see chapter 1). Despite these differences (lack of code switching and double quotatives), Garnet's use of English resembles Keeper's more clearly than it does that of his siblings. In fact, toward the end of the novel, his narration even begins to pick up some of the rhythm and cadences of Keeper's speech, including his roaring laughter (see table 4.2).

TABLE 4.1 EXAMPLES OF THE USE OF EVIDENTIALITY IN *KEEPER'N ME*

KEEPER	GARNET
Old man told me one time he said, the very last time you got up in the mornin' and said a quiet prayer of thanks for the day you been given was the very last time you were an Indyun. *Then he said,* the very last time you got handed some food and bowed your head and said a prayer of thanks and asked for the strength you got from that food to be used to help someone around you, well, that was the very last you were an Indyun too. *And he told me he said,* the very last time you did something's for someone without bein' asked, being thanked or tellin' about it was the very last time you were an Indyun. (38)	Something caused by distance and time and a quiet yearning of magic we all carry around inside us. *That's what Ma says. Says* that magic's born of the land and the ones who go places in life are the ones who take the time to let that magic seep inside them. Sitting there, all quiet and watching, listening, learning. That's how the magic seeps in. Anishanabe are pretty big on magic, *she says.* Not so much the pullin' rabbit outta hats kinda magic but more the pullin' learning outta everything around 'em. A common magic that teaches you how to live with each other. Seeing them hills breathe, and believing it, is making yourself available to that magic. Like leaving the door to your insides unlocked, *she says.* (8)

TABLE 4.2 SIMILARITIES BETWEEN KEEPER'S AND GARNET'S SPEECH IN *KEEPER'N ME*

KEEPER'S OPENING SPEECH	GARNET'S CLOSING SPEECH
Funny thing is, like I told the boy, the old days never really gone. Not for us. The outside world goes crazy all the time, findin' new ways to do old things, forget the teachin's their own old ones taught. But us we listen all the time. To old guys like me. Always talkin' anyway, might as well listen, eh? Heh, heh, heh. (2)	We still go sit by the edge of Shotgun Bay and watch that big orange drum of a moon flat across the sky. Still walk over through the frost and snow and rain to pray and sing and cook breakfast. Still having adventures and laughter. Still learning. Looking more'n more jake all the time. Be a storyteller, he told me. Talk about the real Indyuns. About what you learned, where you travelled, where you've been all this time. Tell them. Tell them stories on accounta them they all need guides too. Hmmpfh. Guess we're all Indians really. Heh, heh, heh. (214)

Evidently, by the end of his narration, , Garnet has indeed come home. The various stages of Garnet's homecoming are reflected on the content level: he starts spending time with Keeper, performing a sunrise ceremony every morning (book 2); he finds his grandparents' cabin in the bush (book 3); he goes on a vision quest, returning with an eagle feather (book 4). Meanwhile, the very fact that Garnet is telling this story using a particular variant of Anishnaabe English—if one that lacks the code switching, Anishnaabemowin pronunciation, and double quotatives of the previous generation—foreshadows the successful homecoming he describes in the novel. In telling his story, he gives back to his community, particularly the younger generation—and he does so using the *voice* of the people.

Let us pause here for a moment to briefly summarize the discussion above. Wagamese varies the particular uses of language for his Anishnaabe characters in *Keeper'n Me* in order to create a subtle Anishnaabe English base; he has all the characters, regardless of age and personal history, use pronoun copying and subject dropping, both of which are echoes of Indigenous verb complexity—a central indirect holophrastic trace. In the case of the novel's two narrators, Wagamese also includes the holophrastic traces of evidentiality and figurative uses of language. Depending on a character's age, he then adds to this holophrastic base further markers of Anishnaabemowin, most notably code switching and eye vernacular, as in the cases of Keeper and Garnet's mother. What Wagamese achieves with this nuanced portrayal of Anishnaabe voices is quite unique: he claims rhetorical sovereignty, the right to use language and discourse as it suits his particular purpose of continuing Anishnaabe storytelling traditions, and he simultaneously documents and critiques government policies that have sought to assimilate Aboriginal people, thus further destroying the people's ancestral language. The subtle differences among the various Anishnaabe voices portrayed in *Keeper'n Me* thus account for the novel's double intention: to empower Anishnaabe and other Aboriginal people and to critique the colonial regime. That the novel addresses both Aboriginal and non-Aboriginal people (as evident most notably in Keeper's opening speech) makes sense, then, once one considers the novel's complex goal.

MARIA CAMPBELL'S *STORIES OF THE ROAD ALLOWANCE PEOPLE*

The story behind Maria Campbell's seminal collection of Métis stories, *Stories of the Road Allowance People*, differs considerably from that of Wagamese's first novel. Wagamese's use of Anishnaabe English in *Keeper'n Me* may be interpreted as an act of *reclaiming* something lost—a language, an identity, a whole life—and while Garnet's story may be loosely based on Wagamese's own life, the community of White Dog depicted in *Keeper'n Me* is fictional. In *Stories of the Road Allowance People*, by contrast, the Michif English used by Campbell serves to *preserve* the traditional Métis stories of her home community on its own terms, that is, in the people's own voice. Both texts, then, exercise rhetorical sovereignty—the right of peoples to determine their rhetorical needs and to decide on the specific form and language of discourse—but the contexts of the two texts differ considerably, and these differences are also felt at the narrative level. *Keeper'n Me* features two fictional first-person narrators whose voices begin to resemble each other more and more as the story progresses but nevertheless remain distinct. In contrast, *Stories of the Road Allowance People* is a collection of stories performed by different Métis elders, but the stories throughout the collection are told using the same Michif-inflected English—a code that Campbell created specifically for the purpose of publishing the elders' stories. What readers hear in Campbell's collection, then, is essentially the voice of a community—Campbell's own home community in northern Saskatchewan—as mediated through her work as translator.

In collections such as *Stories of the Road Allowance People*, oral narratives are put into print and thus made accessible to a larger audience, although this growth in readership is not usually the main incentive for the writing down and publishing of oral stories. In the case of *Stories of the Road Allowance People*, Campbell's motivation was to make her community's stories accessible in English to the next generation of people in her community, who (unlike Campbell) speak neither Michif nor Cree or Saulteaux.[20] Campbell's role in *Stories* is thus not so much that of author or editor as that of mediator and translator of the collective memory of her people.[21] These are local stories that Campbell gathered for this project. Whether they are humorous in tone (in "La Beau Sha Shoo," for example, a fiddler drinks wine with Jesus in heaven; in "Good Dog Bob," a boy hides under another man's bed to avoid being detected as an adulterer, yet the latter has sex with the boy's lover) or address issues of colonialism (related to residential school trauma, in "Jacob," or the Riel Resistance of 1885, in "Joseph's Justice"), the elders' stories speak to the resilience of their com-

---

20 Campbell, "'One Small Medicine,'" 188; Maria Campbell, "Maria Campbell," interview by Hartmut Lutz and Konrad Gross, in *Contemporary Challenges: Conversations with Canadian Native Authors*, comp. Hartmut Lutz (Saskatoon: Fifth House, 1991), 48.

21 See Campbell, "'One Small Medicine,'" 200.

munity—the people's ability to continue into the future despite the history of colonialism that has so strongly affected their lives.

Maria Campbell recorded the elders' stories in Michif, the language of the Métis people, and translated them for publication using what she describes as "the dialect and rhythm of my village, and my father's generation" (4)—a "dialect" heavily inflected by Michif. Michif is what linguists call a mixed language, a language that is derived from two different source languages—in this case, Cree (most of the verbs in Michif are Cree) and French (most of its nouns are French). Campbell's recreation of Michif in an English-language text was a very conscious act. It was only when she started translating the stories using the voice of her father and other community members that the stories began to work for Campbell. The result as published is a Michif English code that reads and sounds as in the following passage (quoted from the revised edition of *Stories*, which was published in 2010).

One time we had a red-headed woman come to our country to buy fur.
Oh *he* was a hell of a looker.
But *he* was a bigger cheat *den* all *dah res* of *dem.*
An us
we can do *nutting*
cause *we was gentlemans an he was a lady.*
During *dis* time too
we gots dis guy living *wit* us.
He come from down *sout* someplace when he was a young man
an he marry up *wit* one of *our womans an dey* raise a family.[22]

As this excerpt (taken from "Dah Red-Headed Fur Buyer") illustrates, Campbell has translated the stories as they are "pronounced 'à la mitchif.'"[23] This is how critic Pamela Sing describes the particular use of language in *Stories of the Road Allowance People*. Rather than following standard English orthography, the words in English are spelled as they are

---

22 Campbell, *Road Allowance People*, 8; emphases mine.
23 Pamela V. Sing, "Intersections of Memory, Ancestral Language, and Imagination; or, the Textual Production of Michif Voices as Cultural Weaponry," in "For the Love of Words: Aboriginal Writers of Canada," ed. Renate Eigenbrod and Jennifer Andrews, special issue, *Studies in Canadian Literature* 31.1 (2006): para. 23. http://journals.hil.unb.ca/index.php/scl/article/view/10202/10552.

pronounced by Métis storytellers and other members of Campbell's community (see table 4.3).

TABLE 4.3 ORTHOGRAPHY/PRONUNCIATION IN *STORIES OF THE ROAD ALLOWANCE PEOPLE*

LANGUAGE FEATURE	CAMPBELL'S MICHIF ENGLISH	EXAMPLE
voiced and voiceless dental fricatives ("th")	spelled either "d," "tt," or "t"	"dah" (for "the"); "dis" (for "this"); "nutting" (for "nothing"); "sout" (for "south")
homophones (words that are pronounced the same but have different meanings and spellings)	spelling is harmonized	"dere" (for all of the following: "their," "there," "they're"); "your" (for both "your" and "you're")
consonant clusters in word-final positions	reduced or altered	"han" (for "hand"); "can" (for "can't"); "don" (for "don't"); "tole" (for "told"); "ole" (for "old")
verb conjugation	past-tense endings are dropped; the subject verb concord in English is violated	"dey start" (for "they started"); "he ask" (for "he asks")

The language of *Stories of the Road Allowance People* is more than just standard English transcribed à la Michif, however. Campbell's collection also contains further non-standard features of English. Some of these features are unique to Michif, such as the possessive constructions and the irregular adjective-noun agreement, both very characteristic of the Métis language (see table 4.4). These Michif-specific influences are important in that they clearly distinguish the Indigenous English code used by Campbell from related codes based on Cree and other Algonquian languages, such as Anishnaabemowin. Readers of *Stories* will not be able to see this nuanced difference unless they have some knowledge of Michif. What they can easily make out, however, using the holophrastic heuristic introduced in chapter 2, are other non-standard uses of English that qualify as holophrastic traces. These holophrastic traces are just as much a part of the rhetorical sovereignty claimed through Campbell's choice of language as are the Michif-specific influences.

TABLE 4.4 MICHIF–SPECIFIC INFLUENCES IN *STORIES OF THE ROAD ALLOWANCE PEOPLE*

LANGUAGE FEATURE	MICHIF	CAMPBELL'S MICHIF ENGLISH
possessive constructions	possessor / possessive pronoun / possessed Example: *"mŭ pči garsŭ sŭ pči žwal"* (my-little-boy his-little-horse) my son's pony*	"a dog hees tail" (a dog's tail) "dah Prees hees book" (the priest's book)
adjective-noun agreement	prenominal adjectives agree with the nouns in number and gender; most postnominal adjectives do not†	both "dah udders mans" and "dah udder mans" "La Beau Sha Shoo" (instead of "Le Beau Sha Shoo" or "La Belle Sha Shoo)

* Peter Bakker, *A Language of Our Own: The Genesis of Michif, the Mixed Cree-French Language of the Canadian Métis*, rev. ed. (New York: Oxford University Press, 1997), 88.

† Ibid., 106.

Holophrastic traces in *Stories of the Road Allowance People* are almost entirely of an indirect nature and include evidentiality, as suggested by the strikingly frequent use of quotatives throughout the collection, such as in the following excerpt from "Jacob" (quotatives are marked in italics).

Jacob *he say*
he look at dat lil baby
an he start to cry and he can stop.
He say he cry for himself an his wife
an den he cry for his Mommy an Daddy.[24]

Quotatives indicate the nature of evidence for a given statement; in *Stories of the Road Allowance People*, they are used primarily in narratives that recount the personal story of someone other than the storyteller. In other words, they are a more or less direct indicator of the ancient Aboriginal copyright system discussed in chapter 1: whenever someone told another person's story, the storyteller would frequently remind his/her audience in the storytelling process that the story was actually someone else's. Campbell's use of quotatives therefore serves very similar functions as

24   Campbell, *Road Allowance People*, 90; emphases mine.

evidentiality in Indigenous oral traditions; in fact, given the particular makeup of her collection and the ways in which the stories are set up, quotatives in *Stories of the Road Allowance People* are a direct indicator more of Indigenous traditions of storytelling than of much contemporary Indigenous fiction—including those texts that feature particularly oral voices, such as that of the Anishnaabe Elder Keeper in Wagamese's *Keeper'n Me*. The novel's main narrators, Keeper and Garnet, occasionally include short stories-within-stories and thus rely on evidentials, but given the length of these stories, this particular feature of Indigenous narrative traditions is less "overt" or evident than in Campbell's collection of stories.

Another type of indirect holophrastic trace featured in *Stories of the Road Allowance People* is echoes of Indigenous verb complexity, as evident in the following passage from "Good Dog Bob" (echoes are italicized):

> One time we stop at a small settlement for dah night.
> Dere was only womans an kids
> cause dah mans dey was all out on dah traplines.
> Well *dis one woman*
> *he* keep on coming aroun our camp
> an *he* keep on making signs for me to follow *him*.[25]

In contrast to *Keeper'n Me*, Indigenous verb complexity in *Stories* is suggested not only through pronoun copying or subject dropping but also through third person equality. Not only does Campbell add a pronoun after the subject or object noun, evoking the expressivity of Indigenous verbs, as in "dah ole womans / dey sing"; she also restricts the use of personal pronouns to male forms, creating a discourse that sounds very odd in sections featuring female characters or words that would be rendered neuter in English, such as "dog." Some Indigenous languages, particularly those in the Algonquian language family (e.g., Blackfoot, Cree, Anishnaabemowin, Mik'maq), distinguish nouns, pronouns, and verbs based on animacy, that is, based on different ways of being in the world (animate vs. inanimate). Hence, there are no pronouns reflecting gender in Algonquian languages, nor are there any gendered personal pronouns in Michif, since they are all derived from Cree, the Algonquian parent language of Michif. In *Stories of the Road Allowance People*, the third person equality of Cree is reflected in its use of pronouns, which are restricted to male pronoun

---

25 Campbell, *Road Allowance People*, 18; emphases mine.

forms that express all relevant genders: masculine, feminine, and neuter (i.e., "he," "she," "it"). The function performed by third person equality in *Stories* can actually be related to the tendency of many Indigenous languages for holophrasis; in order to make sense of Campbell's Métis stories, one often has to read entire sentences, sometimes even whole series of sentences, as if they were one single unit.[26] For example, the lines "I go wit dis *woman* to *hees* shack. / *Hees man* was gone trapping so *he* tole me not to worry / just get in dah bed wit *him*" have to be read together in order to determine who invites the narrator to sleep with her/him (the woman or her husband?).[27] In many Indigenous languages, the interrelatedness of component parts that activate a larger image takes place on the word level—thus the notion of holophrases. Maria Campbell's use of pronouns creates the same function and effect in *Stories*, not on the word level, of course—English grammar does not allow this—but on the sentence level. The third person equality suggested by the uniform use of personal pronouns in *Stories of the Road Allowance People*, while not being Michif-specific, is a holophrastic trace strongly associated with Algonquian languages, such as Cree, one of the two parent languages of Michif.

Using an English code that both "michifizes" and "holophrasticizes" standard English, *Stories of the Road Allowance People* allows the voices of the Métis elders and their community to come alive in English. The language in which Maria Campbell has put her community's stories onto the page successfully captures the voice of the people from whom the stories originate; as Campbell noted in an interview with Susan Gingell, she "has been told" by Métis people "that the way [she] used the language freed them, that it was healing to be able to laugh about something that we'd once been punished for and made to feel ashamed of. Seeing and reading the language in a book gave our stories and our use of English a whole different meaning was the cause of lots of discussion."[28] The stories shared in Campbell's collection are local, then, not just in terms of their content but particularly with regard to their language, and having their form and content match was a conscious act. Campbell refers to her translations in *Stories of the Road Allowance People* as "putting the Mother back in the language," that is, into English, a language that, according to one of her elders, was motherless.[29] What Campbell needed to do, the elder advised

---

26 Renate Eigenbrod, *Travelling Knowledges: Positioning the Im/Migrant Reader of Aboriginal Literatures in Canada* (Winnipeg: University of Manitoba Press, 2005), 150.

27 Campbell, *Road Allowance People*, 20; emphases mine.

28 Campbell, "'One Small Medicine,'" 190.

29 Campbell, "Maria Campbell," 49.

her, was to tell the stories from a position of being fully grounded in her own place and to realize that her language had originated in that very place, her homeland, northern Saskatchewan.[30] By recreating in English the language of her community, Campbell embraces Métis language and discourse traditions while simultaneously undermining the hegemony of standard English, a language fraught with colonial history and values. Campbell's use of English is not antagonistic, however. Rather, it demonstrates that discourse is always social. Language serves particular functions, and any one particular use of language may be adequate in one context but utterly inappropriate in another. In performing Métis rhetorical sovereignty against dominant forms of public discourse, *Stories of the Road Allowance People* is a prime example of the salient role that language plays in performances of Indigenous peoplehood.

HARRY ROBINSON'S "CAT WITH THE BOOTS ON"

A similar case can be made about the collected stories of Okanagan storyteller Harry Robinson. His first collection of stories, *Write It on Your Heart*, contains a retelling of "Le Maître Chat, ou le Chat Botté," the famous European folktale of a cat who, through a series of tricks, gains power, wealth, and a wife for his poor master, a miller's son, as first published by Charles Perrault in 1697. I end this chapter with a discussion of Robinson's "Cat with the Boots On" (the title Robinson gives to the story in its opening line) so as to emphasize, more clearly than I have done thus far, how a reading of Indigenous literatures can never separate form from content.

As noted above, the Okanagan language clearly inflects Robinson's use of English. The lack of differentiation between third person singular and plural as well as the use of equative constructions that lack any form of the verb "to be" not only are direct ancestral language influences, but also count as indirect holophrastic traces in Robinson's texts. "Cat with the Boots On" is much more than a text that has the "sound" of an Okanagan narrative; Robinson's story is Okanagan also because it communicates an Okanagan worldview and, in fact, becomes part of Okanagan oral tradition. However, if translator Wendy Wickwire had rendered Robinson's stories into plain English, readers would likely not notice the differences between his "Cat with the Boots On" and Perrault's "Puss in Boots." In short, I believe that paying close attention to Robinson's use of language ultimately points readers to the realization that this story it is not a rhetorically naive text but, as so many early Indigenous works of the eighteenth

---

30 Campbell, "'One Small Medicine,'" 188–89.

and nineteenth centuries, is "calculated and negotiated with a specific audience, and a specific goal, in mind."[31] For as both apart from and a part of the original story, "Cat with the Boots On" marks an act of decolonization that, whether intended by Robinson or not, reclaims Indigenous notions of peoplehood—the "tribal web of kinship rights *and* responsibilities" linking people, land, and the cosmos.[32]

Though Robinson's retelling of Perrault's story remains relatively true to the original, there is one unique structural difference between the two. In "Cat with the Boots On," the cat sets out to regain the ranch for the rancher, adding an important theme: the undoing of forced oppression. A man arrives at another man's doorstep and, by threat of force, demands that the latter leave his home. Fearing the death of his family, the man does as requested. He builds a new home across the creek but is not able to continue his old life as a rancher. This, in a nutshell, is the story of the colonization of Indigenous peoples in North America. And yet, in his retelling of Puss's story Robinson unmistakably sets the story in Europe (282, 283) and stresses that the two ranchers featured in the story are white men (283, 286). I believe that these facts do not so much contradict a reading of "Cat with the Boots On" as criticizing the colonization of Indigenous peoples as demonstrate the story's rhetoric of unfixity of meaning. This rhetoric, which is based on symbol and allows for the story to be both an Okanagan story and an Okanagan-inflected retelling of a European story, becomes apparent when reading "Cat with the Boots On" in the context of Okanagan oral tradition.

Despite differences in the internal makeup of Robinson's three collections, there is a clear narrative thread connecting one publication to the next: the dispossessing of Indigenous peoples by European colonizers based on the power of a piece of paper. This piece of paper is introduced in "Twins: White and Indian," one of the Coyote stories in *Write It on Your Heart*. "Twins" features a pair of twins, the older of whom will eventually become Coyote and is the ancestor of "the Indian" (46), while the other twin is the ancestor of "the white man" (45). At the end of the story, the younger twin is banished to a land across a huge body of water because he steals a piece of paper with written instructions that the Creator has given to the twins for use by both. "Twins" explains the significance of the written word as the source of power for Euro-Westerners, and it describes

---

31 Malea D. Powell, "Sarah Winnemucca Hopkins: Her Wrongs and Claims," *American Indian Rhetorics of Survivance: Word Medicine, Word Magic*, ed. Ernest Stromberg (Pittsburgh: University of Pittsburgh Press, 2006) 69.

32 Justice, *Our Fire Survives*, 24.

them as prone to telling lies.[33] In a later story, called "Prophecy at Lytton," the Creator evokes this piece of paper by repeating his prophecy that the "white man" will return to North America with the help of the piece of paper, but the Creator also stresses that the white people will come to North America to "to live here with you. / But this is your place" (187). "Twins" does not end with the younger brother's banishment, however. The older twin is allowed to stay in their land of origin, receives the name of Coyote, and—equipped with God's power—travels across the land, making the earth inhabitable for the First People by, for example, slaying monsters.

Coyote's adventures are told in the stories succeeding "Twins" as well as in the opening tales of *Living by Stories*, Robinson's third collection. One of these stories, called "Coyote Makes a Deal with the King of England," moves forward in time to the moment when the younger twin returns to his land of origin. Upon their arrival in North America, the descendants of the younger twin kill the descendants of the older twin, steal their lands, and conceal the content of the "paper," although God had instructed them to share it with the older brother. As a result, Coyote travels to visit the King of England in order to draw up a treaty. They agree on a set of rules of conduct to be followed by both European and Indigenous peoples; the rules are written down in a big book, copies of which are given to both groups. The paper, which turns from a mere piece of paper in "Twins" and "Prophecy" into a treaty and a book in "Coyote Makes a Deal," is anything but fixed.

The same paper found in these Coyote stories also found its way into "Cat with the Boots On." The rancher's son and the other rancher travel across the country in a buggy. The cat runs ahead of the party and instructs the workers in the fields to tell the rancher that the owner of the land on which they are working is the other rancher's son. This land happens to be where the son's family had lived before the gorilla stole it from them. The people working the field, then, are telling not a lie but the truth when they say that the King is "the owner" of the land where they work: "By God, he put it down on the paper" (304). When the son moves into his late father's house after the gorilla's death, he is thus returning to his original home. Building on three other stories told by Robinson, "Cat with the Boots On" thus becomes an integral part of the whole that is Okanagan oral tradition

---

33 Wendy Wickwire, "Stories from the Margins: Toward a More Inclusive British Columbia Historiography," *Journal of American Folklore* 118.470 (2005): 462.

as passed down by Robinson, underlining the ever evolving nature of oral tradition.

But how can a cat possibly be a coyote, you may wonder? How do ranches in Europe suddenly turn into ranches in the Okanagan? In order to weave a European folktale into his body of Okanagan stories, Robinson relies on the use of a series of symbols. In "Symbol as Figure," E. F. Dyck has, referring to the work of Charles Peirce, pointed to "unfixity," or "the iterative process of the growth of a literary symbol," as the symbol's "central characteristic."[34] Symbol may be said to come into being the moment a sign turns into a *signifier for an infinite chain of new signs* at the level of connotation, thus preventing any final meaning.[35] It is this unfixity of meaning that distinguishes symbol from metaphor (e.g., Shakespeare's "All the world's a stage, and all the men and women merely players")— whose meaning is fixed through the interaction or likeness between tenor ("world") and vehicle ("stage")—and, by implication, allegory, a form of extended metaphor. Although it narrates the undoing of forced oppression, "Cat with the Boots On" is not an *allegory* of the decolonization of Indigenous peoples. Rather, it is both a *story* of the decolonization of Indigenous peoples and an Okanagan-inflected retelling of Perrault's "Puss in Boots." What makes the incorporation of European story into Okanagan tradition possible is the use of symbol, as opposed to allegory or metaphor, as the text's main rhetorical design. It is only through employing a series of symbols that "Cat with the Boots On" is able to produce an unfixity of meaning that allows the text to shift between Okanagan story and Okanagan-inflected retelling of a European story. Take, for example, the cat. Robinson's cat is all of the following: He is, of course, a cat. But he also is the cat in Perrault's story; as such, he is the animal helper found in so many traditions of orature, including Okanagan tradition (see, for example, Robinson's *Nature Power*). Moreover, given his use of language, his role as animal helper, and his transformatory powers, Robinson's cat is also Coyote in Okanagan oral tradition.[36] In short, the possible meanings of Robinson's cat remain indeterminate; he is not this or that but all these different people at one and the same time. Thus, the cat functions as a symbol: it has various symbolic values that allow us to associate this sign with a whole series of other signs. Similarly, the rancher's son in "Cat with

---

34   E. F. Dyck, "Symbol as Figure," *Semiotic Inquiry* 14.3 (1994): 54–55.

35   See Roland Barthes's discussion of the different levels of signification, in *Elements of Semiology*, trans. Annette Lavers and Colin Smith (London: Jonathan Cape, 1967) 89–92.

36   Also see Wendy Wickwire, introduction to Robinson, *Write It on Your Heart*, 28.

the Boots On" functions as a symbol. He is, first of all, a rancher's son. He also is a white man. He is the miller's son in Perrault's story. At the same time, he is a member of a family that includes a cat; as the cat's "relative," the son is a descendant of the older twin in Robinson's "Twins." That is to say, he is Okanagan. The other rancher in Robinson's story, on the other hand, is a rancher and a white man. He is also the King in Perrault's story, the sovereign in late medieval feudal society. As such, the rancher is one of the King of England's children who are now living across the ocean, but he is also a descendant of the younger twin in Robinson's "Twins." That is to say, this other rancher is indeed a "white man." One way of reading the two ranchers in "Cat with the Boots On," then, is as representing Indigenous peoples on the one hand and Euro-Western peoples on the other.

That Robinson refers to both ranchers as white men does not so much contradict this reading as underline the subtle ways in which he creates an unfixity of meaning in the text. The symbolism of Robinson's story is more complex, however, than to suggest simply an Indigenous/Euro-Western dichotomy. First, the rancher in Robinson's story, although oblivious to the cause of the other rancher's plight, helps him out by allowing one of his workers to assist him in building a new home (287–89). Second, the rancher is not the one who steals the other rancher's land; it is the gorilla who does this. The gorilla is described as half bear, half human (284). Robinson's gorilla is not just a gorilla but also a shape-shifter who will engage in a power contest with the cat at the end of the story. In addition, the gorilla fills the role of Perrault's story's ogre, whom he resembles in both physical appearance and viciousness. As such, the gorilla is also one of the monsters in Robinson's stories, like the Owl, who devours the First People until Coyote comes along to put an end to it (66–74). The gorilla does not actually eat the rancher and his two sons, but he threatens to kill them if they do not leave (285). As a result, the rancher and his sons move away and settle a few miles from their original home, on the other side of a creek (286).

The rancher's new land and the creek function as another set of symbols. These symbols differ from the others in that they do not have any connection to Perrault's story. The rancher's new land is "good land" (286), but the home he eventually builds is makeshift: it is not a ranch but a cabin. In the course of colonization, Indigenous peoples were forced to move onto reserves, losing their traditional lands. Thus, the cabin in Robinson's story is a cabin, but this sign's symbolic values also include a house on a reserve. Similarly, the creek that runs between the rancher's new land and that of the other rancher is, first of all, a creek, but it is also the slough water in Robinson's "Twins" that becomes a huge mass of water once the younger twin jumps across after having stolen the paper (47–49). The symbolic values of the creek include the Atlantic Ocean and the friction that separates the older twin's descendants from those of the younger twin, or Indigenous peoples from Euro-Westerners. All of this is to say that Robinson's gorilla is not just a gorilla, an ogre, or a shaman who joins the cat in a power contest; one of the gorilla's symbolic values is that of colonialism in person.

Depending on the meaning readers assign to the signs that function as symbols in the story—whether, for example, the cat is read as Coyote or as an animal helper, the gorilla as colonialism in person or as an ogre with shamanic powers—"Cat with the Boots On" shifts between Okanagan story and Okanagan-inflected retelling of "white people stories." The unfixity of meaning marks "Cat with the Boots On" not just as a retelling but also as a parody, an "imitation with critical ironic distance."[37] This critical ironic distance—using a colonizer's tale to critique the colonization of Indigenous peoples while placing the narrative in Okanagan traditions of story and thought—is subtle. Robinson's story remains relatively close to the original, but this makes the rhetoric of "Cat with the Boots On" all the more powerful.

Leaving the European story relatively unharmed, and using a series of symbols to create an unfixity of meaning, "Cat with the Boots On" uses a colonizer's story to perform an act of decolonization. Yet Robinson's story also points out a reading of the colonizer's story that Euro-Western audiences—Wickwire and the readers of *Write It on Your Heart*—would not have imagined themselves. The critical ironic distance produced by Robinson's repetition of "Puss in Boots" also lies in stressing the validity and meaning of a moral lying outside Euro-Western thinking, one that relies on Indigenous notions of the web of kinship rights and responsibilities that make up peoplehood: to treat one's cat, and by implication one's relations, well. Thus, "Cat with the Boots On" is also an Okanagan offering to the world, a teaching in living *and*, I would argue, also in reading, particularly. For it is ultimately Robinson's peculiar but sophisticated use of the English language that points to the performance of rhetorical sovereignty embodied by his story and signals to his readers that there is something else going on in his retelling of a popular European folktale, something

---

37   Linda Hutcheon, *A Theory of Parody: The Teachings of Twentieth-Century Art Forms* (New York: Methuen, 1985) 37.

more subtle than meets the eye, something that warrants our absolute attention as readers. Form, in other words, mirrors content, and vice versa.

Ancestral language influences in English are more widespread than most readers of Indigenous literatures will realize; what is more, these influences are actually very easy to detect in an Indigenous text, as long as readers know what to look for. The trick is not to assume one is reading just another English-language text. Reading for holophrastic traces helps readers pay attention to the nuances of Indigenous discourse and thus serves as a very useful technique in uncovering ancestral language influences and, at the same time, the expressions of rhetorical sovereignty they constitute. As evident in the discussion of Richard Wagamese's *Keeper'n Me* and Maria Campbell's *Stories of the Road Allowance People*, holophrastic traces are important indicators of ancestral language influences in Indigenous discourse in English, however general they may be. Depending on the text in question, reading for holophrastic traces may even create the starting point for more specialized studies that highlight the specificities of these ancestral language influences, as in the case of Campbell's collection. And as suggested in the discussion of Harry Robinson's "Cat with the Boots On," paying attention to the language-specific features of an Indigenous text may lead to a more comprehensive inquiry into Indigenous discourse structures, traditions, and worldviews. The heuristic for holophrastic traces introduced in chapter 2 can be applied to a variety of Indigenous texts (contemporary fiction, textualized oral traditions), but of course not all Indigenous texts invite a reading for holophrastic traces, as their engagement with Indigenous English codes and discourse patterns naturally varies. As the formal manifestations of the holophrase, holophrastic traces focus attention to questions of language, grammar, style, and voice and the roles played by these elements in the production of meaning. What specific discourse functions holophrastic traces perform in individual Indigenous texts needs to be determined by the readers, however. Holophrastic traces are an integral part of an Indigenous poetics because they *help generate* readings of Indigenous literatures, but they never constitute these readings. While holophrastic traces provide evidence of performances of rhetorical sovereignty in Indigenous writing in English, these performances vary and are contextualized differently. In *Keeper'n Me*, exercising rhetorical sovereignty is part of one fictional character's project of reclaiming his identity, particularly in relation to his home community; in *Stories of the Road Allowance People*, it is part of an effort to preserve peoplehood for a specific Métis community in northern Saskatchewan and for the Métis people more generally; in "Cat with the Boots On," performing rhetorical sovereignty amounts to an act of ingenuity that allows an Indigenous people to continue into the present.

I began this chapter by summarizing the rather bleak situation of Indigenous languages in contemporary North America. By focusing the attention of this chapter on ancestral language influences in Indigenous uses of English and urging readers to acknowledge and respect Indigenous English codes as valid forms of language, in no way do I mean to downplay or negate the primary importance of Indigenous language revitalization. Rather, I concur with Gingell, who urges teachers (and, one may add, readers) to question how particular Indigenous English codes are "*functioning.*"[38] It is important that we ponder the various social, cultural, political, and other contexts that determine the particular functions performed by non-standard varieties of English in a given discourse. Indigenous English codes, Gingell aptly notes, "may provide a stepping stone to learning and ultimately acquiring fluency in the speaking and writing" of ancestral languages: these "interlanguages" create language confidence in speakers and thus may indirectly facilitate language revitalization. Keeper's and the Ravens' mother's code switching in *Keeper'n Me*, for example, may eventually encourage Garnet to start speaking Anishnaabemowin himself. Equally important, as Gingell further observes, Indigenous English codes in Indigenous writing and storytelling perform important rhetorical and political functions.[39] Rhetorical sovereignty is no minor achievement; it is the prerequisite for yet other forms of sovereignty because it allows people to perform peoplehood—in their own voices and in their own traditions. Audience becomes crucial. Many Aboriginal texts are indeed read primarily by non-Aboriginal readers, but this doesn't mean that they are the author's intended audience. Campbell published *Stories of the Road Allowance People* not to entertain or inform non-Native people but to capture the stories and voices of her own people. Campbell's community is her audience, and it will hear itself speak when reading the stories on the page; this is what matters, not whether the language adheres to standard English or is intelligible for non-Aboriginal readers. That many Indigenous storytellers and storywriters now compose in English is no proof of the superiority of the colonizer's tongue and discourse practices, for the English we read in Indigenous texts is used with a specific *Indigenous consciousness* in mind. It is the task of readers to see and understand this Indigenous consciousness, which lies beyond the surface of the English used

---

38 Gingell, "Lips' Inking," 39.
39 Ibid., 40.

by Indigenous writers and storytellers. One possible approach by which readers can accomplish this task is holophrastic reading.

FURTHER READING

William L. Leap's *American Indian English* (Salt Lake City: University of Utah Press, 1993) offers a detailed introduction to Indigenous English codes used in North America. For an excellent survey of Michif and its genesis, see Peter Bakker's *A Language of Our Own* (New York: Oxford University Press, 1997). A short but also very accessible introduction to Okanagan language and discourse is provided by Anthony Mattina and Clara Jack in "Okanagan Communication and Language" (in *Okanagan Sources*, ed. Webber and En'owkin Centre, Penticton, BC: Theytus, 1990). Susan Gingell ("Lips' Inking," *Canadian Journal of Native Education* 32 [2010]) and Pamela V. Sing ("Intersections of Memory, Ancestral Language, and Imagination," *Studies in Canadian Literature* 31.1 [2006]) have offered detailed discussions of Cree and Michif English codes in contemporary Cree and Métis poetry and storytelling. I have discussed the relationship between ancestral language influences and rhetorical sovereignty in "The Marriage of Mother and Father" (*Studies in American Indian Literatures* 22.1 [2010]) and "The Rhetoric of Harry Robinson's 'Cat with the Boots On'" (*Mosaic* 44.2 [2011]).

CHAPTER 5

INDIGENOUS NARRATOLOGY

Narratology is the study of narrative—all those cultural productions that tell a story of some kind. More specifically, narratology is interested in narrative structures and the ways in which these influence our interpretations of both narrative texts and (because ours is essentially a storied existence) the world around us. One of the premises of narratology, therefore, is that narrative forms influence the production of meaning because they guide readers in the processing of narrative. As a particular theory of literary criticism, narratology has always been dominated by Euro-Western traditions of thinking. Wayne Booth, Roland Barthes, Algirdas Julien Greimas, Gérard Genette, Tzvetan Todorov, Seymour Chatman, Jonathan Culler, Peter Brooks, Mieke Bal, the Russian formalists—though based in different countries, all of these are Euro-Western critics trained in Euro-Western discourses of knowledge who tend to work with texts that grow out of Euro-Western cultural traditions. In other words, the various different narrative paradigms and theorems developed by narratologists have been formulated within the study of almost exclusively Euro-Western texts.

Anyone who has ever picked up a novel or short story collection by an Indigenous writer will know that Indigenous stories often don't work in the same way that Euro-Western stories do: narrative lines are flatter, avoiding the ubiquitous climaxes of Euro-Western literatures, moving them to a different part in the narrative, or denying readers any form of denouement (see, for example, Gwich'in writer Robert Arthur Alexie's *Porcupines and China Dolls*, discussed in chapter 6); moreover, Indigenous narratives will often avoid linearity, instead taking on circular or web-like forms. In short, the narrative conventions of Indigenous oral traditions differ from those in Euro-Western traditions of literature, and this difference is also apparent in Indigenous texts written in the so-called "colonizer's genres," such as the novel or short story. What is needed, then, to study the different narrative conventions of Indigenous narrative traditions is an *Indigenous narratology* that is part of a larger Indigenous poetics. If we think of Indigenous poetics as the art of reading Indigenous discourse, a way to map Indigenous texts for meaning, then one central component of these poetics is the question of how Indigenous narratives are structured—how, in other words, Indigenous texts are built so that they can tell their story. When I call this inquiry "Indigenous narratology" I am not referring to a theory of narrative as developed by Indigenous critics, although such a theory would without doubt be a major contribution to the field of Indigenous literary studies. Rather, I define Indigenous narratology as the study of Indigenous narratives and narrative structures in order to determine how they affect our readings and interpretations of Indigenous texts. This Indigenous narratology is concerned with the study of Indigenous rather than Euro-Western writing, by grounding Indigenous narratives and narrative structures in the discourse traditions from which they emerge.

Why should readers of Indigenous literatures be interested in narrative structures? Narrative structures influence the production of meaning in narrative and guide our readings and understandings of texts; they are, in other words, the formal clues to making sense of story. Moreover, Indigenous narratology helps readers to develop an appreciation for Indigenous texts in their own right, as these structures serve to continue ancient Indigenous language and discourse traditions in English. Readers need not be narratologists to develop this appreciation. Reading Indigenous texts for relational word bundles may be sufficient for readers to recognize and acknowledge the basic structures of Indigenous narrative texts and thus to develop a deeper understanding of what they are reading. Relational word bundles are a particularly important tool of Indigenous narratology for two reasons: first, they are the functional equivalents of the holophrase, the central structure of much Indigenous-language discourse; and second, they provide a *holistic approach* to the study of Indigenous narrative structures.

Let me explain these two observations in more detail. Like holophrases in Indigenous-language discourse, relational word bundles express complex ideas and perform significant narrative functions, thus contributing to the narrative grid of a given text. More specifically, relational word bundles are figures of speech that involve a change in the meaning of a word and therefore carry a large bundle of meaning. Metaphor, synecdoche, and irony are different figures of speech, but they share the ability to express a surplus of meaning. Not only are figures of speech word bundles; they may also be used in discourse as significant narrative units. However, no single figure of speech can form a narrative grid on its own. Multiple figures, functioning as significant narrative units, are needed to hold a narrative together. In the end, it is the connections between these figures that produces meaning. Figures that also function as significant narrative units are, therefore, always *relational* word bundles, which, in their interdependence, constitute a given text's narrative grid—what I have described in chapter 2 as *synecdoche writ large* (the narrative grid standing for the narrative). It is their relational and synecdochic nature that makes relational word bundles such holistic tools; they allow readers to study different parts of a text's structure not in and of themselves but in relation to each other, thus avoiding a "chopping up" of the narrative. In short, relational word bundles are such salient structures because they concern both the arrangement of text (they perform narrative functions) and its argument (they are figures of speech); relational word bundles are both form and content.

Because they focus attention on narrative forms, relational word bundles help readers of Indigenous literatures to *map the narrative*, to explore its structure in order to make sense of the text in question. Relational word bundles are based in language, but reading Indigenous narratives for relational word bundles always goes beyond a mere reading for style or form, primarily because relational word bundles often also point readers to the cultural, historical, social, political, spiritual, or other contexts that inform a given text. For example, in *Arctic Dreams and Nightmares*—a collection of short stories by the late Inuk writer Alootook Ipellie (discussed later in this chapter)—the relational word bundles "the great White Ghost" and "the bubble of our life-blood" evoke Inuit traditional knowledge: one is a circumlocution for polar bear that Inuit would have used during the hunt out of respect for the animal; the other includes the word "bubble," which Inuit shamans used to describe the human soul. Aside from forming part of the collection's narrative grid (they are part of the opening section that frames the narrative), these two relational word bundles in *Arctic Dreams and Nightmares* also establish important spiritual contexts that inform Ipellie's collection.

Indigenous narrative structures are so varied and complex that it would take more than a chapter in a book to give them due credit. Rather than providing a comprehensive introduction to Indigenous narratology, this chapter will focus on two texts that, despite their generic differences, share a seemingly "loose" narrative structure, enabling a discussion of the important role played by relational word bundles in the production of meaning in narrative. These texts are *Ceremony*, a novel by Laguna Pueblo writer Leslie Marmon Silko, and Alootook Ipellie's *Arctic Dreams and Nightmares*. I could have picked a number of other texts for this purpose. I have chosen Silko's *Ceremony* not only because it is an often-taught novel but also because Robert Nelson has undertaken a comprehensive analysis of its narrative structure (in *Leslie Marmon Silko's* Ceremony: *The Recovery of Tradition*), on which I can build in my own discussion. Ipellie's *Arctic Dreams and Nightmares*, on the other hand, is a lesser known but equally powerful text that provides a nice counterpoint to the discussion of Silko's novel because of its genre. In both texts, Euro-Western genres are indigenized: Silko's novel functions much like traditional Laguna Pueblo storytelling, while Ipellie's collection of short stories continues Inuit traditions of story cycles. The following discussion will focus on how reading for relational word bundles may ground a study of the narrative structures of *Ceremony* and *Arctic Dreams and Nightmares* in the narrative traditions within which these works originate.

LESLIE MARMON SILKO'S *CEREMONY*

Leslie Marmon Silko's debut novel, *Ceremony*, has become a classic of contemporary Indigenous writing. Together with the work of other prominent Indigenous writers published in the 1970s and 1980s—including N. Scott Momaday (Kiowa), James Welch (Blackfeet-Gros Ventre), Simon J. Ortiz (Acoma Pueblo), Gerald Vizenor (Anishnaabe), and Louise Erdrich (Anishnaabe)—*Ceremony* brought Indigenous literary traditions to the attention of both mainstream and academic readers. This movement is sometimes referred to as the "Native American Renaissance," a term Kenneth Lincoln coined in 1983 in order to refer to the growth in production of literary writing by Indigenous authors that followed N. Scott Momaday's Pulitzer Prize in 1969 for his novel, *House Made of Dawn*.[1] Lincoln's term

---

1   Kenneth Lincoln, *Native American Renaissance* (Berkeley: University of California Press, 1983).

is controversial and has been critiqued for its troubling implications: that there were few or no significant Indigenous literary texts worth studying prior to this "renaissance"; that contemporary Indigenous writing had no roots or connections to earlier traditions; that oral traditions were inferior to written traditions.[2] Such observations, though they may be inferred from the term "Native American Renaissance," simply do not hold. This issue of terminology notwithstanding, Silko's *Ceremony* helped pave the way for many other contemporary Indigenous authors in North America and may be regarded as a seminal work of twentieth-century Native American writing. Published in 1977, it is still a frequently taught novel at universities across North America and beyond, and it is one of very few Indigenous literary works to have received a book-length study (the work by Robert Nelson mentioned above).

Ceremony tells the story of Tayo, a mixed-blood Laguna Pueblo veteran of World War II who faces two challenges upon his return to the Laguna Pueblo reservation: overcoming the post-traumatic stress disorder caused by his war experiences, and ending the drought that is affecting his people. Tayo's story is a journey toward healing. The shell shock from which he suffers cannot be cured by white medicine; nor is returning home enough to heal him, as his community has never fully accepted him because of his mixed-blood heritage. In the course of the novel, Tayo realizes that what he needs to do—in order both to overcome his own struggle and to help his community—is to reconnect with tribal traditions through ceremony. "The purpose of a ceremony," Paula Gunn Allen (Laguna Pueblo) writes, "is to integrate: to fuse the individual with his or her fellows, the community of people with that of the other kingdoms, and this larger communal group with the worlds beyond this one. . . . The person sheds the isolated, individual personality and is restored to conscious harmony with the universe."[3] Tayo's quest toward healing passes through various stages. The scalp ceremony performed on him by the traditional healer, Ku'osh, has no effect, so Tayo seeks the help of the mixed-blood medicine man, Betonie, who conducts a recovery ceremony over Tayo. Betonie also provides him with further guidance once Tayo sets out to complete the ceremony on his

2   James Ruppert, "Fiction: 1968–Present," in *The Cambridge Companion to Native American Literature*, ed. Kenneth M. Roemer and Joy Porter (Cambridge: Cambridge University Press, 2005), 173; A. Robert Lee, "Introduction," *Loosening the Seams: Interpretations of Gerald Vizenor*, ed. A. Robert Lee (Bowling Green, OH: Bowling Green State University Popular Press, 2000), 2.

3   Paula Gunn Allen, *The Sacred Hoop: Recovering the Feminine in American Indian Traditions* (1986; reprint, Boston: Beacon, 1992), 62.

own; the signs Betonie has seen in his vision—stars, cattle, mountain, and a woman—direct Tayo as he moves from one stage of the ceremony to the next. He makes his way to the foot of Mount Taylor (Tse-pi'na in Laguna). Here, Tayo meets the woman Ts'eh, who further guides him toward recovery. On their first night, she points out the stars to him and Tayo realizes they have the same pattern as the stars Betonie saw in his vision. The next day, Tayo goes farther up the mountain and finally finds his uncle Josiah's lost cattle. Having found the stars, cattle, mountain, and woman, Tayo is finally prepared to complete his ceremony. At an abandoned uranium mine, Tayo must watch how his friend Harley is tortured by Emo, Pinky, and Leroy. Though war veterans like Tayo himself, these men are engaged in nothing but self-destruction and violence and have become agents of Ck'o'yo witchery, which threatens their people's well-being by destroying their relationship to the land. Realizing that he must restrain himself from killing Emo in order to save Harley and himself, Tayo transforms rather than destroys the Ck'o'yo witchery; he does not let it destroy him and his people by succumbing to further violence and destruction. It is with this that his ceremony is completed. The drought has ended, and Tayo returns home to tell the story of his quest to the elders, who give him their blessings. As Tayo learns to renew his relationship to the land, with the guidance of Betonie and Ts'eh, he is healed, and so is his community.

Tayo's story is told in one continuous prose narrative interspersed by thirty smaller texts, which are taken from Laguna and Navajo oral traditions and woven into the postwar narrative of Tayo, set on the page as verse. These embedded texts, as well as their printed ethnographic sources, are the focus of Nelson's book on *Ceremony*, which will form the basis of my own discussion of Silko's novel. My analysis will, however, extend Nelson's by pointing out the relational word bundles that constitute the novel's narrative grid or, as Nelson calls it, its backbone.[4] Nelson adopts the backbone metaphor in his reading of *Ceremony* to suggest the novel's groundedness in traditional Keresan storytelling practices.[5] As he points out, a Keresan discourse marker used to indicate the closing of a story is "*to me ts'itc^c*," whose longer variant, "*to me ts'itc^{ca} s'ak'o 'ya k'ayo tsecpi t'its^c*," is rendered in English as "that long is my aunt's backbone." Silko does not make use of this particular discourse marker, but as Nelson notes, just as she marks the opening of the novel for her readers, she indicates its closing

---

4   Robert M. Nelson, *Leslie Marmon Silko's* Ceremony: *The Recovery of Tradition* (New York: Peter Lang, 2008), 4.

5   Keresan refers to (the language of) the Keres Pueblo peoples in New Mexico, which include the Laguna and Acoma Pueblos as well as the Rio Grande Pueblos.

through another discourse marker in English. Equally important, she uses narrative threads from Laguna Pueblo traditions to form the backbone of the modern story of Tayo. The notion of a story's backbone underlines Keresan understandings of stories as living entities, Nelson further writes; he points to an early example in *Ceremony* of the intimate relationship between story and life.[6] Still in the opening of the novel, the narrator describes a male storyteller who "rubbed his belly. / I keep them [the stories] here / [he said] / Here, put your hand on it. / See, it is moving. / There is life here / for the people" (2).

Nelson's use of the backbone metaphor is not restricted to the novel as such, however, but can be found in at least three contexts:

1. to refer to "the spirit backbone of story"[7]—the "long story of the people" Silko speaks of in her story collection *Storyteller*;[8]
2. to explain the role of embedded texts in *Ceremony* more generally; these texts serve, he argues, as the "backbone—the spinal column—of the novel, the skeleton of story that Tayo's story, the prose narrative, takes shape upon and fleshes out";[9] and
3. to discuss Silko's use of one particular embedded text in *Ceremony*: the story of Pa'caya'nyi and Hummingbird Man that Nelson refers to as the novel's "backbone series" or "backbone story."[10]

Nelson thus distinguishes the backbone of story from the backbone of the novel and the novel's backbone story, and he does so in order to illustrate Silko's use of traditional Keresan storytelling devices, contextualizing in Laguna fashion the modern Laguna story of Tayo into traditional Laguna story.[11] More specifically, then, Nelson's study of *Ceremony* is concerned with Silko's use of intertexts, how these intertexts determine the novel's narrative structure, and how this structure, in turn, influences the ways in which we read and understand Silko's novel.

The various stages of Tayo's quest in the prose narrative are reflected, or mirrored, in the intertexts from Laguna and Navajo ethnographic

---

6   Nelson, *Silko's* Ceremony, 22–23.
7   Ibid., 30.
8   Leslie Marmon Silko, *Storyteller* (New York: Arcade, 1981), 7.
9   Nelson, *Silko's* Ceremony, 23.
10 Ibid., viii, 18.
11 Ibid., 14, 19, 25–26.

materials that are embedded in *Ceremony*. As Nelson notes, the six sections in the prose narrative of the novel follow the same pattern of departure and recovery as do the concatenations of embedded texts.[12] Moreover, Nelson shows at length how each embedded text, or series of embedded texts, forms what he calls a "*homological* relationship" with a particular episode in the prose narrative of Tayo's journey. What he means by this is that both the embedded "ethnographic" texts and the prose narrative about Tayo derive from "the long story of the people," that spirit backbone of story central to Laguna peoplehood.[13] Why, then, does Nelson read the embedded texts, and not the prose narrative, as the novel's backbone? This reading is based on mapping the narrative space of the novel and locating the thirty embedded texts in relation to the narrative line of the modern story of Tayo, arriving at a narrative map that reveals a structure very much resembling a body's spinal column. As Nelson further points out, in three instances, embedded texts connect important episodes in the prose narrative, and the narrative space of embedded texts gradually decreases over the course of the novel at about the same rate as that of the episodes in the prose narrative, which tend to occupy less and less space toward the end of the novel.[14] It is the embedded texts, then, that seem to hold the novel together, much like a backbone holds a body together.

To stay within the imagery used by Nelson, if the prose narrative fleshes out the backbone formed by the embedded texts, muscles are needed to keep the flesh from slipping away from the bone. The homological connections made by Nelson between embedded texts and prose narrative take place on the level of character, function, cultural context, and motif, but these relationships ultimately have to be established in the text through *language*.[15] More specifically, the connections between the various different narrative threads of *Ceremony* are produced with the help of relational word bundles. These act as signposts to the readers, so that as they read the novel they are able to recognize the interdependence of narrative threads that creates "a novel wordweb,"[16] that web of words forming a meaningful whole, the novel we have come to know as *Ceremony*. To illustrate the role of relational word bundles in establishing the narrative structure of Silko's novel, I will focus on two series of embedded texts, which are also analyzed by Nelson: the opening as well as closing series, which form the novel's narrative frame; and

---

12   Ibid., 16–17.
13   Ibid., 29.
14   Ibid., 15.
15   Ibid., 29–31.
16   Ibid., 18.

the Sunrise series, also part of the narrative frame. In other words, rather than aiming for an exhaustive reading for relational word bundles in *Ceremony*, I will offer a thorough discussion of a few of the novel's relational word bundles as they concern two central series of embedded texts.

Opening and closing frames are characteristic of traditions of orature around the world. In some of these traditions, these frames are signalled through specific discourse markers or formulae—sets of words whose narrative function is to indicate to the audience the beginning or end of the story performed. The narrative frames thus created are integral parts of the storytelling performance because they provide much of the interpretative context for listeners, including, for example, the story's generic classification, which may be indicated by a formula or through the use of quotatives.[17] In Keresan traditions, the phrases used to signal a story's opening and closing include "*hama-ha*" (translated by Franz Boas as "long ago— eh")[18] and "*to me ts'itc^{ca} s'ak'o 'ya k'ayo tsecpi t'its^c*" ("that long is my aunt's backbone"), respectively. As noted above, Silko does not frame *Ceremony* with these traditional Keresan formulae. Instead, she relies on other narrative strategies to achieve a narrative frame that carries much of her novel's interpretative context (see fig. 5.1).

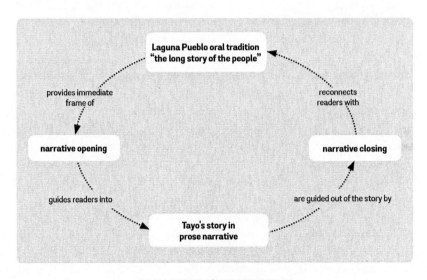

FIG. 5.1 *CEREMONY'S* NARRATIVE FRAME

---

17   See Richard Bauman, *Verbal Art as Performance* (Prospect Heights, IL: Waveland, 1984), 9, 11, 15.

18   Nelson, *Silko's* Ceremony, 58.

The opening of *Ceremony* is formed by four isolated embedded texts, each of which is assigned a separate page. These four embedded texts appear before the prose narrative of Tayo's journey begins, so it makes sense to read them as forming a separate unit—embedded not into the prose narrative but into the novel as a whole.[19] Together with the embedded texts that constitute the closing, the four embedded texts of the novel's opening serve to frame—or, as Nelson sometimes puts it, bracket—the novel and hence the story performed therein. However, the point of this frame is not so much to establish a border between the story told in the novel and the outside world as it is to create and define a relationship between Laguna oral tradition and this novel by a contemporary Laguna Pueblo writer. It is this relationship that gives *Ceremony* its unique interpretative context. Readers are asked to see the modern story of Tayo in the context of the "long story of the people," not separate from it.

Nelson traces four texts within *Ceremony*'s narrative opening, each of which seems to be narrated by an omniscient narrator who, we may assume, also tells the story of Tayo in the prose narrative as well as the stories in the other embedded texts. The first embedded text resembles the sacred narratives in Laguna Pueblo tradition. It evokes Ts'its'tsi'nako, Thought-Woman, the Laguna Pueblo creator and culture hero, and her role as creator of the universe and of stories, including the one the reader is about to read: "I'm telling you the story / she is thinking" (1). The next embedded text of the opening, entitled "Ceremony," features a male storyteller's monologue about the interdependence of story, ceremony, and life; this monologue is presented in the first person but is marked as reported speech through the quotative "[he said]," which is repeated twice (2). The monologue is followed by a much shorter text: three lines spoken by a female voice, who insists emphatically that "The only cure / I know / is a good ceremony" (3). While the monologue that precedes the woman's speech is marked by poetic language, this particular embedded text is more conversational in style, as is the text framing the woman's speech: "what she said." Finally, the last embedded text in the novel's opening, centred and printed in the middle of the page, is the word "Sunrise" (4)—the shortest and, I concur with Nelson, also the most ambiguous text in *Ceremony*'s opening.[20]

At a first glance, these four embedded texts of the novel's opening seem to be too different, both in content and style, to amount to anything meaningful, but in fact they could not be any more meaningful. These texts are

---

19   See also ibid., 39.
20   Ibid., 50.

actually connected, and not just because anything that follows after the first page is, according to the narrator, Thought-Woman's creation. As Nelson puts it, these four embedded texts are part of the four-stage transformation through which readers of *Ceremony* have to go to move from their own reality to the story of Tayo that lies beyond the novel's opening[21]; that is, readers need to realize the interdependence of creation, story, and ceremony that is central to Laguna traditions of thought and that also marks the central theme of the opening. How does *Ceremony* succeed in arguing for the central relationship between creation, story, and ceremony? Or, to put it differently, how does the text help readers to make sense of it? The interdependence of creation, story, and ceremony is suggested by relational word bundles that establish relationships between the four texts as well as with Laguna oral tradition and the novel's prose narrative, through foreshadowing and backshadowing. In other words, all that readers have to do to gain a deeper understanding of what they are reading is to pay attention to the relational word bundles that form the novel's opening.

The first embedded text introduces Thought-Woman as ur-creator— "whatever she thinks about / appears"—and as the creator of stories, including the story told in *Ceremony*—"I'm telling you the story / she is thinking." In its reference to Thought-Woman's presence in both Laguna Pueblo narrative tradition ("whatever she thinks about / appears") and Silko's novel ("I'm telling you the story / she is thinking"), the first embedded text of *Ceremony* establishes two important narrative movements. First, there is the intertextual reference to Laguna Pueblo narrative tradition, that backbone of story, or what Silko refers to as the "long story of the people," which is not part of *Ceremony* but forms the novel's immediate literary context. Second, there is foreshadowing to an inside text: the story told in *Ceremony* (that is, both the prose narrative and the book's other embedded texts). At this point in the novel, this last movement is still rather general. "I'm telling you the story / she is thinking" links to the whole text but doesn't have specific connectors—not yet, that is.

The first textual connector for Thought-Woman's story follows directly in the second embedded text, which ends as follows: "And in the belly of this story / the rituals and the ceremony / are still growing." The two metaphors implied in these lines ("belly of this story" and "rituals and the ceremony / are still growing") establish a link back to Thought-Woman's story in the first embedded text, for "this story," we may assume, is "the story / [that] she is thinking" and that will be told in whatever follows

---

21   Ibid., 39.

the opening. A similar but more general connection to the first embedded text is established much earlier in the monologue, when the male story-teller quoted therein observes that "You don't have anything / if you don't have the stories" and that, moreover, "There is life here / for the people"— "here" referring to the belly of the storyteller, where he keeps the stories. Stories, in other words, are survival; they keep the people alive as long as the stories are protected. The interdependence of *life* and of *creation* with *stories*, as suggested in the figure of Thought-Woman, is hence picked up and elaborated in the storyteller's monologue. Reinforcing and building on the metaphor of stories as living entities, the storyteller's monologue also foreshadows the central idea evoked in the very last embedded text of the novel's opening, "Sunrise," which functions as a symbol of life and creation.

The storyteller's monologue centres on the connection between life, creation, and stories, but also introduces another idea, namely, their re-lationship to ceremony. It does so by way of its title, "Ceremony," and its closing lines—"And in the belly of this story / the rituals and *the ceremony* / are still growing" (emphasis mine)—which frame the monologue by introducing the notion of ceremony as a central component of life. Cere-mony, Allen argues, aims at integration and connection of individuals with their communities and of communities with the world around them, as noted earlier. If the belly of stories houses ceremonies, keeps them strong and alive so that the people can reconnect with one another and the world, then stories are repositories of survival. This is one way of read-ing the storyteller's closing lines, as referring to the responsibility of story-keepers to carry the life of the people. As Nelson observes, however, a less generic reading is also possible, namely, of the storyteller as Tayo, where "this story" refers more specifically to Tayo's story. In other words, not only does Tayo's ceremony in the prose narrative heal him and his com-munity, but his very story also carries the power of ceremony for others; it continues its healing beyond the pages of the novel.[22] We may therefore say that, through its very frame, the second embedded text establishes yet another connection: to the prose narrative and Tayo's journey toward healing through ceremony as well as to the third embedded text and the woman's speech about ceremony as cure. The second embedded text, then, contains both backshadowing and foreshadowing.

The same may be said of the third embedded text, the conversational observation of a woman that "the only cure / [she] know[s] / is a good

---

22   Ibid., 45.

ceremony." Her observation establishes links both with the prose narrative, by evoking the ceremony Tayo will complete, and with the storyteller's monologue about the relationship between life, story, and ceremony. What is more, by the time readers hear the woman speak, they will be prepared for her claim because they have already heard the argument about the potency of ceremony offered in the two preceding embedded texts. A good ceremony is alive and growing—not just anywhere, but sheltered in the belly of a story, which in turn ensures the survival of the people (as suggested by the male storyteller in his monologue) and connects the people with all creation, since stories, just like anything else, originate with Thought-Woman (as implied in the first embedded text about Thought-Woman).

Thus, by connecting outside reality with the story told in the novel, the opening of *Ceremony* gradually leads readers into the novel. The mythic narrative of Thought-Woman in the first embedded text teaches readers that story is part of creation and evokes Laguna oral tradition, the immediate literary context of the novel. Next, readers learn about the vibrant power of story for the survival of the people, which is released, as the third text argues, through ceremony. Finally, the third embedded text helps establish the link back to creation—the central idea of the novel's first embedded text—by providing the bridge to the last embedded text of the opening, the one-word text: "Sunrise." For, if ceremony is a cure, then it ensures health—in other words, life—and life is one of the symbols evoked by this last text of the opening.

"Sunrise" may read like a stage direction in the script of a play, but it can also be seen as the symbol of a (new) beginning.[23] A beginning, you may ask, of what? For one thing, this last embedded text suggests the beginning of Tayo's story, which unfolds on the succeeding pages and happens to begin with the dawning of a new day: "He [Tayo] lay there in the morning and watched the high small window above the bed; dark gray gradually became lighter until it cast a white square on the opposite wall at dawn" (6). The beginning of the story told in the novel is the beginning of Tayo's journey toward healing, which will end with a prayer to Sunrise. Of course, first-time readers of *Ceremony* will not be aware at this particular narrative moment of the role of sunrise as the novel's central motif and frame. And yet, the mere word "Sunrise" is also a foreshadowing of what is to come. It is a figure of anticipation, of something that is not yet but will

---

23   The notion of stage direction as one of functions performed by this particular embedded text is suggested by Nelson (ibid., 50).

be in the future. The one-word text ending the novel's opening, "Sunrise," may also be read as a symbol of life and creation; as such, it functions as backshadowing to the three embedded texts preceding it as well as to the Laguna Pueblo narrative tradition evoked by the first embedded text, because all of these texts concern creation and life in one way or another.

At this point, it might be helpful to briefly summarize our findings thus far. The opening of *Ceremony* comprises four isolated texts that appear in succession. These texts may be seen as forming a larger whole because of thematic associations. Creation marks the origin of peoples, who are kept alive through stories, which in turn house and nurture ceremonies that ensure the peoples' continuity. Story and ceremony, in other words, are components of the larger cycle of creation and ultimately life itself. The interconnectedness of the four texts forming the narrative opening of *Ceremony* is established by way of narrative units acting as either intertextual or intratextual references, thus providing textual connectors between what may otherwise appear to be entirely separate texts. Following the heuristic outlined in chapter 2 (see table 2.4), we may say that these narrative units qualify as relational word bundles:

1. They take the form of two central figures—of anticipation, in the case of foreshadowing, and of recollection/recovery, in the case of backshadowing. In other words, these narrative units mean what they mean (for example, that a good ceremony is the only cure for a lost individual, such as Tayo), and yet, they also carry meaning beyond their literal meaning (for example, by evoking the reason why a good ceremony is the only cure for a person who is lost in the world). Moreover, some of these narrative units are not just flashbacks or examples of foreshadowing but also involve further rhetorical figures, such as metaphor and symbol.

2. These central figures, moreover, perform significant narrative functions, as they help constitute the novel's narrative opening, which gradually leads readers into the novel, helping them understand its interpretative context: the interdependence of creation, story, and ceremony that is so central to Laguna thought.

3. Finally, all these narrative units are interconnected: they establish links between one another, thus forming the novel's opening, which, in turn, is part of the novel's narrative grid that holds together the story told therein (see fig. 5.2).

The narrative opening in *Ceremony* is just one of various narrative components that make up its narrative grid, but the opening plays a significant role in the novel because it makes readers "jump through hoops," as Nelson puts it. In Laguna and Navajo traditions, hoops have traditionally been associated with wholeness and the people's continuity, but they may also be understood as vehicles for transformation.[24] In the prose narrative, the traditional healer Betonie has Tayo move through a series of five hoops during the recovery ceremony he performs (141–44); in the process, Nelson notes, Tayo migrates back "into the Fifth World [of Laguna creation] awaiting his return," thus "mov[ing] from a state of complete lost-ness to a state of [re-]centered-ness."[25]

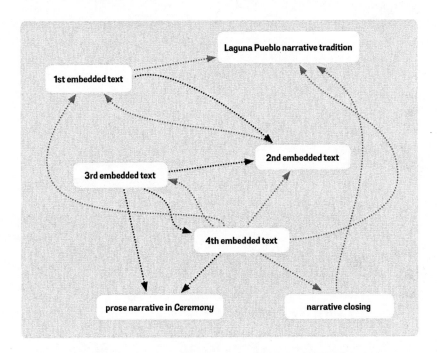

FIG. 5.2 THE NARRATIVE GRID CREATED BY *CEREMONY*'S OPENING

Similarly, Silko has her readers migrate through four initial hoops, or texts, before they enter the prose narrative of Tayo.[26] In the process, Silko gradually outlines the interpretative context of the novel, thus preparing

---

24   Ibid., 50–51.
25   Ibid., 54.
26   Ibid.

readers for the world of the novel; specifically, Tayo's story and the embedded texts forming its backbone should be read as grounded in the context of Laguna story and Laguna notions of story. The homological relationship Nelson points out between the opening hoop series and Betonie's hoop series is intriguing, not only because it provides us with a Laguna context with which to understand the opening. The recovery ceremony performed by Betonie marks a reference point for some of the opening's relational word bundles, particularly those in the second and third embedded texts, which are concerned with the potency of ceremony and, ultimately, story. Though subtle, the relationship between the novel's two hoop series is, then, an example of the connections that exist between backbone and prose narrative. These connections are vital to ensuring the fleshed-out story of Tayo does not slip off the novel's skeleton.

Connections between backbone and prose narrative are numerous, and I shall focus here on but one example, partly because it allows me to direct the analysis back to *Ceremony*'s narrative frame, of which the opening is but one component. The last element in the opening, the one-word text, "Sunrise," overlaps with another series of embedded texts, what Nelson calls "the three-part Sunrise series." This series moves from the discourse marker "Sunrise" in the opening to the traditional song about two-thirds of the way through the novel and finally to the prayer that ends the novel.[27] As noted above, the one-word text in the novel's opening is as much stage direction as it is a symbol for creation and life. Its function and meaning are eventually commented on, in the second text of the Sunrise series, a traditional Sunrise song repeated by Tayo one morning as he watches the sunrise from the foot of Mount Taylor:

> Sunrise!
> We come at sunrise
> to greet you.
> We call you
> at sunrise.
> Father of the clouds
> you are beautiful
> at sunrise.
> Sunrise! (182)

---

27   Ibid., 57.

The framing lines "Sunrise" in this song link directly back to the one-word text ending the novel's opening, but the song is also connected to two episodes within the prose narrative of the novel. First of all, the Sunrise song is both embedded text and part of the prose narrative as Tayo "repeated the words [of the song] as he remembered them." The connection between embedded text and prose episode is further suggested by the lines "the sun came over the edge of the horizon" and, more specifically, through a metaphor: "The power of each day spilled over the hills in great silence. Sunrise" (182). The Sunrise song also provides a connection to earlier points in the prose narrative: the story's very beginning one morning at dawn (5–6), as well as another episode about one-third of the way through the novel. In this particular episode, Tayo remembers the summer before the war when, during another dry spell, "he got up before dawn" to ride down to a spring in the canyon (93). This last episode is not just the link back and forward to the last text of the opening and to the Sunrise song that Tayo repeats later in the novel; it also provides connections to still other narrative threads in the novel. As Tayo watches life around the spring, he remembers the story of how "Spider Woman had told Sun Man how to win the storm clouds back from the Gambler"—a direct link to one of the embedded texts forming the novel's backbone (170–76). Moreover, upon leaving the canyon, Tayo sees "a bright green hummingbird shimmering above the dry sandy ground" (94–95)—an equally direct link to the nine-part story of Humming Bird and Pa'caya'nyi that mirrors Tayo's quest toward healing.[28] The Sunrise song thus links to all of the following: the end of the novel's opening; three episodes in the prose narrative, one of which, in turn, establishes connections with other series of embedded texts; and the Kapauta motif and the Humming Bird and Pa'caya'nyi series, both of which are taken from Laguna Pueblo literary tradition. The result is a beautifully crafted example of foreshadowing-within-backshadowing: the Sunrise song in the Sunrise series provides a reference backward within the prose narrative to Tayo's memory of another dry spell, which eventually ended with the appearance of the hummingbird when he went to greet the new day by the spring in the canyon. Within this narrative moment, the evocation of the story of Humming Bird and Pa'caya'nyi foreshadows a future event in the prose narrative: the eventual end of the drought at the end of the novel. Thus, Silko links sunrise and water, two elements essential to the continuity of the people, and she also emphasizes the progress Tayo is making on his journey toward healing: while in the earlier episode

---

28　See Silko, *Ceremony*, 46–49, 53–54, 71–72, 82, 105–106, 113, 151–52, 180, 255–56.

he did not remember the Sunrise song, he does so now, shortly after Betonie has performed the recovery ceremony.

The final text in the Sunrise series is the prayer that ends the novel: "Sunrise, / accept this offering, / Sunrise" (262). Like the Sunrise song, this prayer is framed by the word "Sunrise," which functions again as a symbol, though in this particular case, it is also a form of address, to "Sunrise, understood as a living entity."[29] Thus, this last text in the novel establishes links back to the two other texts in the Sunrise series, which also feature the same one-word symbol. Moreover, just as the first Sunrise text is the final stage of the novel's opening, the Sunrise prayer at the end of the novel serves as its closing, leading readers out of the novel, but not without reconnecting them with Laguna Pueblo traditions of narrative and prayer (see fig. 5.1). This way, the novel releases its readers with the knowledge that what they have just read is not just a series of events but one single event—the recovery of Tayo and his community—that happens in the timespace between two sunrises, between opening and closing the book, between beginning to read and finishing *Ceremony*.[30] Moreover, by harking back to the opening of the novel, its closing reminds readers yet again that this single event, the modern story of Tayo, is embedded in the "long story of the people" (as mentioned earlier).

The relational word bundles that help constitute the Sunrise series in *Ceremony* are very particular, then: they all take the form of a single word, "Sunrise"—a symbol that serves as a significant narrative unit, functioning as backshadowing, as foreshadowing, or as both. As such, the relational word bundles in the Sunrise series stress the central imagery of the novel— sunrise as life and creation—and produce a narrative structure that is modelled on traditional Laguna traditions of performance: opening, story as prayer, closing. (In the third Sunrise series text, "this offering" refers essentially to the novel, *Ceremony*, as a whole.)[31] Further, the relational word bundles in the Sunrise series also establish narrative relations to other parts in the novel, including two other series of embedded texts taken from Laguna Pueblo narrative tradition. The resulting structure, the novel's narrative grid, is an intricate pattern of relationships: within and outside the series; between different sections of the prose narrative; and between different narrative threads of prose narrative and embedded texts. The complexity of this pattern of relationships in *Ceremony* is suggested in figure 5.3.

---

29 Nelson, *Silko's* Ceremony, 57.
30 See ibid., 62.
31 Ibid., 61–62.

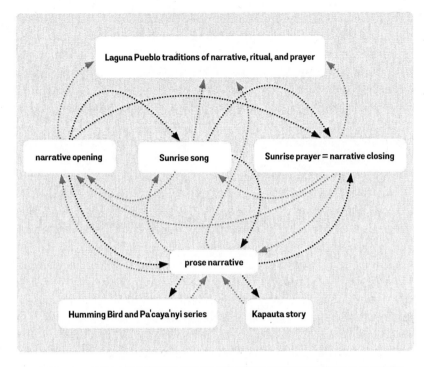

FIG. 5.3 THE NARRATIVE GRID CREATED BY NARRATIVE FRAME AND SUNRISE SERIES IN *CEREMONY*

This figure is based on the narrative frame and Sunrise series alone and does not include internal relationships within the narrative opening and the prose narrative. It is therefore only an approximate illustration of the intricate web of relationships established within *Ceremony* between different elements of its narrative structure. What figure 5.3 shows quite clearly, however, is the extent to which *Ceremony* is indeed contextualized by Laguna Pueblo verbal traditions, whether they concern ritual, song, or narrative. Into the contemporary, but fictional, Laguna story of Tayo, the novel directly weaves Laguna ethnographic texts; simultaneously, it grounds the resulting text into the "long story of the people." Silko once described Pueblo discourse and storytelling as "resembl[ing] something like a spider's web—with many little threads radiating from a center, criss-crossing each other. As with the web, the structure emerges as it is made and you must simply listen and trust, as the Pueblo people do, that meaning will be made."[32] Pueblo people, moreover, "don't think of words as being alone"; as

---

32   Leslie Marmon Silko, "Language and Literature from a Pueblo Indian Perspective," in *English Literature: Opening up the Canon*, ed. Leslie A. Fiedler and Houston A.

Silko further explains, "words are always with other words, and the other words are almost always in a story of some sort."[33] Though not a spiderweb per se, figure 5.3 does suggest the web-like structure of *Ceremony*, in which various seemingly unrelated embedded texts criss-cross one another and the various threads in the prose narrative, creating the whole that becomes the novel. What this carefully woven narrative structure underlines is that Tayo's story is part of "the long story of the people"; it is never separate from it. *Ceremony* is deeply grounded in Laguna Pueblo traditions not just in terms of content but, particularly, also in terms of its form.

By unravelling the complex narrative relationships in *Ceremony*, readers gather a deeper understanding of the story of Tayo as well as the relevance of the ceremony he sets out to perform in the timespace of Silko's novel. Readers are invited to read Tayo's story in relation to traditional Laguna stories, that is, to understand contemporary Laguna writing by way of Laguna literary traditions. For example, just as Sun Man (in the traditional story of Kapauta) realizes that he cannot kill the Ck'o'yo magician Kapauta, Tayo realizes that he cannot destroy Ck'o'yo witchery; he can only transform it.[34] Just as Tayo is guided by Betonie and Ts'eh, two knowledge keepers, readers are urged to recognize the important connections between, on the one hand, Laguna history and, on the other, contemporary Laguna life and the potency of traditional knowledges. In so doing, readers will ultimately come to understand that Tayo's quest toward healing contemporarizes the fragmented traditional Laguna stories as much as these stories traditionalize Tayo's contemporary experience in the novel.[35]

The reading of *Ceremony* offered here can do justice neither to the complexity of Silko's novel nor to the insightful and comprehensive analysis of this complexity by Nelson. What my discussion does illustrate, however, is that a narratology grounded in Indigenous linguistic and discursive traditions has much to contribute to the study of Indigenous literatures. Nelson discusses the intricate narrative pattern of *Ceremony* without reading the novel for relational word bundles—that is, at least not consciously so. Many of the narrative connections he points out in his study—for example, the framing and Sunrise series—do indeed mention words, lines, and phrases that, I have argued, constitute relational word bundles. Apparently, reading for relational word bundles is more intuitive than it

---

Baker Jr. (Baltimore: Johns Hopkins University Press, 1981), 54.

33   Ibid., 55.
34   Nelson, *Silko's* Ceremony, 132.
35   Ibid., 25.

may seem. For when we read, we always also map what we read: we try to establish connections between different parts of the narrative, between characters, between the text we are reading and outside texts, and so on. Reading for relational word bundles is, then, simply a more conscious way of reading. It focuses readers' attention on those structures that hold a text together, the signposts on the map that is the text—not just any text, however, but an Indigenous text. And this is why relational word bundles serve as such important tools in Indigenous narratology: they are grounded in Indigenous, as opposed to Euro-Western, discourse traditions.

ALOOTOOK IPELLIE'S *ARCTIC DREAMS AND NIGHTMARES*[36]

Where Silko's novel *Ceremony* continues Laguna Pueblo storytelling traditions, Alootook Ipellie's story collection *Arctic Dreams and Nightmares* continues Inuit traditions of story cycles. Yet there is one crucial difference between the two texts, other than the respective Indigenous narrative tradition that each continues: where *Ceremony* may initially appear to be one long concatenation of words without any inherent structure, *Arctic Dreams and Nightmares* may seem to the untrained reader like a series of unrelated stories. In *Ceremony*, Silko manages to tell a story without dividing the text into chapters. Her novel is a continuous flow of words, some contemporary, some traditional. By arranging these words into larger parts, and connecting these larger pieces with one another, she is able to produce an intricate and coherent web of words. Ipellie's story collection, *Arctic Dreams and Nightmares*, works exactly the other way around. The collection gathers together twenty clearly demarcated stories; each bears an individual title and is further distinguished from the others by an accompanying black-and-white pen-and-ink drawing, which acts as a visual summary of that story. Thus, while the challenge of reading *Ceremony* is to put together what clearly must belong together, given the book's physical form, the challenge for readers of *Arctic Dreams and Nightmares* is to find the narrative line in a series of stories that seem unrelated, aside from the fact that they apparently share a narrator. Of course, Ipellie's stories may be read independently, and they would still make sense. When read sequentially and in relation to one another, however, they gain far deeper

---

36 The following discussion of Alootook Ipellie's *Arctic Dreams and Nightmares* is by no means a complete ethnographic survey of Inuit cultural and sacred traditions; nor is it possible to sketch in a short overview all of the regional differences in traditions among Inuit groups across the Arctic. Where possible I have attempted to rely on Inuit sources, such as the *Interviewing Inuit Elders* series published by Nunavut Arctic College, to guide my analysis of Ipellie's text.

meanings. As with *Ceremony*, connections between individual stories in *Arctic Dreams and Nightmares* may be established by reading the text for relational word bundles.

At first, the narrative line in *Arctic Dreams and Nightmares* appears to be rather loose. The stories, which involve episodes of Inuit life after first contact with Europeans, are held together by one recurrent first-person narrator, "a powerful shaman" (xix) who has recently passed away, as revealed in the first four stories of the collection. The remainder of his narrative represents a kind of travelogue of the narrator's living soul as he recalls his adventures travelling across the Arctic. As such, *Arctic Dreams and Nightmares* shares many features with the Qayaq story cycle, an epic narrative known in various versions throughout the circumpolar world.[37] Like Qayaq, the shape-shifting narrator in *Arctic Dreams and Nightmares* travels across the Arctic, meeting all kinds of interesting, often highly curious, people and animals. However, whereas Qayaq is a restless wanderer in search of his lost brothers, the narrator-shaman of *Arctic Dreams and Nightmares* is journeying on the traditional Inuit seasonal rounds in search of food, to provide for his family. With the exception of the first four stories, the events that inspire his stories are not presented in chronological order. From the descriptions of the seasons, readers may gather only that these events stretch over several years, even centuries. In fact, the narrator-shaman seems to have been a contemporary of both William Shakespeare and Brigitte Bardot at the same time, which has only one possible explanation: he seems to have been reborn again and again. His stories concern either hunting or sex or, in some cases, both. The question of survival (through sustenance or procreation) hence features prominently in the narrative, providing a thematic focus for the twenty stories. Ultimately, however, *Arctic Dreams and Nightmares* is held together not by recurring theme and narrator alone but also through an intracately designed narrative opening and closing that frames what essentially acts as a story cycle. The narrative frame in Ipellie's collection is less obvious than that in *Ceremony*, but it is just as important. For it is this opening and closing frame that contextual-

---

37 Ann Chandonnet, preface to *The Epic of Qayaq: The Longest Story Ever Told by My People*, by Lela Kiana Oman, ed. Priscilla Tyler and Maree Brooks (Ottawa: Carleton University Press, 1995), viii. For retellings of the Qayaq cycle, see, for example, Oman, *The Epic of Qayaq*; Catherine Attla, *K'etetaalkkaanee, the One Who Paddles among the People and Animals: The Story of an Ancient Traveller*, trans. Eliza Jones (Fairbanks: Alaska Native Language Center, 1990); and Ticasuk, *The Longest Story Ever Told: Qayaq, the Magical Man*, 2nd ed. (Fairbanks: University of Alaska Press, 2008).

izes Ipellie's stories as a celebration of Inuit traditional beliefs (particularly shamanism), and this narrative celebration relies on two conventions of Inuit literary and rhetorical traditions: satire and the story cycle form.

The narrative opening of *Arctic Dreams and Nightmares* is formed by the first four stories, which introduce the story cycle's narrative situation. That these stories differ from the remaining ones in the collection is also suggested by the narration, which switches from the experiencing self to the narrating and reflecting self. The opening also tells a much deeper story, which sets the theme and mood for the remainder of *Arctic Dreams and Nightmares*. It is not until story 4 that readers discover that the first-person narrator is "one of the most powerful shamans living in the Arctic" (22); yet there are clues that suggest he may be a shaman well before he admits to being one. In story 1, "Self-Portrait: Inverse Ten Commandments," the narrator wakes up in the middle of the night to find himself face to face with the devil, whose hands are outstretched, an ugly little face on each finger. Eventually, the narrator realizes that this frightening image is, in fact, an incarnation of himself; he begins to fight the image, but it is only when it disappears that he realizes his soul has just gotten rid of its own devilish being, and that if he hadn't done so, he would not have been granted a happy afterlife (8–9).

Given its references to Satan, the Ten Commandments, the Garden of Eden, and life in the afterworld, this first story appears to have a very Christian tone. This impression extends to story 2, "Ascension of My Soul in Death," which describes the journey of the narrator's soul into the supernatural world. But this story takes an unexpected turn when the narrator suddenly states, "There is no truth to anyone being able to live for an eternity" (15). According to the narrator, one's soul is indeed granted a life in the afterworld, but apparently only for the period of time that one has spent on earth; once this period has passed, one's soul is reborn. Here is the first hint that the apparently Christian context of the narrator's account is not very Christian after all, but instead is informed by a mixture of Inuit spiritual beliefs, the Caribou Inuit belief in reincarnation, and other Inuit groups' beliefs in an afterlife.

In story 3, "Nanuq, the White Ghost, Repents," the narrator finally reveals the circumstances of his death. While he and his father were out on the ice, hunting seal, a polar bear had come upon them. "With a few powerful swipes of its claws and life-ending bites from its hungry jaws, the great White Ghost had cut through our flesh and burst open the bubble of our life-blood" (17). The "great White Ghost" evokes the expression "great white one," a direct translation of *qakurturjuaq*, which is a common synonym for "polar bear" (usually *nanuq* in Inuktitut) and is used during hunting or by "shamans & hunters in Inuit song and myth."[38] *Nanuq* often also functions as an animal helper of shamans, and the polar bear is a very strong one at that, due to his "special status . . . among the animal species."[39] The narrator uses variations of the expression "great white one" throughout story 3, including in its title: he is referred to as "Nanuq, the White Ghost," the "great white Nanuq," (17) and the "Great White Ghost" (17, 18, 19). These phrases provide the first indication of the narrator's involvement with shamanism. The second indication follows in the second part of the phrase quoted above, "the bubble of our life-blood." The narrator's use of the word *bubble* to refer to his soul might not prove that he is a shaman, but it is nonetheless a strong indication, as this is the word that Inuit shamans use to describe the human soul.[40] *Arctic Dreams and Nightmares* can be read as the narrative of an Inuit shaman who shares with his fellow Inuit (and potential non-Inuit readers) his knowledge of death and the journey of his soul into the afterworld.

Given the allusions to shamanism in story 3, the first two stories need to be reconsidered from a new perspective: they may seem Christian in tone but are, in fact, deeply embedded in Inuit spiritual traditions. The narrator-shaman initially describes the apparition in front of him as an "**incarnation** of myself" (5; emphasis in original). Indeed, when the ugly faces on the fingers of his incarnation start telling him stories about "Hell's **Garden of Nede**" (5; emphasis in original)—the devil's version of the Garden of Eden—the narrator realizes that it is the "image of myself as Satan incarnate" that he sees and that the "ten squalid heads represented the Inverse Ten Commandments in Hell's Garden of Nede." What puzzles the narrator even more is that this is happening despite his adherence to the advice of the "so-called Christian minister," to be good so as to "be assured a place in God's Heaven" (6). Ever since the first arrival of missionaries in

---

38 *Inuktitut: A Multi-Dialectal Outline Dictionary,* comp. Alex Spalding (Iqaluit: Nunavut Arctic College, 1998), s.v. "qakurturjuaq."

39 Bernard Saladin d'Anglure, "Nanook, Super-Male: The Polar Bear in the Imaginary Space and Social Time of the Inuit of the Canadian Arctic," in *Signifying Animals: Human Meaning in the Natural World,* ed. Roy Willis (London: Unwin Hyman, 1990), 183.

40 Inuit believe that their souls reside in their living bodies, in the form of a bubble. Most Inuit refer to the soul as *tarniq,* whereas shamans call it *pullaq* or *pullakuluujaaqtuq* ("that which looks like a little bubble"). Even Inuit who knew the meaning of pullaq did not usually use it to refer to the soul (Mariano Aupilaarjuk et al., *Cosmology and Shamanism,* vol. 4 of *Interviewing Inuit Elders,* ed. Bernard Saladin d'Anglure [Iqaluit: Nunavut Arctic College, 2001], 9, 19).

the Canadian Arctic, Christian propaganda has read Inuit shamanism as an act of the devil and has worked towards eliminating it entirely, thus robbing Inuit people of "the foundation of [their] entire system of . . . beliefs and practices before the coming of the Whites."[41] Strictly speaking, then, it is not the devil per se that the narrator fights but the Christian reading of Inuit shamanism as a deed of the devil. Being a shaman, the narrator represents (in the eyes of Christians) the devil, who challenges the Christian religion by inverting the Ten Commandments into a "Garden of *Nede*"—a place that is seemingly in *need* of Christian proselytizing (one possible interpretation of the Nede/Eden anagram in *Arctic Dreams and Nightmares*). Therefore, when the narrator's soul "finally acquires the distinction of being the 'free spirit' it had longed to be" (14), it has escaped both the struggles of human life on earth and the Christian propaganda intended to eradicate Inuit shamanism, itself just one of the severe effects of colonialism on Inuit communities. The narrator's eventual "ascension of my soul" (11, 13) in story 2 may refer to both of these escapes, since "ascension," with its Christian connotation, puts the narrator on an almost equal level with God, thereby reversing the Christian misreadings of shamanism. Indeed, when the narrator in story 4, "I, Crucified," sees himself "hanging from a cross, crucified" (21)—his hands, feet, and side punctured and his head crowned with thorns—the analogy between the narrator-shaman and Jesus is made explicit. The story ends with the narrator's "slow death hanging from the whalebone crucifix. Crucified" (25). Given the obvious symbolism, the narrator's earlier use of the phrase "**incarnation** of myself" is highly ambiguous; it might refer to the narrator's multiple lives on earth, and/or it might refer to him as the embodiment of a deity in human form. What happens in the course of the narrative opening in *Arctic Dreams and Nightmares* is this, then: the narrator moves from the status of devil to that of deity as he defends shamanism against Christian misinterpretations. It is from this position, that of an Inuit shaman, that he remembers and tells his life stories, thus producing a narrative that aims to reinforce Inuit spiritual beliefs and to carry traditional knowledge of shamanism into contemporary times.

---

41 One of the first missions in the Canadian Arctic was located on the east coast of Labrador, founded in 1771 by German Moravians (Inge Kleivan and Birgitte Sonne, *Eskimos: Greenland and Canada* [Leiden, The Netherlands: E.J. Brill, 1985], 2). Bernard Saladin d'Anglure, "An Ethnographic Commentary: The Legend of Atanarjuat, Inuit, and Shamanism," in *Atanarjuat, the Fast Runner: Inspired by a Traditional Inuit Legend of Igloolik*, by Paul Apak Angilirq (Toronto: Coach House /Isuma, 2002), 203, 209, 225–27.

Arctic Dreams and Nightmares is very clearly more than the sum of its individual stories. It is a story cycle with a coherent narrative line that becomes visible for readers who are willing to read between the lines. Ipellie's narrator never explicitly states the purpose or interpretative context of his stories. These are slowly revealed, however, in the collection's opening (and closing; see below). Instead of using specific discourse markers to signal its narrative frame, *Arctic Dreams and Nightmares* relies on other textual clues to indicate to its readers the status of a particular part of the text (e.g., the first four stories) and its relation to others (e.g., the closing story). As in the case of Silko's *Ceremony*, these signals consist of relational word bundles, and indeed, the phrases I have discussed above qualify as such word bundles. First, they are essentially figures of speech; second, they serve as significant narrative units because they constitute the collection's narrative opening; and third, this opening forms part of the narrative grid that holds Ipellie's text together.

More specifically, the relational word bundles in the opening are self-contained, but as figures of speech—functioning as symbol, metaphor, or metonymy—they also include a subtext that is left for readers to uncover. The "great White Ghost" and "the bubble of our life-blood" function as indicators of Inuit shamanism and evoke Inuit traditional knowledge. The phrases "image of myself as Satan incarnate" and "Inverse Ten Commandments in Hell's Garden of Nede" describe the narrator's apparition and point to Christian misreadings of Inuit shamanism. The phrase "the distinction of being the free spirit it had longed to be" has a double meaning; it describes the narrator's soul having attained its freedom by leaving behind the often perilous life on earth, while simultaneously pointing to the narrator-shaman's successful fight against the image of himself as the devil, an image propagated by Christian missionaries to the Arctic. This fight is also suggested in the phrases "ascension of my soul," "hanging from a cross, crucified," "hanging from the whalebone crucifix. Crucified," and "I, Crucified"—all carry strong intertextual significance as references to *the* Euro-Western master narrative, the Bible, and thus draw an implicit comparison between the narrator-shaman and Jesus. Ironically, the crucifixion in story 4 is the narrator's death. In one stream of Inuit spirituality, however, as practiced by groups of Caribou Inuit, a soul can be reincarnated.[42] So the narrator's death at the beginning of *Arctic Dreams and*

---

42   Zebedee Nungak and Eugene Arima, "A Review of Central Eskimo Mythology," in *Unikkaatuat sanaugarngnik atyingualiit Puvirngniturngmit/Eskimo Stories from Povungnituk, Quebec, Illustrated in Soapstone Carvings,* ed. Zebedee Nungak and Eugene Arima (Ottawa: National Museums of Canada, 1969), 124.

Nightmares does not necessarily imply the end of his story. In fact, this story is only now ready to be told. The importance of the phrases given above, then, lies not just in providing readers with the narrative situation of the collection (i.e., a narrator-shaman who has recently passed away is about to remember and share his adventures on earth). These phrases also define the spiritual and historical contexts of *Arctic Dreams and Nightmares*—Inuit shamanism and its eradication as pursued by Christian missionaries—and thus provide readers with the narrative's interpretative context: celebration of Inuit shamanism, against all odds. We may say that the relational word bundles forming the narrative opening in *Arctic Dreams and Nightmares* invite readers to see the first four stories as forming a larger, self-contained section within Ipellie's text, which turns what may seem to be a series of unrelated stories into a story cycle empowering Inuit people by affirming shamanism as a legitimate and vital part of the people's traditional knowledge.

The degree to which the celebration of Inuit shamanism is asserted in *Arctic Dreams and Nightmares* really becomes clear only toward the end of the cycle. The narrative's closing starts with the title story, "Arctic Dreams and Nightmares" (story 15), as here we find the first instances of backshadowing to the narrative's opening. "Arctic Dreams and Nightmares" marks a break in the narrative in many ways. It is the most reflective story in the cycle. Instead of telling a story, the narrator-shaman meditates on the harshness of Arctic life. The tone of the story is rather sombre; even the stories narrating his previous deaths seem more cheerful. Further, the title story marks the first time in the narrative that the narrator opens up to the reader emotionally: he shares his dreams and nightmares, admits that he suffers from alcoholism, and dies yet again (this time, however, his death is figurative). Despite the sombreness of "Arctic Dreams and Nightmares," the narrator-shaman walks out of the the story in a strengthened position. He overcomes alcoholism by using his spiritual powers, and with that, he changes the course of the narrative—a narrative, readers ought to remember, that seeks to reaffirm Inuit traditional knowledge and cultural values against all odds, be it Christianity (one of the facets of colonization) or alcoholism (one of its consequences).

Indeed, the remaining stories in the collection contain few references to Euro-Western cultures, particularly when compared with the earlier stories, which are full of Euro-Western elements (e.g., Shakespeare, eau de cologne, ballet, Frankenstein, Brigitte Bardot). In "Love Triangle" (story 16), the "wrestling" match between a man and his wife's lover—a means suggested by the narrator of solving their conflict—resembles traditional

"Inuit 'boxing,'" a socially recognized and traditional solution to issues in Inuit communities.[43] In what might be perceived by most Euro-Western readers as a bizarre and shocking story, "Hunting for Skins and Furs" (story 17) evokes the lack of taboos around sex in pre-Christian Inuit society and the need for a mixing of blood to prevent degeneration.[44] "The Agony and the Ecstasy" (story 18) involves traditional gender roles, including the Inuit construction of a "third gender."[45] "The Woman Who Married a Goose" (story 19) is a variation on a traditional Inuit story that tells of an ancient past when humans and animals would marry and have sexual intercourse with each other. In short, the stories framed by the title and the closing story embrace Inuit cultural traditions, including the lack of sexual taboos, making possible the shift from the implied criticism of Christianity in "Arctic Dreams and Nightmares" to its overt criticism in the closing story, "The Exorcism." This story describes a shamanic ritual, the chasing away of a *tupilak* (an evil spirit), and thus paves the way for an explicit (re) embracing of Inuit shamanism.

The narrator-shaman admits that the ritual described in "The Exorcism" is unusual, even for the powerful shaman that he is. It takes him ten days to free a family of ten "possessed by the demon of a recently deceased shaman" whose name is Guti. Shaman Guti is described as an evil shaman: he takes advantage of his position and abuses many women in his camp "in return for his shamanic services, which were usually total failures" (177). One night, Guti and Kappia, a man in Guti's camp, get into a fight; Kappia kills Guti, who puts a curse on Kappia's family before dying (178). Because his family proves to be heavily affected by the curse, Kappia calls on the narrator for help in performing an exorcism (179). That the narrator-shaman uses the term "exorcism" to describe his shamanic ritual is ironic, because much in his narration points to the ritual being a *tupilanniq*, the killing of a *tupilak* (evil spirit) by an Inuit shaman.

---

43   Saladin d'Anglure, "Ethnographic Commentary," 223.

44   See Makka Kleist, "Pre-Christian Inuit Sexuality," in *Me Sexy: An Exploration of Native Sex and Sexuality*, ed. Drew Hayden Taylor (Vancouver: Douglas and McIntyre, 2008), 16.

45   In "The 'Third Gender' of the Inuit," Bernard Saladin d'Anglure argues that there is a tripartite system of gender in Inuit cultures: male, female, and in between. Further, Inuit who were given names typical of the opposite sex tended toward transvestism. This system of gender invited shamanism because it caused "genuine crises of identity, which opened the way for the emergence of a shamanic vocation." Indeed, some former "transvestites" eventually became shamans. Saladin d'Anglure thus reads Inuit shamanism as a continuation of what he calls the "third gender" (Saladin d'Anglure, "The 'Third Gender' of the Inuit," *Diogenes* 52.4 (2005): 143, 144n3).

During this particular ritual, the narrator arouses "Shaman Guti's demons" in order to drive them away from Kappia's family (179). Since the
demons, or *tupilait*, have affected all members of the family, a ritual must
be performed for each one. When it is Kappia's wife's turn, the narrator
must strip her naked "so that the demon would have nothing to cling onto
when it was being pulled out." The scene conjures images of childbirth:

> The first thing I saw were the horns of the demon as its head began
> to come out of Kappia's wife's vagina in the manner of an infant be-
> ing born! As the head came out it was hissing like a snake with its
> mouth wide open. I was surprised to learn that the demon was wear-
> ing a chained cross around its neck.
>
> Kappia's wife screamed with the kind of pain she had never felt be-
> fore. The excruciating pain didn't even compare to pains of child-
> birth. (180–81)

The narrator does not mention how bloody the ritual is, but the comparison
with childbirth suggests that it is indeed bloody, as is also typical of *tupilanniq*.[46] The references to the "horns of the demon," its "hissing like a snake,"
and its "wearing a chained cross around its neck," however, mark the demon
as Christian—as does the shaman's name, Guti, which is an Inuktitutized
version of "God." It is the Christian God himself, then, whom the narrator
exorcises in the final story of *Arctic Dreams and Nightmares*. What is more,
the descriptions of Satan and the story of the fall in Genesis evoked by the
horns and the demon's snake-like behaviour suggest that this God is in fact
an evil shaman who resembles the devil: "After all, Shaman Guti's name
meant 'God'" (181). To put it even more bluntly, the closing story of *Arctic
Dreams and Nightmares* equates the Christian God with the devil. Because
the story deals with evil shamanism, it associates the latter with Christianity. What the narrator-shaman is fighting is not the Christian notion
of shamanism as devilish but Christianity itself. Indeed, the demons that
befall Kappia's *family of ten* are the *ten faces* mocking the narrator in story
1 ("Self-Portrait: Inverse Ten Commandments"). The reversal that began

---

46 The killing of a tupilak—called *tupilanniq* in Inuktitut—is described as follows:
"There is an enormous amount of blood when the *tupilaq* is killed. The *angakkuq*'s
[shaman's] hands become covered in blood while he is killing a *tupilaq* which cannot be seen by ordinary people. This blood can only be washed off by human urine"
(Aupilaarjuk et al., *Cosmology and Shamanism*, 255).

with the narrator's "ascension" to a Jesus-like position—suggested in the description of his crucifixion (story 4)—is thus completed when the narrator-shaman of *Arctic Dreams and Nightmares* equates the Christian God with both the devil and an evil shaman. As Christianity is exorcised from contemporary Inuit cultures with the help of an ancient shamanic ritual, Inuit shamanism is restored as the main spiritual and social reference point for Inuit people. That the narrator describes the ritual performed to expel God from the Arctic as an exorcism doubles the irony in this last story; the techniques and rituals of exorcism taught to Canadian Inuit by Christian missionaries were meant for exorcising their shamanic beliefs, after all, not Christianity.[47] In its use of irony and mockery, the reading of Christianity with which *Arctic Dreams and Nightmares* closes is both radical and satiric—a circumstance that is all the more interesting when one considers that traditional Inuit poetry includes "derisive poems" as a prominent subgenre, known for its satirical or ironic elements.[48]

The closing story of *Arctic Dreams and Nightmares* is only one component of the cycle's narrative closing, but it is arguably the most important because it sheds new light on all the stories that precede it. The description of "Shaman Guti's demons" associates God with the devil and simultaneously links back to the first story in the collection, "Self-Portrait: Inverse Ten Commandments." The description of the demon that befalls Kappia's wife—"horns of the demon," "hissing like a snake," and "wearing a chained cross around its neck"—evokes the story of Adam and Eve's expulsion from the Garden of Eden but also provides a shadowing back to story 1's "Garden of Nede." The description of the demon's necklace as "a chained cross around its neck" connects "The Exorcism" with "I, Crucified," the last story in the narrative's opening, which tells the story of the narrator's crucifixion and contains intertextual references to the Bible. The phrase "After all, Shaman Guti's name meant 'God'" completes the equation of Christianity with the devil and evil shamanism already alluded to in the phrases describing Shaman Guti's demons. As such, this phrase simultaneously provides a link

---

47 Bernard Saladin d'Anglure points out that the arrival of Pentecostal preachers in the Arctic in the 1960s "strengthened the polarization between the forces of good and the forces of evil—between God and the Devil. Everything before Christianity was depicted as the Devil's work and any relationship with spirits, other than Christian ones, became cases of demonic possession. Specialists were brought in from the South to teach Inuit techniques and rituals of exorcism" (Saladin d'Anglure, "Ethnographic Commentary," 225, 227).

48 Robin McGrath, *Canadian Inuit Literature: The Development of a Tradition* (Ottawa: National Museums of Canada, 1984), 48.

to story 1, which now more clearly than before reads as an embracing and celebration of Inuit shamanism. In short, all of these phrases not only function as figures of speech but also perform the significant narrative function of establishing the cycle's closing, which in turn completes its narrative frame, a central component of the text's narrative grid.

The stories in *Arctic Dreams and Nightmares* make sense when read in isolation; yet, by framing these stories within an opening and closing that symbolically exorcise Christianity from the Arctic, Ipellie has invested them with additional meaning. If it weren't for the opening and closing frame in *Arctic Dreams and Nightmares*, the book would indeed be a collection of loosely arranged stories rather than a celebration of Inuit shamanism as a integral aspect of Inuit continuance. The narrative frame, in turn, is signalled to readers by way of relational word bundles. In the opening, these word bundles build a more or less coherent narrative line and indicate the cycle's interpretative context through intertextual references to both Inuit traditional knowledge and the Bible. In the closing story, which marks the last and most crucial component of the narrative closing, these word bundles link to Genesis (intertextual), on the one hand, and to the cycle's opening (backshadowing), on the other, thus perfecting the cyclical narration of *Arctic Dreams and Nightmares*. Recognizing this narrative frame is crucial, because it allows readers not only to find the narrative line in a collection of seemingly unconnected stories, but also to fully appreciate the depth of Ipellie's use of satire and construction of what is essentially a story cycle. That satire and story cycles are two narrative conventions of Inuit literary traditions only further underlines the significant role played by the study of narrative structures in reading Indigenous literatures.

On the surface, Leslie Marmon Silko's *Ceremony* reads like a "traditional" novel and Alootook Ipellie's *Arctic Dreams and Nightmares* like a "traditional" short story collection—"traditional," that is, from a Euro-Western generic point of view—when in fact the particular narrative structures of these texts reveal both to be continuations of distinct narrative traditions, one Laguna Pueblo, the other Inuit. To realize where these two texts stand, generically speaking, readers need to know each respective narrative tradition and, further, must be aware of the ways contemporary Indigenous authors bend Euro-Western generic forms in order to incorporate them into their Indigenous traditions. Thus, to return to the notion of Indigenous narratology I outlined at the beginning of this chapter, we can see why such a narratology is an important component of Indigenous poetics: because Indigenous narratology grounds studies of narrative structures in the language and discourse traditions from which they emerge. Holophrastic reading provides readers a tool with which to see beyond the generic conventions of Euro-Western literatures. Within Indigenous narratology, it is relational word bundles that serve as a particularly important tool. Not only are relational word bundles concerned with questions of narrative form, but they also derive from a significant Indigenous language structure, the holophrase, and thus allow us to think about Indigenous narrative structures in English by thinking outside of English. Indigenous narratology is an important sub-field of Indigenous literary studies in its own right. Paying attention to the more formal questions of reading narrative may inform various inquiries into Indigenous literatures, whether traditional or contemporary, and relational word bundles prove to be an integral component of Indigenous narratology because they allow readers to map Indigenous narrative and thus discover some of these texts' deeper meanings. However, the questions of how narratives are structured and how these structures affect meaning can never really be the end goal of reading and interpreting Indigenous texts, as much as holophrastic reading is just one of many components of Indigenous narratology.

FURTHER READING

For a comprehensive study of the Laguna and Navajo intertexts that inform Leslie Marmon Silko's *Ceremony,* as well as their ethnographic sources, see Robert M. Nelson's *Leslie Marmon Silko's* Ceremony (New York: Peter Lang, 2008). Silko has commented on Pueblo traditions of storytelling, in "Language and Literature from a Pueblo Indian Perspective" (in *English Literature: Opening up the Canon,* ed. Fiedler and Baker Jr., Baltimore: Johns Hopkins University Press, [1981]). An excellent discussion of Inuit shamanism is offered in *Cosmology and Shamanism* (Iqaluit: Nunavut Arctic College, 2001), a volume in the *Interviewing Inuit Elders* series edited by Bernard Saladin d'Anglure.

CHAPTER 6

HISTORICAL TRAUMA AND HEALING

In *Taking Back Our Spirits: Indigenous Literature, Public Policy, and Healing*, Métis scholar Jo-Ann Episkenew argues that the historical trauma from which Aboriginal people in Canada suffer—physically, mentally, spiritually, emotionally, and socially—is the result of centuries of ill-devised and ill-intentioned public policy. In a discussion of the work of Anishnaabe writer and scholar Gerald Vizenor, Episkenew further observes "that when historical trauma is not publicly acknowledged and honoured in story, subsequent generations inherit and display the effects of that trauma."[1] Two important means by which to heal the wounds inflicted by colonialism on Aboriginal people and their communities, therefore, are language and story—traditional medicines whose "healing power" Aboriginal peoples have trusted "since time immemorial."[2]

Indeed, narrative plays a crucial role in contemporary writing therapy more generally. According to Jeff Park, narrative is used to communicate ideas and knowledge, but it also "act[s] as a site of self-construction, . . . one of the dominant ways people in the modern world create a sense of

---

1   Jo-Ann Episkenew, *Taking Back Our Spirits: Indigenous Literature, Public Policy, and Healing* (Winnipeg: University of Manitoba Press, 2009), 9.

2   Ibid., 12.

who they are, and how they relate to others."[3] Writing allows individuals suffering from a painful experience to construct a new, life-affirming self through the transformative powers of language and story. Writing therapy research shows that while "the use of writing for health-promoting emotional disclosure is well-documented," the exact "mechanisms or elements at the heart of healing or recovery remain unclear."[4] This is why the space of transformation through writing is sometimes referred to as the "black box" of writing therapy.[5] Something must happen in this space to turn a hurt, wounded individual into a transformed individual; however, just what brings about this transformation is not really known. Whatever the exact mechanisms and processes that make this transformation possible, the *reclaiming of story* is crucial in Indigenous contexts, particularly given the central role of narrative in Indigenous epistemologies and the severity with which Indigenous storied knowledges have been disrupted and destroyed by colonialism. Equally important for the process of healing through narrative is the *reclaiming of voice*, because voice implies presence.

Yet this last observation leads us to the following conundrum: if Indigenous literatures indeed help Indigenous writers, their communities, and readers to heal from the effects of what Episkenew calls "postcolonial traumatic stress response," then they do so using one of the colonizer's languages, which for many Indigenous authors in North America is English. Episkenew admits that "writing in English is simultaneously a political act and an act of healing." However, in a discussion of the seminal publication of Gloria Bird (Spokane) and Joy Harjo (Muskogee Creek), she adds— and quite rightly so—that Indigenous writers' use of English features a *reinvented* language, to allow for healing to occur.[6] As discussed in chapter 4, holophrastic traces may be used to read and identify performances of rhetorical sovereignty, which is arguably an important component in the process of healing from the effects of colonialism. To tell one's story and thus to transform one's pain and wounds is one thing; to tell this story while also determining one's own language, content, style, and forms of discourse is yet another. Holophrastic reading cannot answer the question of what is happening in the black box of healing through Indigenous

---

3   Jeff Park, *Writing at the Edge: Narrative and Writing Process Theory* (New York: Peter Lang, 2005), 3.
4   Reinekke Lengelle and Frans Meijers, "Mystery to Mastery: An Exploration of What Happens in the Black Box of Writing and Healing," *Journal of Poetry Therapy* 22.2 (2009): 57–58.
5   Ibid.
6   Episkenew, *Taking Back*, 12.

writing. However, as part of an Indigenous poetics that is informed by Indigenous language and discourse traditions, holophrastic reading can help readers pay attention to and understand the subtle nuances of language that document and problematize healing from historical trauma in all its complexities, processes, trials and tribulations, failures—not in just any texts, however, but in those whose very choice of language is also a grim reminder of what has caused the healing to be necessary in the first place.

With *Porcupines and China Dolls* (2002) by Gwich'in novelist Robert Arthur Alexie and *The Lesser Blessed* (1996) by Dogrib writer Richard Van Camp, this chapter discusses two Aboriginal novels that are set in the Canadian North and examine issues of the residential school system whose legacy still impacts Aboriginal communities across Canada today.[7] Dating back as early as the 1870s, Indian residential schools were established by the federal government in order to separate Aboriginal children from their parents, thus further assimilating Aboriginal people into mainstream Canadian society. All across Canada, Aboriginal children were removed from their families, often forcefully, and put into these schools, where they were forbidden to speak their ancestral languages and practice their spiritual beliefs. Health and sanitary conditions in the schools were often well below standard, and many children suffered physical, sexual, emotional, and mental abuse by the priests and nuns running the schools. It is estimated that about 150,000 Aboriginal children in Canada attended these schools. Approximately 80,000 residential school survivors are still alive today, but the physical, emotional, mental, and spiritual trauma of former students has been passed on to subsequent generations of Aboriginal people and is therefore felt by entire communities, being the cause of numerous social problems ranging from poverty and high suicide rates to drug abuse and domestic violence.[8]

Awareness of the disastrous damage done by residential schools began to spread when the schools were eventually closed down in the 1960s, but it was not until the early 2000s that residential school survivors sued the Canadian government and the churches, resulting in the Indian Residential Schools Settlement Agreement of 2006.[9] Part of this agree-

---

7   *Porcupines and China Dolls* was published by Stoddart in 2002, shortly before the publisher went bankrupt. The novel was eventually republished by Theytus Books in 2009. All references in this chapter are to the original edition.

8   "Residential Schools," Truth and Reconciliation Commission of Canada, accessed January 14, 2012, http://www.trc.ca/websites/trcinstitution/index.php?p=4.

9   "Indian Residential Schools Settlement Agreement," official court notice, May 8, 2006, http://www.residentialschoolsettlement.ca/IRS%20Settlement%20Agreement-%20 ENGLISH.pdf.

ment is the establishment of the Truth and Reconciliation Commission of Canada (TRC), which began its work in June 2008, the same month that Canadian Prime Minister Stephen Harper apologized in Parliament to former students, their families, and their communities for the federal government's role in the operation of residential schools across the country.[10] Over a five-year period, the TRC will document what happened in Canada's residential schools, in part by hearing testimony from residential school survivors. Most commentators agree that the reconciliation process is, as Episkenew puts it, of "monumental importance" for Aboriginal peoples but also for settler descendants and new immigrants to Canada.[11] At the same time, much doubt exists as to whether reconciliation will indeed work towards the decolonization of Aboriginal peoples in Canada. As Jennifer Henderson and Pauline Wakeham note, Harper's apology in Parliament did not include the word "colonialism"; therefore, they interpret Harper's subsequent denial of Canada's colonial history (in a Reuters interview during the 2009 G20 Pittsburgh summit) as part of "a strategic isolation and containment of residential schools as a discrete historical problem of educational malpractice rather than one devastating prong of an overarching and multifaceted system of colonial oppression that persists in the present."[12] Harper's apology has been further criticized as being framed entirely within a Euro-Western context that ignores Indigenous perspectives and ways of knowing and as a nation-state conception seeking closure rather than what Taiaiake Alfred (Kanien'kehá:ka) argues is really needed, namely, restitution, without which "reconciliation will permanently absolve colonial injustices and is itself a further injustice."[13]

---

10   See Canada, *House of Commons Debates,* June 11, 2008 (Right Hon. Stephen Harper, Prime Minister, CPC), http://www.parl.gc.ca/HousePublications/ Publication.aspx?DocId=3568890&Language=E&Mode=1&Parl=39&Ses=2.

11   Jo-Ann Episkenew, "Afterword," in "Reconciling Canada," ed. Jennifer Henderson and Pauline Wakeham, special issue, *ESC: English Studies in Canada* 35.1 (2009): 193.

12   Jennifer Henderson and Pauline Wakeham, "Colonial Reckoning, National Reconciliation?: Aboriginal Peoples and the Culture of Redress in Canada," in "Reconciling Canada," ed. Henderson and Wakeham, special issue, *ESC: English Studies in Canada* 35.1 (2009): 1–2.

13   Jill Scott, "Conditions of Possibility for Apology: Toward an Indigenous Framework of Redress," paper presented at the annual conference of the Canadian Association for Commonwealth Literature and Language Studies, University of New Brunswick, Fredericton, May 28, 2011; Taiaiake Alfred, "Restitution is the Real Pathway to Justice for Indigenous Peoples," in *Response, Responsibility, and Renewal: Canada's Truth and Reconciliation Journey,* ed. Gregory Younging, Jonathan Dewar, and Mike DeGagné (Ottawa: Aboriginal Healing Foundation, 2009), 181.

Alexie's and Van Camp's debut novels address the residential school legacy and also work as powerful arguments against forgetting. Alexie makes stories of residential school survivors the focus of *Porcupines and China Dolls*, which traces a fictional Gwich'in community's coming to terms with the disclosures of sexual abuse by three community members. Van Camp deals with the issue of residential schooling far more indirectly in *The Lesser Blessed*, as he tells the story of a Dogrib teenager facing the consequences of having caused the death of his abusive father, himself a residential school survivor. *Porcupines and China Dolls* and *The Lesser Blessed* demonstrate the extent to which the residential school legacy affects Aboriginal communities, and they document both the necessity of healing for these communities as well as the struggles and failures that healing so often implies. Both are powerful yet also very dark novels, particularly *Porcupines and China Dolls*, which is less hopeful in tone than *The Lesser Blessed*. Despite their difference in tone, both novels persuade by creating empathy, not just by displaying the wounds inflicted on Aboriginal people, their families, and their communities by the federal government and the churches but also by denying readers the forms of resolution that are so characteristic of Euro-Western novelistic traditions. In her analysis of *Porcupines and China Dolls*, Keavy Martin notes that "although the telling of the survivors' stories is linked to the process of healing, [Alexie's] narrative also works paradoxically to keep wounds open, as the characters continue to stumble under the weight of their history and the readers are required to bear witness."[14] *The Lesser Blessed* works in slightly different ways: it traces Larry's transformation from a buried to an unburied self through an embracing of story as traditional knowledge; at the same time, however, the novel refrains from giving readers the gratification of knowing how Larry's future will unfold. By conceptualizing "healin' [a]s a journey—there is no end!"—Jake Noland's main message in *Porcupines and China Dolls* (170, 188, 203)—Alexie's novel and arguably also Van Camp's "thus work to problematize or resist the amnesia that so often accompanies movements toward reconciliation."[15]

Porcupines and China Dolls and *The Lesser Blessed* are "hard but good medicine," to borrow a phrase from Van Camp's review of Alexie's novel.[16]

---

14 Keavy Martin, "Truth, Reconciliation, and Amnesia: *Porcupines and China Dolls* and the Canadian Conscience," in "Reconciling Canada," ed. Jennifer Henderson and Pauline Wakeham, special issue, *ESC: English Studies in Canada* 35.1 (2009): 49.

15 Ibid.

16 Richard Van Camp, "Review of *Porcupines and China Dolls*," Hanksville website, accessed June 3, 2015, http://www.hanksville.org/storytellers/VanCamp/writing/

Yet they persuade not just through appealing to their readers' emotions (*pathos*) or tracing their characters' transformation (*ethos*); they are particularly powerful also in their use of language (*logos*). In fact, studying the language employed by these writers, including the very question of how they "build" their narratives, allows us to trace Alexie's and Van Camp's nuanced portrayals of historical trauma and healing and the crucial role that art plays in building paths to healing and empowerment.

ROBERT ALEXIE'S *PORCUPINES AND CHINA DOLLS*

At first glance, Robert Alexie's *Porcupines and China Dolls* offers a quite linear and straightforward narrative. The novel starts with a prologue in which an unnamed male character stands beside a highway, attempting to commit suicide. What follows is a 280-pages-long flashback that explains what drove this man to want to end his own life: readers are presented with a short history of his people, the Gwich'in or Blue People, named after the Blue Mountains they call their home; readers then learn about the arrival of the first explorers, the first settlers, the missionaries, and eventually residential schools; and they witness how attending these schools has destroyed the lives of former students, their families, and the whole community of Aberdeen, a small hamlet in the Northwest Territories. About two-thirds into the text, the novel reaches its climax when three residential school survivors—the man of the prologue, James Nathan; his friend, Jake Noland; and Chief David William—disclose in front of the gathered community how they were sexually abused by Tom Kinney, one of the teachers at what community members have long referred to simply as "the hellhole" (8). The climax takes the form of a hyperbolic, "almost-apocalyptic battle scene,"[17] in which the three survivors become "Warriors of Old" who fight their "demons, dreams, and nightmares" (185) in front of the other community members, some of whom run to their assistance, thus turning personal struggles into a communal battle for healing. What happens after this climax, however, is an even more desperate portrayal of a dysfunctional, wounded community. The traditional drums of the Blue People return to the community, if only for one night; the community revives the old tradition of burning the recently deceased to return them to the mountains; and yet people are still hurting. They continue to struggle with their demons, dreams, and nightmares—and not just the three men who disclosed their suffering. The narrative now also reveals how the

---

Porcupines.html.

17   Martin, "Truth, Reconciliation, and Amnesia," 48.

sexual abuse suffered by some in residential school is passed onto the rest of the community. The drinking and the violence continue; in fact, it feels as though things may have gotten worse since the big battle scene of disclosure. "Despite the characters' powerful attempts to put their pasts behind them," Martin observes, "they are unable to find a reliable cure for memory. History, it seems, cannot be so easily dissuaded."[18] Indeed, the novel refuses to offer readers a happy ending; instead, it ends with an almost verbatim repetition of the prologue (284–85; cf. 1–2): the man standing beside the highway is now identified as James Nathan, and readers finally learn that his suicide attempt, one of many depicted in the novel, remains an attempt after all. Louise, the love of his life, intervenes and brings him back: "James, I love you. I've always loved you. I'll always love you . . . forever. We'll get through this" (286). Whether James and Louise will indeed succeed in finally putting to rest their "demons, dreams, and nightmares," the narrator doesn't disclose. They may not.

To summarize the novel's narrative line, then, we may say that *Porcupines and China Dolls* takes the form of one very long but chronological flashback to a short first scene, which is repeated at the end of the novel but never really elaborated. This narrative line not only makes for a very unsatisfying read, but also appears simplistic. Of course, everything in that big flashback works towards explaining the scene from the prologue. In fact, bits and pieces in this two-page scene actually appear verbatim or in some form throughout the main narrative of the novel, as do other phrases first introduced within the prologue. In other words, the narrative is not linear at all but in fact repeatedly refers back onto itself. What appears to be a "minimalist, repetitive style"[19] is actually a style based on formulae, resulting in an extremely intricate and beautifully crafted narrative structure that may sound "heavy" and repetitive to non-Indigenous readers. The formulae I have mentioned are, of course, relational word bundles: they involve figures of speech (that is, enhanced uses of language that create a bundle of meaning), they perform the significant narrative function of producing an intricate narrative that carries much of the novel's argument, and in their interdependence, these formulae hold Alexie's novel together, forming its narrative grid. Before discussing some of these relational word bundles in more detail, let us examine why Alexie may have chosen this particular narrative structure for his novel.

---

18   Ibid., 49.

19   James Grainger, review of *Porcupine and China Dolls*, by Robert Alexie, *Quill & Quire* (May 2002): 25. http://www.quillandquire.com/review/porcupines-and-china-dolls/.

Porcupines and China Dolls provides a brutal and bleak, but honest and sometimes even humorous portrayal of a dysfunctional Aboriginal community in Canada's far North. Focusing on James Nathan and his friend Jake Noland, the novel tells the story of their individual struggles. As their battle of disclosure suggests, and the remainder of the narrative confirms, however, individual pain, anger, and sorrow never remain personal but affect other people, their families, and ultimately the whole community. There is, first of all, the immediate losses brought onto this community by residential schooling—the losses of language, culture, traditional knowledge, and most of all, the "skill [of] parenting" (17), the ability to be responsible parents, raising children and giving them what they need to live their lives and contribute to the community. Then comes the personal pain, the anger, the hurt from being abused in residential school—mentally, physically, sexually, spiritually—creating demons so powerful that only alcohol seems to be able to drown them, at least temporarily. Not surprisingly, the first time readers meet James (that is, knowing he is indeed James) is during one of his drinking adventures in the local saloon, a haven for all the hurting people of the community and, coincidentally, also the most prominent setting of the first two-thirds of the novel. Interestingly enough, however, while the narration before the climactic battle scene focuses primarily on James, Jake, and David, the remainder of the narrative shifts the attention to other, more peripheral characters in the novel, characters equally affected by residential schooling. Another one of Tom Kinney's victims, Michael Lazarus, commits suicide in the hills—but not before raping Louise (223, 274), who lives in an abusive marriage with Daniel, another abuse victim—though whether because he attended residential school or suffered at the hands of his parents is left unclear (211). Angie, James's former lover, is also a rape victim, and so is the sister of George Standing, one of the local bootleggers and another former hostel attendee; she is molested by her brother (243). Daryl and Larry Hunter, brothers in their mid-twenties whose mother left when they were children to escape an abusive husband, accidently kill Mutt and Jeff, the two town drunks in search of a party (82), when driving down the local highway well above the legal limit. In a rage the next day, Larry guns down their own father, Sam Hunter, another local bootlegger (111–12). Booze is readily available in the community, and not just in the saloon, so it is hardly surprising to read the statistics about people put in jail for underage drinking and other alcohol-related charges the Christmas after James, Jake, and David's disclosure (253–54). In Aboriginal notions of community, the relationship between its members and the community is seen as that of parts to a whole.[20] Thus, if individual members, for some reason or another, do not fulfill their responsibilities, the whole balance is interrupted and the community at large is affected. This interdependence between individual members and the larger community can be observed in *Porcupines and China Dolls*— the personal struggles and hurt of individual members become a struggle for a whole community—but it is also mirrored on a formal level, in the narrative's very structure as a tightly knit, self-referential whole that is based heavily on formulae and repetition. The novel's references to itself are more than examples of foreshadowing and backshadowing; some of these self-references are repeated, turning them into formulae that give the novel its unique narrative structure and "cast . . . an incantory, almost numbing spell on the reader."[21] This makes reading the novel—and maybe even my analysis of it—feel a *million years* long, to borrow one of *Porcupines and China Dolls* most frequently used formulaic constructions. Life for people in Aberdeen is monotonous; it lacks fun, not to mention hope (see 114–15), and consists of nothing but drinking and sex, both of which serve as means by which to *numb* the pain, the anger, the sorrow, so as to avoid having to deal with them. In other words, the formulaic narrative structure in *Porcupines and China Dolls* not only mirrors the interdependence of people in the community but also the state of numbness in which many community members find themselves—a feeling that readers may easily share as they read through the monotony that the novel depicts. In other words, the novel's formulaic self-references, or relational word bundles, are instrumental in giving the novel its peculiar shape, which in turn moulds its general mood and tenor and ultimately its effect on readers.

Let us look at some of the more central formulae in the novel. Probably the most prominent and obvious is the repetition of the prologue at the end of the novel, which marks the end of the almost three-hundred-page flashback. As I said, this repetition is almost verbatim, but there is one major difference between the prologue and the closing: in the prologue, the man standing by the side of the highway, getting ready to put a gun in his mouth, is not identified. Readers will, of course, suspect that he is the same character walking into the Aberdeen saloon, wearing a worn-out "black leather jacket" some thirty pages later (1, 33). Strictly speaking, however, this man could also be Chief David William—he too has attempted to commit suicide in the past (153, 159)—or Jake Noland, or any of the other

---

20 Weaver, *That the People Might Live*, 39.
21 Grainger, review of *Porcupines and China Dolls*, 25.

male abuse victims in the community. In fact, the suicide scene in the prologue is repeated almost verbatim in the scene describing Larry Hunter's attempt to turn a gun on himself after shooting his father (see table 6.1).

TABLE 6.1 COMPARISON OF THE ATTEMPTED SUICIDE DESCRIBED IN THE PROLOGUE AND LARRY'S ATTEMPTED SUICIDE IN *PORCUPINES AND CHINA DOLLS*

SUICIDE ATTEMPT IN THE PROLOGUE	LARRY'S SUICIDE ATTEMPT
Then it came to him. He'd always been alone. He'd always be alone. He *then did something he'd thought about* and tried for a million years. But this time, he knew he'd do it.	Larry *then did something he'd thought about* many times. He pushed and pulled the lever action then turned the gun on himself. He put the barrel in his mouth and put his thumb on the trigger. He closed his eyes and *pushed the trigger.*
All in a smooth motion he got down on one knee, put the barrel in his mouth, then *pushed the trigger.* He watched the hammer fall and closed his eyes. He tensed, waiting for the explosion. After *a million years, he heard it: metal on metal.* It was the loudest sound he'd ever heard. It shook his whole body and deafened him.	He waited for one millionth of a second that lasted *a million years.* Then *he heard it:* the sound of *metal hitting metal.* It was like the sound of the Big Bang that created the universe and eventually all living things therein. Boom!
He took a deep breath, dropped the gun, then exhaled. He heard it: the peace and the silence.	He waited for the bullet to enter his mouth and scatter his brains to the four winds and into oblivion. *He waited for his inevitable journey to hell* right behind his fat fuck of a father. He waited and waited.
He waited for his ultimate journey to hell.	
(2; emphases mine)	(111–12; emphases mine)

That the novel's closing eventually offers a more specific rendering of the scene, filling in the gaps of the prologue, does not reduce the ambiguity of the initial scene. James is just one of many people who cannot put to the rest the "demons, dreams, and nightmares" of residential school. In other words, the suicide scenes framing the novel are generic and non-generic at one and the same time; they suggest both James's story and ultimately the story of his whole community.

Within the suicide scene of the prologue, there exist further formulae that are picked up in the long flashback between prologue and closing. "He'd always be alone" expresses a feeling that becomes one of the main features of James's emotional state as the novel progresses. The phrase reappears almost verbatim in two other instances, the only change being a shift from third to first person ("*I'll always be alone*"; 119, 135). In the prologue, the narrator's observation is entirely without context; readers do not know why this man feels he'll always be alone. By the time they reach the closing, they do. More importantly, readers are pointed directly to the reasons for James's desolate mental and emotional state when, using this formula, the novel draws a direct connection between James's present emotions, his experience in the hostel, and the suicide scene in the prologue.

Another formulaic self-reference encountered in the narrative that is framed by prologue and closing is the phrase "his ultimate journey to hell," which is repeated when James tries to commit suicide in the Blue Mountains shortly after his disclosure: "He positioned his thumb on the trigger and prepared for *his ultimate journey to hell*" (213; emphasis mine). Of course, for any Christian, suicide means reserving a sure spot in hell. However, the phrase has other connotations that readers will not yet have gathered when they first see it in the prologue. The name used by the Blue People to refer to the mission school and the hostel in Aberdeen is "hell-hole" (8), but hell is also a good description of the life James has been living ever since he first stepped into the hostel in the 1960s: "He had cried enough in his dreams and in the privacy of his own hellhole. Today he would make his demons, dreams and nightmares pay" (189; see also 146). And so James gathers all his courage and discloses to the whole community that he was sexually abused in the hostel, but his suffering does not end here. He continues to struggle, even when he eventually becomes sober and builds a life for himself as an artist. When Jake and his wife, Mary, get lost on the river one day, James loses all hope and finds himself out alone in the mountains again.

By using two almost identical suicide scenes, one generic, the other specific, *Porcupines and China Dolls* suggests two stories in one—James's story and the larger community's story—as well as the ways in which these stories intersect. The ambiguity thus implied as well as the gradual movement from generic scene, without context, to specific scene, with much context, is made possible through a series of formulaic self-references that function as relational word bundles, establishing relations between different parts in the narrative. Moreover, it is with the help of some of the relational word bundles in the prologue and closing—specifically, those repeated in the flashback narrative ("He'll always be alone" and "his ultimate journey to hell")—that readers are guided through the text, that they are able to gradually fill the opening scene of the novel with context and meaning, and that they are able to connect James's story of suffering with Larry's, the children's suffering with the community's desolate state, history with the present. It is through getting involved in the narrative—by putting in the missing pieces, by making connections between different parts of the narrative, as trivial as those connections may appear—that readers are able to gain a deeper level of understanding both of the novel and of the disastrous impact of residential schooling on Aboriginal communities. Readers are meant to *feel* the pain, not just read it. Despite his disclosure, James is still hurting; he is still very much a wounded human being. Indeed, the most notable difference between the novel's prologue and its repetition in the closing is that all of the gaps in the prologue are now finally filled. James does not commit suicide, thanks to Louise's intervention and the sense of hope she instills in him, and yet the feeling of pain and sorrow suggested in the prologue remains largely intact in the closing scene. One of the functions performed by the novel's narrative frame, then, is to emphasize the notion that the wounds of history have to be left open and unhealed. The novel's appeal to pathos, to the readers' emotions, is hence carried by both its content *and* its form.

Now, you will probably have noticed that this narrative construction in *Porcupines and China Dolls* would be of little use were the scenes framing the flashback narrative not connected to the issue of residential schools. In order to establish the link between outer frame and inner narrative, Alexie again appeals primarily to pathos, allowing readers to make this connection on their own. The flashback narrative is divided into three parts. Set during a period of two-and-a-half weeks in September and October 1999, "The Awakening" tells the story of how the Gwich'in community of Aberdeen attempts to deal with the sexual abuse disclosure of three of its members. "The Real World" then traces the lives of James and Jake as they deal with the aftermath of their disclosure and attempt to begin a new life with their partners in Yellowknife. The most crucial part in the novel, however, is arguably the one preceding both "The Awakening" and "The Real World." Following directly after the prologue, "The Dream World" gives readers a very brief history of the Blue People, in the first chapter, and then depicts the world of residential school, from both the children's and their parents' points of view, in the remaining three chapters. Thus the stage is set for the two remaining parts of the novel: the long flashback.

Thomas King (Cherokee) observes that "this briefing [on the Blue People's history] is too little to do much good" for non-Aboriginal readers. For Aboriginal readers, on the other hand, "who know . . . the history and the way the weight of this knowing settles over the rest of the book, it is simply a way saying 'once upon a time.'"[22] King's description of the open-

---

22 Thomas King, *The Truth about Stories: A Native Narrative* (Toronto: Anansi, 2003), 116.

ing chapters of *Porcupines and China Dolls* is part of a larger argument, namely, that Aboriginal writers increasingly write "primarily for a Native audience, making a conscious decision not so much to ignore non-Native readers as to write for the very people they write about."[23] Alexie's choice of style—the minimalist, paratactic sentences; the various kinds of repetition, including anaphora and parallelism; the formulaic storytelling—is borrowed from oral storytelling techniques. So, it seems plausible that most readers who are familiar only with Euro-Western traditions of writing will indeed find *Porcupines and China Dolls* a difficult read. At the same time, however, the historical briefing at the beginning of the book includes enough anchors even for non-Aboriginal readers to develop a sense of the weight of history King mentions—enough to at least *bear witness* to how this history weighs on the Blue People's shoulders, provided readers involve themselves in the unfamiliar storytelling. These anchors again take the form of formulaic self-references that function as relational word bundles and are part of Alexie's reliance on oral storytelling techniques. Of these anchors, the more prominent are those that have inspired the novel's title, as these formulae are also repeated in two other parts in the novel. There are yet other formulae that, though restricted to "The Dream World," also suggest the overwhelming, terrible weight of history affecting the community. I will discuss these formulae first and then end this reading of Alexie's novel on those formulae that are also picked up later in the novel, including the porcupine and china dolls.

"The Dream World" consists of four chapters. The first and third chapters provide readers with a short history of the Blue People (one before and shortly after contact, as just mentioned; the other well into the twentieth century), whereas the second and fourth chapters depict life in residential school. Interestingly enough, the two residential school chapters mirror the movement of the opening and closing suicide scenes from generic to specific. The first residential school chapter is generic, telling the story of two siblings, a boy and a girl, as they attend the mission school for the first time. They aren't given names, thus reinforcing the generic rendering of the chapter produced by the use of present and future tenses: this girl and this boy represent every girl and every boy that ever attended the school. The second residential school chapter is a more specific rendering of the first chapter: the children are now identified, as the main characters in the two remaining parts of the novel (James, Jake, Louise, David), and so are their parents. Other than that, however, the second chapter is a direct, if

23   Ibid., 117.

more elaborate repetition of the first chapter. In content, structure, tense, and the generally dark and bleak mood conveyed, the two chapters are essentially identical.

TABLE 6.2 RELATIONAL WORD BUNDLES IN THE RESIDENTIAL SCHOOL CHAPTERS OF "THE DREAM WORLD" IN *PORCUPINES AND CHINA DOLLS*

FIRST RESIDENTIAL SCHOOL CHAPTER (9–16)	SECOND RESIDENTIAL SCHOOL CHAPTER (21–29)
"They don't know it, but . . ." (10, 11) "The young boy doesn't know it, but . . ." (12)	"They don't know it, but . . ." (27) "Something is happening to them, but they don't know it" (29) "only she doesn't know it" (26)
"Their parents, and grandparents don't know it, but someone or something has ripped out their hearts. They watch as their hearts slowly stop beating" (10)	"No unseen force is going to rip their hearts out." (23) "It is at this moment that some unknown force thrusts itself into his chest, seizes his heart, and rips it out. . . . He looks down at his heart and watches as it slowly stops beating." (25–26)
	"Joseph is not watching. He's looking at the ceiling and is screaming and demanding answers." (24) "He [Matthew] looks at the ceiling and screams." (24) "He [Edward] looks at the ceiling for an answer, but none will come and he knows it." (26)

Adding to the overwhelming sense of trauma, these chapters contain more direct forms of repetition in the form of formulae, some of which are encountered in both chapters (see table 6.2). In fact, of all the chapters in the novel, the self-references in "The Dream World" are the most repetitive and formulaic and create the most numbing effect on readers. Some of these formulae use dramatic irony—they forebode evil, unbeknownst to the children and their parents—yet all of them communicate the position of powerlessness in which the characters find themselves, facing an "enemy" that allows neither defence nor escape.

Those readers willing to continue beyond "The Dream World" will re-encounter two relational word bundles central to this first part of *Porcupines and China Dolls*: the porcupines and china dolls formula and the dream formula. The first of these is introduced in the first residential school chapter, when the narrator describes how the children's hair is sheared off and they are deloused using a white powder, turning them into porcupines and china dolls (11), so when the children lie in their beds at night "it sounds like a million porcupines crying in the dark" (12). This imagery is a powerful description of the horrific experience of residential school and is one of the most heartbreaking lines in the novel. Equally powerful is the frequent use of this imagery in the form of different formulae throughout the remaining parts of *Porcupines and China Dolls* (see table 6.3). These formulae serve as powerful reminders of the two residential school chapters in the opening part of the novel. Even before the big disclosure scene, readers will draw the connection between the horrible experience of residential school and the bleak life of the characters thirty years later, their "demons, dreams, and nightmares," their suicidal thoughts, and the dysfunctional state of their community more generally. The porcupines and china dolls formula is not only a repeated reminder of the origin of all the damage, hurt, pain, and sorrow but also an indicator of their horrible reach.

This bleakness is further emphasized by the dream formula scattered throughout the novel. In both residential school chapters, the children, the parents, or both are left wondering if their terrible experience of separation may just be a dream (10, 15, 28); they eventually realize, of course, that it is not a dream, that what they are experiencing is real.

TABLE 6.3 PORCUPINES AND CHINA DOLLS FORMULA IN *PORCUPINES AND CHINA DOLLS*

PORCUPINES AND CHINA DOLLS FORMULA	CONTEXT
"It sounds like a million porcupines crying in the dark." (12)	children lying in their beds in mission school
"They sound like a million porcupines crying in the hills." (15)	parents crying over the passing of their children in mission school
"No one heard the little china doll that night, but if she were given a voice, it would've sounded like a million porcupines screaming in the dark." (80)	Angie remembering the night she was raped as a teenager by two men
"It sounded like a porcupine crying." (87)	James having a nightmare
"He reached for the china doll that he would never reach." (100)	Jakes breaking down when he first tells Mary he was sexually abused in the hostel
"Jake opened his eyes and there was the china doll staring at him." (103)	Jake waking the morning after his confession to Mary

PORCUPINES AND CHINA DOLLS FORMULA	CONTEXT
"He stood, looked to the sky and screamed, and it sounded like a million porcupines crying in the dark." (127)	David being reminded of his own abuse after Jake's confession
"Jake dreamed of a little china doll standing on the bank waving as they drove by. He didn't look at her and she was crying." (165)	Jake having a dream during a hunting trip
"It was knowing they [your children] were going to cry that night. It was knowing it was going to sound like a million porcupines screaming in the dark." (283)	James breaking down upon learning about Jake and Mary's fatal accident

And yet the chapters narrating the terrible experience of residential school are titled "Dream World." The same phrase is used in the remainder of the narrative every time one of the characters is brought back, in one way or another, to his or her experience in the hostel thirty years earlier (see table 6.4).

TABLE 6.4 DREAM FORMULA IN *PORCUPINES AND CHINA DOLLS*

DREAM FORMULA	CONTEXT
"They wonder if this is a dream. Maybe it's a dream." (10)	the parents' reaction when their children are first picked up for mission school
"He wonders if it was a dream." (15)	the boy's reaction to arriving in mission school (first residential school chapter)
"They'll open their eyes and realize it wasn't a dream. It was real." (28)	the children's reaction to arriving in mission school (second residential school chapter)
"Did she go into the Dream World?" (62)	James time-travelling while drunk
"Louise. What's she doing here? Is 'is a dream? . . . Hello, Dream World." (76)	James time-travelling while drunk
"He sat motionless until the face returned to the *Dream World*." (95; emphasis mine)	James time-travelling while drunk
"He closed his eyes and tried to drive the memory into the *Dream World*." (136; emphasis mine)	James trying to drown his memories of residential school during another suicide attempt
"James woke up and looked at Brenda, then let the dream slip back into the *Dream World*" (146; emphasis mine)	James waking up after another night of nightmares

DREAM FORMULA	CONTEXT
"I can't remember one damned thing about those years. Where are they? In the Dream World?*"* (162)	James trying to remember the summers he spent with his parents in their cabin by the Redstone River
"Jake saw a nightmare on television and brought it back from the *Dream World.*" (232; emphasis mine)	a description of Jake's initial confession to Marry
"Louise watched as he drifted off into the *Dream World*, then she covered him with a blanket and went to sleep with Caroline." (257; emphasis mine)	Louise watching James fall asleep
"Or maybe this was the *Dream World* and tomorrow they'd wake up and everything would be back to normal." (258; emphasis mine)	James, Jake, and Mary learning about George's death
"He looked at Angie, but she too had disappeared into the *Dream World.*" (269–70; emphasis mine)	James waking up after Tom Kinney's first appearance in court

Although, thirty years after their experience, James, Jake, David, and all the other residential school survivors have moved on with their lives, they are still controlled by the dream world, by the nightmares that the hellhole continues to give them. It is only by beginning the journey of healing, which they initiate through their disclosures in the aptly titled "The Awakening," that they slowly enter "The Real World," which is not so much reality than it is a symbol of belonging—to the land, to family, to community, to one's people's traditions:

> He looked out over the land of his People: the land of his father and his grandfather. He wondered if this was still a dream. He felt her hand on his arm and turned. She was real and this wasn't a dream.
>
> James' journey had come full circle, and the future had unfolded as it should. (286)

Thus the novel ends with both the awareness that healing may only now really begin for James and the hope that the Blue People will find strength in the old days. Whether this does indeed happen *Porcupines and China*

Dolls leaves open, and with this, the question of whether James and the community will eventually find peace will forever remain unanswered.

One reviewer of *Porcupines and China Dolls*, Madelaine Jacobs, has described Alexie as "a blacksmith pounding the English language until it can be put to his own purposes."[24] Alexie's decision to use a storytelling mode that is characteristic of oral traditions is as much an act of rhetorical sovereignty as it marks a rhetorically ingenious move, as the formulaic self-references that characterize his storytelling also carry much of the novel's argument. Because these self-references involve repetition, they help create a feeling of empathy and make readers bear witness to the weight of history that lies heavy on the novel's characters (*pathos*). Ironically, the two-page repetition of the prologue at the end of the novel also emphasizes what turns out to be the main difference between the two renderings of this scene, thus suggesting *hope* for transformation, namely, the sense that a re-embracing of traditional ways may hold the key to healing from the historical trauma of residential school (*ethos*). Finally, the formulaic self-references produce the novel's tight-knit, self-referential narrative structure, which holds the novel together and enables its appeals to pathos and ethos (*logos*). In fact, the very repetitiveness of Alexie's storytelling instills in his readers the very trauma suffered by James, Jake, and others. Thus, *Porcupines and China Dolls* may be regarded as a powerful reminder of Cree elder Lyle Longclaws's notion that "before the healing can take place, the poison must first be exposed."[25] Alexie's choice of form—the novel's language and narrative structure—ensures that readers feel rather than just read of the pain residential schools have inflicted on Aboriginal communities. His novel is also testament to the significance of language in the process of healing.

RICHARD VAN CAMP'S *THE LESSER BLESSED*

In many ways, Richard Van Camp's debut novel, *The Lesser Blessed*, reads like a negative image of Alexie's *Porcupines and China Dolls*. When James finally reunites with Louise at the end of Alexie's novel, he is still very much suffering from the trauma inflicted on him; he has not yet had a chance to transform. In contrast, *The Lesser Blessed* closes with the narrator's

---

24 Madelaine Jacobs, "Hell Will Not Prevail," review of *Jacob's Prayer*, by Lorne Dufour, and *Porcupines and China Dolls*, by Robert Arthur Alexie, *Canadian Literature* 206 (2010): 110–11. http://canlit.ca/reviews/hell_will_not_prevail.

25 Longclaws's statement is quoted in the epigraph to Tomson Highway's play *Dry Lips Oughta Move to Kapuskasing*.

experience of unfulfilled love, an experience that, ironically, marks the end of the narrator's transformation and helps the narrator to unbury himself; after all, you cannot love others unless you love yourself, and you cannot heal yourself unless you love yourself.

The Lesser Blessed tells the story of Larry Sole, a sixteen-year-old Dogrib living in the fictional town of Fort Simmer, Northwest Territories. The novel consists of three narrative strands. In the "main" narrative strand, Larry befriends Johnny Beck, a Métis and newcomer to Fort Simmer, and tells—so it seems—the story of losing his virginity. In the "psychological" narrative strand, which frequently interrupts the main narrative "through a number of finely crafted, fragmented flashbacks,"[26] Larry unwillingly revisits what in the main narrative strand he refers to cryptically as "the accident" (58): he witnesses his father rape his mother and aunt, and when one day his dad rapes him, too, by demanding oral sex, Larry finds a hammer and slams it down on his passed-out father. It is not clear how seriously Larry has injured him, but when a fire breaks out in their house—which Larry seems to have lit after having sniffed gas with his cousins—his father dies in the inferno, while Larry and his cousins are able to flee, albeit with serious burns. Larry is transferred to the burn victim wing of the children's hospital in Edmonton and undergoes psychological treatment. The main narrative strand, then, really tells the story of Larry's coming to grips with his accident, bits and pieces of which are revealed in the psychological narrative strand. The key to Larry's future is finally provided in the "mythological" narrative strand, which consists of a series of traditional Dogrib stories. These stories are retold at various points in the novel and, together with yet another story-within-a-story, about the Blue Monkeys, function as allegories in the novel, though on different levels. Whereas the Blue Monkeys story is part of the psychological narrative strand and points to Larry's guilty conscience, the four traditional stories that make up the mythological narrative strand provide Larry with lessons that outline the path of healing that he will eventually begin to walk in the main narrative strand.

Readers of *The Lesser Blessed* may trace this journey of healing on two levels: in Larry's very use of language, and in the novel's complex narrative structure. Larry's language moves from that of negation to that of affirmation, as well as from a rather harsh prose to poetic prose and eventually free verse. While there is nothing holophrastic per se about poetic uses

---

26   Geary Hobson, review of *The Lesser Blessed*, by Richard Van Camp, *Studies in American Indian Literatures*, 10.4 (1998): 79.

of language, they are nonetheless reflective of the high degree of imagery and figurativity in Indigenous-language discourse that correlates with the tendency of Indigenous languages to use holophrases (see chapter 1). By the end of the novel, Larry begins to heal from his wounds as he finds a reason to carry on with his life. What makes his particular story of healing so interesting is that, for him, the process of healing is supported by storytelling. (His narration is repeatedly marked as the performance of a story in front of an audience.) How this journey toward healing unfolds, and what makes it possible, can be reconstructed by the reader through studying the novel's narrative structure, as well as by reading for relational word bundles. Larry finds the key to personal healing in Dogrib tradition; interpreting and using the knowledge gained in this tradition, he discovers a way to help himself. Larry's path to healing is, then, also a road to self-empowerment through a deliberate grounding of oneself in the stories and traditions of one's people. In the following section, I will explore Larry's journey in *The Lesser Blessed* more closely by examining some of the novel's uses of holophrastic traces and relational word bundles.

The Lesser Blessed is framed by two short chapters, both entitled "Me." While the opening chapter tells the story of Larry's figurative death, the closing chapter celebrates his rebirth. The two framing chapters also differ considerably in style: the opening is composed in prose, whereas the closing chapter takes the form of a free verse poem. In this poem, which makes use of symbol and backshadowing, Larry symbolically puts to rest his hurt and pain by burying a dead ptarmigan. Larry's move from prose to poetically enhanced prose is interesting, not so much because lyric tends to be the more "valued" genre in Euro-Western contexts, but rather because the poetic use of language mimics the figurative tendency in many Indigenous languages. "I am my father's scream," "Mommy, your monkey's eating Daddy's banana," and "And listen to my black teeth scream"—all of which anticipate Larry's accident story (the sexual connotations, the violence, the fire)—are examples of figures of speech found in the prose sections of Larry's narrative (38, 3). Larry's narration generally tends to involve figurative speech. On his way from the buried "Me" of the opening chapter to the reborn "Me" of the closing chapter, however, Larry turns to Dogrib tradition for orientation; in the meantime, his language evolves from plain prose to a more enhanced prose that is interrupted by both poetic prose and poems composed in either prose or free verse. Larry's general propensity for figurative uses of language intensifies toward the end of the novel. Figurative language tends to be a rather weak indirect holophrastic trace because figures of speech are a universal feature of language across cultures. In the case of *The Lesser Blessed*, however, this indirect holophrastic trace serves a very important rhetorical function, namely, that of formally recognizing the moment at which Larry begins his journey of healing. Larry needs to find his voice before he can take control of his suffering, and what better source is there than his people's traditions? Whether Larry's increasing use of figurative language in *The Lesser Blessed* is merely an indicator of healing—or even its cause—is a relevant question in this context. A closer study of the novel's narrative structure will show that Indigenous stories and knowledges indeed provide significant sources of healing for Aboriginal people and communities.

Van Camp's novel is framed by an opening and closing that are both marked by the use of relational word bundles. Similarly, the falling together of the various narrative strands at the end of the novel is signalled by relational word bundles. However, central to our understanding of Larry's process of healing are really only three relational word bundles, whose significant narrative function lies either in establishing the novel's narrative frame or in providing connections between the main narrative and the mythological and pyschological narrative strands, thus contributing to the novel's narrative grid. First, the "Blue Monkeys" are a symbol of Larry's guilty conscience and by implication a symptom of his suffering; this relational word bundle constitutes part of the narrative frame but also serves as a connector between narrative strands. Second, the metaphor "busy finding Juliet Hope" suggests the solution to Larry's problems and helps constitute the novel's opening. Finally, "Son of Dog" and "doggy-style" point to the means by which Larry may eventually begin his journey toward healing; they also function as a central seam joining the novel's three narrative strands.

Early in the novel's opening, Larry shares with readers the story about his mother's partner running into the "Blue Monkeys of Corruption." Jed was smoking up with friends in his apartment in India when "eight wonderful monkeys" showed up on his balcony. The monkeys appeared to be harmless until they "turned into the Blue Monkeys" and started hammering at the door. Jed and his friends ended up fleeing their apartment; when they returned, their pipe was gone (4–5). Given the story's plot and the capitalization of their name, the Blue Monkeys are obviously a symbol of someone's guilty conscience rather than monkeys with blue fur. Larry does not comment on why he tells Jed's story at this point in the narrative, nor on how the story relates to his personal situation, but the connection becomes clearer the further the novel progresses. Reacting to the constant abuse by his father, directed against both his family and Larry himself, Larry caused his father's death; ever since, he has been plagued by guilt.

When Larry's new friend Johnny first arrives in Fort Simmer, he arouses a lot of interest among the high school students—not from Larry, however: "I didn't do a thing. I was too busy looking for Juliet Hope" (2). As Larry puts it, "[his] love for Juliet has claimed [him]" (28), so he is "too busy," watching the one person with whom he would like lose his virginity (43) by doing it "doggy-style" (see 22, 25, 27, 101).[27] When Johnny starts dating Juliet, Larry's amorous hopes appear to have become futile. Yet, in the course of the novel, "looking for Juliet Hope" will become more than what its literal meaning suggests. What Larry is looking for is twofold: his own *Juliet*, symbolizing love and a sense of belonging, and *hope*, something to keep him going in life, and he does indeed find all this in the end in Juliet Hope.

These two relational word bundles—"Blue Monkeys" and "busy looking for Juliet Hope"—develop the main idea of the novel: they point to Larry's central problem and its solution. The "Blue Monkeys" are encountered in both the novel's opening and its closing but they also appear repeatedly in the main narrative, namely, every time Larry's narration flashes back to his "accident." These flashbacks become longer and more frequent as the narrative progresses. When Larry is beat up by Jazz the Jackal one night and finally manages to make it home, his flashbacks reach his stay in the burn wing of the hospital in Edmonton. This is when one of the Blue Monkeys comes to visit him once again:

> I could hear myself screaming. I would have continued screaming but I opened my eyes, and a Blue Monkey was sitting on my chest, staring into me.
>
> "Hello, Son of Dog," he said, inches from my face. He punched his stump wrist in my mouth, gagging me. I sat up as Jed rushed into the room and threw on the light. (81)

This scene draws a connection between the story of the Blue Monkeys told in the opening and the Dogrib story of creation, which Larry shares with his readers about halfway through the novel (51–52). For the first time in the text, the psychological and mythological narrative strands not only

---

27 Larry never explicitly says that he wants to do it doggy-style with Juliet, but his fantasies about Juliet and his frequent references to "doing it doggy-style" are suggestive enough.

connect with the main narrative strand but also meet and overlap each other, thus anticipating the final merging of all three narrative strands in the novel's closing. This closing begins with the lovemaking scene between Larry and Juliet, which happens to mark the end of his quest—he has finally found Juliet Hope, if for "one night" only (109).

The lovemaking scene contains numerous allusions to Larry's accident. Juliet becomes a fire that consumes Larry, but he lets it be and rides the waves of pleasure that she is giving him. The monkeys are asleep, and "his secret tusk" is no longer the hammer with which he seals his father's fate (78) but a "tusk puls[ing] inside her," enacting a "sweet violation" (110. The metaphors ("It burned my eyes and mind," "I was on fire," "We went for spice"), the symbol ("the monkeys slept"), the oxymoron ("sweet violation"), the simile ("like flames like blades of a wicked fire"), the run-on lines, and the lack of proper punctuation turn this scene into a prose poem that expresses the emotional intensity of the moment (109–10). Moreover, the fire imagery skilfully connects this scene to the newspaper clipping that reports Larry's father's death in a blaze in the novel's opening. Unlike then, however, the fire can no longer do Larry any harm. The sleeping monkeys, of course, are the "Blue Monkeys of Corruption," who visit Larry each time he experiences a flashback to the accident in the psychological narrative strand (39, 41–42, 77–81). Functioning as a symbol of his guilty conscience, the Blue Monkeys disappear only when Larry "finds Juliet Hope" and is reborn. With the Blue Monkeys asleep, Larry begins his journey toward healing:

> "Look at me," I said. "Look at me, just look at me."
> She did
> and I wasn't alone
> I wasn't forgotten
> I wasn't dead
> There was no small town
> There was no killing
> I wasn't bad I was clean (110)

Here Larry repeats two lines from a poetic prose section immediately preceding this poem, "I was not alone; I was not forgotten." The significance of these lines—"and I wasn't alone / I wasn't forgotten / I wasn't dead"—is heightened further when they are repeated yet again, albeit in variation, in the free verse poem that closes the novel. In this second occurrence, however, the negatives of the litotes-like "and I wasn't alone / I wasn't forgotten / I wasn't dead" are transformed into an affirmative, life-embracing statement: ". . . I knew I had somone / someone to remember my name / . . . I would in time / find one to call my own / mine to disapper in / to be . . ." (119).

By finding his Juliet Hope, Larry is able to put his Blue Monkeys to sleep—but his lovemaking with Juliet is more than simply sexual; it also signals his embrace of Dogrib oral tradition. Larry's retelling of the Dogrib creation story establishes an intertextual allusion to Dogrib oral tradition; at the same time, it also draws an interesting connection to his own asides about doing it "doggy-style" (22, 25, 27, 101). These asides are ultimately pubertal, but they can also be read as Larry's own interpretation of the Dogrib origin myth, according to which the Dogribs originate from the union between a woman and her dog-husband. When Larry finds Juliet Hope at the end of the novel, the act of making love, the "doing it doggy-style"—or rather, "Dogrib-style"—turns him into a new person. Larry is "reborn" through his lovemaking with Juliet and also through the implied embracing of his heritage, which underlines how creation stories are as much for the present and the future as they are about the past. Of course, doing it doggy-style (preferably with Juliet) has been on Larry's mind for most of the main narrative. As pleasurable as sexual intercourse may be, however, for Larry it also implies that he must face the source of his fire nightmares. After all, it has been a series of forced acts of sexual intercourse, either witnessed or experienced, that drove Larry to kill his own father. Sleeping with Juliet is more than just finding Juliet, then; for Larry, it also means finding hope through finding a way to deal with his past. When, in the psychological narrative strand, Larry's narration flashes back to his time in hospital and he imagines one of the Blue Monkeys calling him Son of Dog, this address then forms the "mythological" answer to Larry's "psychological" problem: he needs to connect with Dogrib traditions, with his origins.

Although he has to leave Juliet behind because she is leaving town bearing Johnny's child, Larry walks out of his story having a future, for when he buries the dead ptarmigan after making love with Juliet he also unburies himself:

> I placed the ptarmigan in the snow and covered her.
> I said, "Rest."
> I said, "Sleep."
> I said, "Die." (118–19)

Larry's words as he buries the ptarmigan echo words from a story he told to Juliet just a few evenings before their lovemaking. The story is about a mother who, having caused her son's death, is haunted by his spirit and gains peace only after seeking advice from a medicine woman, who advises her to burn all her son's clothes in a fire (99–100). Unlike the other three Dogrib stories contained in the mythological narrative strand of *The Lesser Blessed*, this story is not explicitly marked as Dogrib, although Larry clearly invents it so as to make it appear as such. By hiding his personal story about the accident in an allegory that both resembles a traditional Dogrib story and anticipates the burning imagery in his lovemaking scene with Juliet, Larry lays down a way to unbury himself. Like the woman in his story, he can escape his "fire nightmares" (71) only by symbolically setting himself on fire (in this case, through the "fire" created between himself and Juliet as they make love), thereby putting the past to rest. When he buries the ptarmigan in the snow, Larry repeats the woman's ritualistic formula, saying, "rest, sleep, die." In doing so, he "buries" once and for all his nightmares, the Blue Monkeys, and his feelings of guilt, as the ptarmigan now takes his place under the earth. Following the teachings revealed in the tradition of his people, including his own embodied understanding of that tradition, and assuming the guise of a contemporary storyteller, Larry is beginning to heal from his wounds. He is finally able to move on with his life, thus ending his story.

Through studying the novel's relational word bundles, it is possible to gain a deeper understanding of the narrative structure of *The Lesser Blessed*—its narrative frame, the relations between its three different narrative strands, and their eventual merging—and, more importantly, of how this very structure affects meaning in the novel. Tracing the novel's central relational word bundles, readers also trace Larry's journey to healing. Interestingly enough, this journey also points to the pivotal significance of art and story in healing from historical trauma. As literary critic Sam McKegney observes in *Magic Weapons*, "the key to safety, healing, and empowerment is not merely gaining precise knowledge of the 'factual' past [of residential school], but is, rather, invoking a personal understanding of that past in the creation of a potentially positive future through art."[28] The process of writing *Porcupines and China Dolls* may be understood as a personal form of empowerment for author Robert Alexie, himself a residential school survivor. In the case of *The Lesser Blessed*, this process of em-

---

28 Sam McKegney, *Magic Weapons: Aboriginal Writers Remaking Community after Residential School* (Winnipeg: University of Manitoba Press, 2007), 177.

powerment is fictionalized: Van Camp has invented a first-person narrator whose very act of telling his story in the novel marks a form of empowerment. That both novels link healing so closely with self-empowerment is not surprising, given that the historical trauma of residential schooling has been inflicted onto Aboriginal peoples by a colonial regime, making healing a central aspect of the process of decolonization. What is noteworthy, however, is that Richard Van Camp's implicit argument for the renewal of traditional knowledges as a prerequisite to healing is made through the voice of a character who represents the current generation of Aboriginal people in Canada. It is this generation that will be the driving force of change for Aboriginal communities across the country.

"Although healing from the trauma of colonialism is a prime function of contemporary Indigenous literature," Episkenew writes, "healing without changing the social and political conditions that first caused the injuries would be ineffectual.... When their testimony reaches a large and diverse audience, it is possible for Indigenous writers to effect healing by advancing social justice."[29] Audience engagement is therefore a central goal of Aboriginal literatures. If writing provides a mechanism toward healing, by offering ways in which a hurt self may transform into a healing self, then so does reading. The implication of the audience in the case of Indigenous literatures, however, goes beyond Indigenous families and communities to also include non-Indigenous readers. Alexie's *Porcupines and China Dolls* and Van Camp's *The Lesser Blessed* are powerful but demanding novels. Despite their differences in tone, both novels imagine healing as an ongoing process, and neither shies away from depicting unpleasant "truths," which they convey in a language that is both powerful and inventive but also challenging for readers unfamiliar with oral traditions or uneasy with explicitly sexual, graphic, or violent uses of language. At the same time, it is through focusing the readers' attention on the formal aspects of narrative that these two novels reveal best what I consider their main argument, namely, that (re)turning to traditional knowledges (including stories and storytelling) is indispensable to healing. This argument is never advanced explicitly in either novel, but it may be gathered from the way both construct their closings, especially in relation to their openings: in *Porcupines and China Dolls*, the closing scene has James awaken to the land, to his family and community, whereas in *The Lesser Blessed*, Larry finds guidance in Dogrib oral tradition and storytelling in order to start building a future

---

29 Episkenew, *Taking Back*, 17.

for himself. In both cases, readers may trace this "hidden" argument for the relevance and resilience of Indigenous traditional knowledges by studying the uses of relational word bundles in both novels. By focusing attention on language and discourse construction, holophrastic reading allows readers to acknowledge and examine the subtle nuances of Alexie's and Van Camp's portrayals of historical trauma and healing. Moreover, as part of an Indigenous poetics that is grounded in the holophrase, the most prominent Indigenous language structure, holophrastic reading invites readers to read and interpret these two novels on their own terms, that is, within Indigenous language and discourse traditions. This is no trivial matter, given the fact that the residential school system is largely responsible for the loss of ancestral languages, with all of the implications of that loss. Reading Indigenous texts in English from the point of view of Indigenous languages encourages readers to discover new perspectives—perspectives that may yet change the way they think about language, poetry, storytelling, colonialism, genocide, and reconciliation.

FURTHER READING

In *Taking Back Our Spirits* (Winnipeg: University of Manitoba Press, 2009), Jo-Ann Episkenew offers an in-depth discussion of the effects of government policies on Aboriginal communities and the roles played by Aboriginal literatures in healing from historical trauma. *Reconciling Canada*, a special issue of the journal *ESC: English Studies in Canada* edited by Jennifer Henderson and Pauline Wakeham (2009), analyzes issues of redress, apology, and reconciliation in Canadian and other contexts.

CHAPTER 7

INDIGENOUS LITERARY SOVEREIGNTY

A
s Niigaanwewidam James Sinclair (Anishnaabe) notes, when Indigenous literatures rose to the attention of mainstream readers
and academics in the 1960s and 1970s, approaches to Indigenous
literary texts tended to be informed by Euro-Western literary
theories. In the course of the 1980s and onwards, more and more Indigenous authors and/or critics as well as some non-Indigenous scholars criticized that these approaches could not adequately engage with the particular concerns and forms of Indigenous literatures, particularly as they relate
to the politics and histories of specific tribal/national communities. One
literary movement that has developed out of these critical discussions is
Indigenous literary nationalism.[1] Although its origins can be traced back
to the 1980s,[2] this movement is often associated with the work of Robert
Warrior (Osage), Jace Weaver (Cherokee), and Craig S. Womack (Muskogee Creek), whose independently authored studies—*Tribal Secrets* (1995),
That the People Might Live (1997), and *Red on Red* (1999), respectively—are
now seminal works on Indigenous literary nationalism.

---

1   Niigaanwewidam James Sinclair in Kristina Fagan et al., "Canadian Indian Literary
    Nationalism?: Critical Approaches in Canadian Indigenous Contexts—A Collab-
    orative Interlogue," *Canadian Journal of Native Studies* 29.1/2 (2009): 20.
2   See particularly Simon Ortiz's seminal essay, "Towards a National Indian Litera-
    ture" (see Introduction, note 9).

The main goal of Indigenous literary nationalism is to "illuminat[e] the intellectual histories, experiences, and knowledge structures" evident in the literary and critical discourses of Indigenous nations and to ground these discourses "in the history and politics of those nations' community existences."[3] It thus helps to "shift the focus of research away from the effects of colonization to the contributions and potential of Indigenous worldviews."[4] In its commitment to the continuance of Indigenous people as *peoples*, Indigenous literary nationalism is by definition political and privileges Indigenous voices in their own intellectual traditions. As Womack,[5] Cherokee scholar Daniel Heath Justice,[6] and other nationalist critics have noted repeatedly, however, literary nationalism is not the only meaningful approach to Indigenous literatures, nor should it be restricted to Indigenous critics. Equally important, Indigenous literary nationalism does *not* operate within the nation-state model of nationalism but is instead grounded in Indigenous notions of nationhood as being

> more than simple political independence or the exercise of a distinctive cultural identity; it is also an understanding of a common social interdependence within the community, the tribal web of kinship rights *and* responsibilities that link the People, the land, and the cosmos together in an ongoing and dynamic system of mutually affecting relationships.[7]

Indigenous nationhood is the political extension of Indigenous peoplehood, which is usually theorized under the model proposed by Tom Holm (Cherokee), Ben Chavis (Lumbee), and J. Diane Pearson, who see peoplehood as "a holistic matrix" of four interwoven and interdependent social concepts: language, sacred history, land/territory, and the ceremonial cycle.[8] *Language* communicates the *sacred history* of a people. This sacred history, in turn, outlines proper social behaviour; describes the people's culture, customs, and laws; defines their relationship with a particular *land* or *territory*; and explains the *ceremonies* that bind the people to this

---

3   Sinclair in Fagan et al., "Canadian Indian Literary Nationalism?," 20.

4   Deanna Reder in Fagan et al., "Canadian Indian Literary Nationalism?," 32.

5   Craig S. Womack, *Red on Red: Native American Literary Separatism* (Minneapolis: University of Minnesota Press, 1999), 2, 4.

6   Justice, *Our Fire Survives*, 10.

7   Ibid., 24.

8   Holm, Chavis, and Pearson, "Peoplehood: A Model" (see Introduction, note 5).

environment.[9] If one follows the argument of Holm, Chavis, and Pearson, then peoplehood—in its nation-specific manifestations—functions as a meaningful matrix for nationalist readings of Indigenous literatures.

Derived from the holophrase, a dominant Indigenous language structure, holophrastic reading is a method that speaks directly to the element of language. This element is often seen as "the most problematic" component of the peoplehood matrix,[10] as the majority of contemporary Indigenous people in North America speak as their first language a non-Indigenous language, most commonly English. It is true that Indigenous languages in North America have suffered immensely from colonial policies targeted at the assimilation of Indigenous people into mainstream society; it is also true that it is difficult to replace what is lost once a language becomes extinct. And yet, to look at Indigenous uses of English from the point of view of the English language is in many ways just another act of colonization, because such a reading is ultimately grounded in the assumption, whether conscious or not, that using the colonizer's language amounts to giving in to the colonizer's language and discourse practices. And, as various Indigenous writers and scholars before me have argued, this assumption is both wrong and dangerous.[11] Throughout this book, I have repeatedly stressed the importance of holophrastic reading for Indigenous poetics because, by challenging readers to approach the English used by Indigenous writers and storytellers from outside that very language, holophrastic reading allows readers to ground their readings of Indigenous literatures in those language and discourse traditions from which these literatures emerge. Granted, the notion of Indigenous poetics I am advocating in this book is generic in focus; there exist, strictly speaking, as many Indigenous poetics in North America as there are Indigenous literatures and languages. In this sense, Indigenous poetics and holophrastic reading provide only a general framework, or context, for the development of nation-specific Indigenous poetics. One such nation-specific poetics will be the focus of this chapter dedicated to the work of Cree poet Louise Bernice Halfe.

Halfe, whose Cree name translates into Sky Dancer, was born in 1953 on Saddle Lake Reserve in Two Hills, Alberta. Since her first appearance as a poet in Jeanne Perreault and Sylvia Vance's *Writing the Circle* (1990),

---

9   Ibid., 13–15.

10   Billy J. Stratton and Frances Washburn, "The Peoplehood Matrix: A New Theory for American Indian Literature," *Wicazo Sa Review* 23.1 (2008): 57.

11   See, for example, Ortiz, "Towards a National Indian Literature"; and Jace Weaver, Craig S. Womack, and Robert Warrior, *American Indian Literary Nationalism* (Albuquerque: University of New Mexico Press, 2006), xv–xxii.

Halfe has been a prominent voice in contemporary Cree poetry. Her first collection, *Bear Bones and Feathers* (1994), shows a strong concern for the continuance of *nêhiyawak* (Cree people), as do her latest two collections. Unlike Halfe's first book of poetry, however, *Blue Marrow* (2004) and *The Crooked Good* (2007) have a very strong narrative quality and therefore lend themselves more easily to holophrastic reading. In her poetry, Louise Halfe frequently switches between English, Cree, and a Cree-inflected English—not to produce polyphony but to create a decidedly Cree voice in the English language. Halfe's poetry marks a use of English in which Nêhiyawêwin (Cree language), *âcimowina* and *âtayôhkêwina* (the two main genres of Cree literature), and Cree discourse practices are ever-present. Her reclaiming of rhetorical sovereignty could fill a chapter in its own right, given her frequent code switching and other ancestral language influences. The point of this chapter, however, is to trace how Halfe's use of language gives birth to poems deeply involved with the continuation of Cree stories on Cree terms through a deliberate grounding of her work in what Cree scholar and poet Neal McLeod calls *mamâhtâwisiwin*, and to demonstrate how holophrastic reading may be applied to trace Halfe's performances of *mamâhtâwisiwin*.

MAMÂHTÂWISIWIN AND PEOPLEHOOD

McLeod describes *mamâhtâwisiwin* as "Cree poetics," a process that he argues is both creative and critical; through poetic dreaming, storytellers keep alive the "ancient poetic pathways" that constitute Cree ancestral knowledge.[12] In other words, Cree knowledge is based not in discourses of science but in "metaphorical discourse, composed of symbolic and poetic descriptions of the world and [Cree] experiences." This metaphorical discourse connects "human beings to the rest of the world through the process of *mamâhtâwisiwin*, the process of tapping into the Great Mystery"—a process that is brought about by history and *wâhkôhtowin*, Cree for "kinship."[13] In Cree contexts, storytelling is therefore intricately linked to the creation and keeping of knowledge, including the people's collective memory. The poetic pathways that constitute Cree knowledge are always "embodied understandings" and are therefore never impartial; rather, they indicate the storyteller's "location in understanding the world and reality."[14] However, because at the heart of this embodied under-

---

12 McLeod, "Cree Poetic Discourse," 117, 113.

13 Ibid., 109.

14 Ibid., 113.

standing of the world lies *wâhkôhtowin*, the process of tapping into the Great Mystery is always a "poetics of empathy"; Halfe and others establish connections with their ancestors through storytelling, thereby fulfilling their "moral responsibility to remember."[15] McLeod describes this process of connecting as "intra-narrative dialogue (âniskwâpitamâcimowin 'the act of inter-textual connecting')."[16] *Âniskwâpitamâcimowin*—connecting through story—is central to *mamâhtâwisiwin* because it marks that process by which Cree poetic and intellectual traditions grow and develop organically; "retravell[ing] and indeed expand[ing]" ancestral knowledge, contemporary Cree storytellers perform kinship and create a future for their people.[17] Interpretation—of the world as much as of story—thus becomes the core of *mamâhtâwisiwin*.

McLeod's use of poetics broadens significantly the common definition of the term, as the art of making, whether of poetry or of literary discourse more generally. Cree poetics result in storytelling, but above all these poetics mark the process of attempting to understand the world. Based on their own embodied understandings, poetic dreamers create descriptions of the world and reality in which they live, McLeod writes. A similar motivation to ponder and to explain is found in Halfe's attempt in *The Crooked Good* "to unravel the . . . philosophy" of the *cihcipiscikwân* (Rolling Head) narrative, "its psychology and spirituality."[18] Cree poetics, then, are always poetry *and* philosophy, storytelling *and* spirituality. In Cree contexts, this ability to understand the world beyond our immediate reality originates with *wîsahkêcâhk*, the Cree elder brother and "first ceremonalist" who *ê-mâmâhtâwisit* ("has the ability to tap into the Great Mystery").[19] When practicing *mamâhtâwisiwin*, Cree storytellers thus ultimately also connect with *wîsahkêcâhk*; they connect in *language* with the *sacred history* of their people and, by implication, with their *ceremonial cycle*, which expresses their unique relationship with the *land*. McLeod's broad conception of Cree poetics results from none other than its embeddedness in a holistic notion of peoplehood defined by the interdependence of language, sacred history, ceremonial cycle, and the land (as conceptualized by Holm, Chavis, and Pearson).

---

15 Ibid., 114, 111.

16 Ibid., 117.

17 Ibid., 117, 121.

18 Louise Bernice Halfe, "Keynote Address: The Rolling Head's 'Grave' Yard," *Studies in Canadian Literature* 31.1 (2006): 73.

19 McLeod, "Cree Poetic Discourse," 112.

By performing *mamâhtâwisiwin*, Halfe performs and celebrates Cree peoplehood. However, even as discourse *and* philosophy, poetry *and* spirituality, *mamâhtâwisiwin* is ultimately always grounded in language because it involves *âniskwâpitamâcimowin*, connecting through story. In *Blue Marrow* and *The Crooked Good*, Halfe connects with her people's poetic pathways in order to recover the voices of Cree women who have become silenced, hidden, and oppressed through colonization. While *Blue Marrow* weaves together, from a female perspective, Cree oral history of the fur trade, *The Crooked Good* engages more intimately with Cree mythical past by reclaiming an ancient sacred narrative that has become distorted by colonialism: the story of Rolling Head. In order to study *mamâhtâwisiwin* in Halfe's poetry, therefore, we must study the specific structures of language that create *âniskwâpitamâcimowin*, and one method of doing so is to read Halfe's work for holophrastic traces and relational word bundles, the two main components of holophrastic reading.

LOUISE BERNICE HALFE'S *BLUE MARROW*

The Cree people traditionally distinguish between two narrative genres: *âtayohkewina* are "spiritual narratives" that are generally considered sacred and relate to "the time when the world was not yet in its present, definite state"; *âcimowina*, on the other hand, are concerned with the present world, particularly with precontact times, and include everything that is not regarded *âtayohkewina*.[20] *Âtayohkewina* are never explicitly or fully told in *Blue Marrow*, but the poem alludes to some of these sacred stories, including the Cree earth diver story and the narrative of Rolling Head. The focus of *Blue Marrow*'s intertextual connecting is on Cree history, through an engagement with *kayâs-âcimowina* ("old-time stories") and *âcimisowina* ("stories about oneself"), two sub-genres of *âcimowina*.[21] In fact, *Blue Marrow* does more than engage with Cree history; it *writes* Cree oral history of the fur trade from the point of view of *iskwêwak*, Cree women. *Blue Marrow* gathers together a long sequence of poems that capture numerous first-person narratives. With one voice floating into another, however, the poem forms only a loosely structured sequence of voices. The women's stories are put down on paper and gathered together by a first-person narra-

---

20   Neal McLeod, *Cree Narrative Memory: From Treaties to Contemporary Times* (Saskatoon: Purich, 2007), 97; Leonard Bloomfield, *Sacred Stories of the Sweet Grass Cree* (1930; reprint, Saskatoon: Fifth House), 6; Wolfart and Carroll, *Meet Cree*, 92.

21   H. Christoph Wolfart, "Cree Literature," in *Encyclopedia of Literature in Canada*, ed. W. H. New (Toronto: University of Toronto Press, 2002), 246.

tor, a contemporary Cree woman, "The Keeper of the Stories" (21). Taking dictation from her ancestors, the narrator takes an intermediary position between the past generations, of her grandmothers and grandfathers, and her children's generation.[22] She is a poetic dreamer who recovers for future generations of Crees the forgotten, silenced, or untold narratives of First Nations and European contact—stories of rape, hunger, loss, and cultural disorientation, as told by her female ancestors.

How does Halfe achieve this intertextual connecting, this telling and interpreting of Cree ancestral knowledge, for the benefit of future generations? Seen as a whole, *Blue Marrow* is a long series of short short stories that achieve their effect only when contextualized. The numerous stories being recovered by the narrator need to be orchestrated; they need to be arranged in such a manner that they are not only told but also heard and understood by the narrator's audience, her own children and future generations more generally as well as the readers of the poem. Halfe has chosen to render all the stories collected in *Blue Marrow* in the first person—arguably to give the stories immediacy, but her choice also further underlines that these stories have grown out of *embodied* understandings. That is, when the ancestors tell their life stories in *Blue Marrow*, they speak from a position of knowledge that brings the present world closer to the readers' understanding and thus sheds light on why and how the history of colonialism continues to affect Crees and other Aboriginal nations. *Blue Marrow* involves not only many stories but also many different narrators, whom the reader must be able to distinguish somehow for the stories to work. Here is where Halfe's main narrator comes in: she orchestrates the various first-person narratives by identifying who is speaking at any given moment or by having the speakers identify themselves. The narrator's use of quotatives is subtle—she never interrupts her ancestors. Once one of the *iskwêwak* begins her story, the narrator waits patiently until she has finished, rather than interrupting her story with further quotatives. And yet, some quotatives are needed for the poem to work, especially given that the narrator, too, speaks in the first person. Evidentiality—the process of identifying and qualifying (the source of) one's knowledge—is often associated with holophrasis. The quotatives, then, are *Blue Marrow*'s first indirect holophrastic trace (see table 7.1)—and an important one, too, because as a structural device they enable the poem's *âniskwâpitamâcimowin*, its connecting through storytelling.

---

22   Méira Cook, "Bone Memory: Transcribing Voice in Louise Bernice Halfe's *Blue Marrow*," *Canadian Literature* 166 (2000): 88.

TABLE 7.1 EXAMPLES OF INDIRECT HOLOPHRASTIC TRACES IN *BLUE MARROW*[23]

INDIRECT HOLOPHRASTIC TRACES		
TYPE	**DEFINITION**	**EXAMPLES IN *BLUE MARROW***
evidential	discourse markers that identify or qualify a speaker's (source of) knowledge	phrases that 1. identify the speaker at any particular moment "kayâs-âcimowin nôtokwêsiw wîhtam" ("ancient story / old woman / she tells it" [25]); or 2. have the speaker identify herself "ohkomipan, *I am she who speaks*" (20)
echoes of Indigenous verb complexity	remnants of the complex structure of verbs in Indigenous languages (what is sometimes referred to as "pronoun copying" or "subject dropping")	*ê-pêcimakik.* I haunt them. My wailing stories. (52)
figurative / descriptive language	particularly high degree of figurative or descriptive uses of language, especially in relation to context and/ or genre	"The bones stand and sing and I feel the weight of them as they guide my finders on this page." (2)
textual silences	a text's deliberate use of silences; intended to draw readers further into the text	opening and closing frame; intertextual references to Cree literary and intellectual traditions

All of the evidentials used in *Blue Marrow* contain some form of a tag. Those passages attributed to the narrator are indicated by way of a formula, the Cree word *âcimowinis*, "small story." The poem uses other formulaic tags, too, which I will discuss in detail below; however, in most other cases, the tags consists of a verb (to tell, to continue a story, to speak, etc.) combined with a personal name. In fact, *Blue Marrow* is a text intricately

---

23 Of the various elements in this table, I will discuss only evidentiality and echoes of Indigenous verb complexity. For a detailed analysis and discussion of indirect holophrastic traces in *Blue Marrow* see Neuhaus, "That's Raven Talk," chap. 5.

woven together with the names of the narrator's ancestors, which appear both in the main part of the poem and in a long list recited by the narrator in the poem's opening. These personal names are based on English, Cree, or a conflation of the two and function as examples of synecdoche (a part standing for the whole) in that they use a person's defining characteristic as his or her name. As such, these names can be read as examples of traditional Indigenous personal names, which tend to be descriptive and very often "not only designated persons but also 'meant,' or alluded to, something else," such as place of birth, astronomical or climatic phenomena, the environment, life events, or a person's outstanding characteristics.[24] An Indigenous personal name becomes a whole phrase, or often even a whole sentence, when translated literally into English; these translations— known as loan translations—usually result in such descriptive names as "She Has Strong Back Strong Wings Woman" or "Night Traveller Woman" (to cite two names used in *Blue Marrow*). This is not to suggest that the personal names in Halfe's collection are indeed direct translations of actual Cree names; rather, they create the *illusion* of loan translations. What is more, these loan translations take the form of complex compounds— ranging from deverbal noun-noun compounds and compound nouns with verbal modifiers to synthetic compounds and quotation compounds—all of which qualify as direct holophrastic traces because they mimic the holistic structure of the holophrase (see table 7.2).

TABLE 7.2 EXAMPLES OF DIRECT HOLOPHRASTIC TRACES IN *BLUE MARROW*[25]

RELATIONAL WORD BUNDLES		
TYPE	**DEFINITION**	**EXAMPLES IN *BLUE MARROW***
quotation compounds	a phrase or complete sentence that can be analyzed as a single word; a compound that looks like quoted speech	*wâpâsôs*: Up at Dawn Woman (3); *kâ-itwêhât*: She Who Says So Woman (6); Count My Blessings Grandmother (57); Born in a Dent Grandmudder (61); Born in Tent Grandmother (63); *sîpi-kiskisiw* Grandmother: Long Term Memory Grandmother (76)

24   David H. French and Kathrine S. French, "Personal Names," in *Languages*, ed. Ives Goddard, vol. 17 of *Handbook of North American Indians*, ed. William C. Sturtevant (Washington, DC: Smithsonian Institution Press, 1996), 214.

25   For a detailed analysis and discussion of direct holophrastic traces in *Blue Marrow*, see Neuhaus, "*That's Raven Talk*," chap. 5.

	RELATIONAL WORD BUNDLES	
TYPE	**DEFINITION**	**EXAMPLES IN *BLUE MARROW***
synthetic compounds	a compound whose head is derived by affixation of a verb	"Watchmaker" in Watchmaker Woman (5); "Night Traveller" in Night Traveller Woman (5); "Lip Pointing" in Lip Pointing Woman (6)
compound noun with verbal modifier	a verb-noun compound whose head is formed by the noun	Fiddler Woman (4); Kingfisher Woman (4); Fire Thunder Woman (6)
deverbal noun-noun compound	a noun-noun compound whose modifier is a deverbalized noun	Frying Pan Woman (3); Sitting Weasel Woman (4); Rolling Head Woman (5); Sparkling Eyes Woman (6); Wandering Stone Grandmother (42, 43, 44, 45, 48); Starved Gopher Grandmother (52)

What does the use of these direct holophrastic traces have to do with *âniskwâpitamâcimowin*, you will rightly wonder? As the narrator orchestrates the stories of her ancestors, she names the speakers to enable their stories to travel smoothly (evidentiality), but also to mark the ancestral knowledge thus communicated as embodied understanding. These are the stories not of nameless people, but of Cree relations. Moreover, by grounding this act of reference in Cree traditions of name giving, the narrator ensures that the voiceless are given a chance to speak on their own terms— a prerequisite for self-empowerment. As McLeod states, "Names define and articulate a place within society and the world. Indigenous names are absolutely essential for the description of Indigenous realities."[26] The indigenized personal names in *Blue Marrow*, then, have a political purpose—one that is even more complex than the mere use of Indigenous name-giving traditions may suggest. The names of the women whose voices are heard in the main part of the poem are particularly interesting in this respect, because the women's stories also reveal the etymologies of the women's names. *Sîpi-kiskisiw* Grandmother (Long Term Memory Grandmother) speaks of the times when her father "*fought with lance and arrow, / rotted behind bars / his treaty coat / a shredded ribbon*" (76). Grandmother Bargain explains in her confession how "*My father saw / my future husband—/ mounds of fur*" and thus tells the story of how she was sold by

---

26 McLeod, "Cree Poetic Discourse," 111.

her father to a white man as part of a bargain to obtain the white man's provisions (54–56). Speaking herself into an angry fit, one woman "*put dem* [white men] *back / on dem big canoe. / Dem go home. / My big family / make dem go home*"—and so becomes Not So Long Ago Granny Wants to Get Even (64–65). Another woman, talking about her birth, tells the reader, "*I can't dell you where I waz born. / In a dent somewhere, / maybe in da bush*"; she becomes Born in a Dent Grandmudder (61).

Although the narrator assigns Indigenized personal names to the women speaking in the main part of her narrative, she claims that she does "not recognize who speaks" (18, 61). This statement may seem contradictory, but in fact it makes sense insofar as the personal names assigned to these women reduce their identities to those of colonized objects conquered and ruled over by white men. The use in *Blue Marrow* of Indigenous traditions of name giving thus marks the narrative as one that carries an implicit political statement—one that "affronts the master narrative of imperialism and commodification by offering, in its place, a vivid account of the dispossessed who, though dead and buried, refuse to be silent."[27] As symbols of the stories of colonization, the women's names in the main part of *Blue Marrow* can be read as "abbreviated texts"[28]: they mark the women who bear these names as colonized objects, yet their stories persist, and so do these women, through the narrator's connecting with them.

The Indigenized personal names in the main part of *Blue Marrow* are not just direct holophrastic traces, however; they also function as relational word bundles, the other main component of holophrastic reading. As symbols, these names take the form of figures of speech; what is more, they also provide structural markers within the poem by allowing readers to distinguish between different stories, all the while letting them see how these stories are all variations on the theme of colonization. Functioning much like chapter titles in longer narratives or stage directions in a play, the women's names facilitate reader understanding as well as providing a summary of the poem. In other words, the ancestors' names ensure that the poem's loose narrative structure does not fall apart.

The same narrative function is also performed in *Blue Marrow* by another set of tags used to identify speakers, namely, the formulaic tags of

---

27 Cook, "Bone Memory," 97.

28 Martha B. Kendall argues that Northern Yuman personal names "must be considered abbreviated texts or allusions to narratives, whose significance is social as well as cultural" (Kendall, "Exegesis and Translation: Northern Yuman Names as Texts," *Journal of Anthropological Research* 36.3 [1980]: 261).

- *nôhkom âtayôhkan,* who is also part of the chorus of voices orchestrated by the narrator (she is usually identified as "The Keeper of the Sacred Legends" [23; see also 34, 39, 77, 78]),

- the chorus of foremothers—"*kahkiyaw iskwêwak, nôtokwêsiwak, câpânak, êkwa ohkomipanak*" (meaning "all women, the very Elderly Women, Great Grandmothers, and Eternal Grandmothers" [22, 30, 34, 49, 54, 59, 63, 67, 72, 77, 85]), and

- the chorus of forefathers—"*kahkiyaw nâpêwak, kisêyiniwak, câpânak, êkwa omosômipanak*" (meaning "all men, the very Elderly Men, the Great Grandfathers, and the Eternal Grandfathers" [77, 78; see also 37, 70]).

These formulaic tags arguably also function as symbols, not of the history of colonization but of *wâhkôhtowin* (kinship). The invocations of the voices of the foremothers and forefathers, and of *nôhkom âtayôhkan,* also qualify as relational word bundles: as symbols of kinship, they carry a huge bundle of meaning; as evidentials, they help give form to the poem, thus fulfilling a significant narrative function; and in their interdependence, they help weave the poem's narrative grid.

To distinguish one ancestor's story from another's is one thing; to suggest connections among these stories is another. In order for the poem to recover collective knowledge rather than piecemeal reminiscences, the ancestral knowledge passed on in *Blue Marrow* needs to be anchored somehow. This anchoring is achieved through a series of strategies, including intertextual references to Cree *âtayôhkêwina,* meta-fictional moments, and an opening and closing that frame the narrator's poem as prayer and ceremony. Different though these strategies are on the surface, they all ultimately involve the use of relational word bundles, as we shall see next.

With very few exceptions, most notably the Cree morning song recited toward the end of the poem (87),[29] intertextual references in *Blue Marrow* are to Cree sacred history alone and are embedded in the poem through the voices of the ancestors, the narrator's parents, or the narrator herself, thus linking different generations of Cree people. The story of *wîhtikow,* the cannibalistic figure of Cree sacred history, is evoked twice: once in an elaborate aside spoken by "one of the *omosômimâwak*" (grandfathers) who remembers his own grandfather "saz da burning of da last *wîhtikow,*"

---

29 See also the poem "Ditch Bitch" in Louise Bernice Halfe, *Bear Bones and Feathers* (Regina: Coteau, 1994), 50–51.

and again in a speech by *sîpi-kiskisiw* Grandmother (Long Term Memory Grandmother), who tells of the time her "Mother buried *wîhtikow*" (36–37, 76). The Cree elder brother, *wîsahkêcâhk*, is alluded to by the narrator's father and mother, both of whom remember the night the narrator was taken away to residential school, when the narrator's mother rubbed her belly and told her the story of "*how* wîsahkêcâhk *tossed his eyes*" (82, 89).[30] The next intertextual reference to the Cree elder brother is made by the narrator herself when she recites part of the Cree creation story in the poem's closing, thus ending *Blue Marrow* with a reminder of the life-giving force of *okâwîmâwaskiy* (Mother Earth) and of woman's significant role in creation.

> We are Star People.
> *wîsahkêcâhk* sang to the Water People
> to bring back to Earth from where we dove.
> She pinched the mud from the exhausted Muskrat
> Blew *yôtin* [wind]. Blew *iskotêw* [fire]. *iskwêw* [woman] was born.
> *pimâtisiwim* [life] fills woman.
> Man is born. (98)

Finally, the narrative of Rolling Head, who is also listed in the enumeration of women in the poem's opening, is evoked by *nôhkom âtayôhkan*:

> *For centuries*
> *I've tumbled through thistles,*
> *charcoal stars and suns,*
> *groaning lakes and rivers,*
> *my hairy skull*
> *a home for mice and snakes.* (23)

These intertextual references to Cree sacred history have a bundle of meaning (they refer to outside texts), but they also add to the intertextual connecting of *Blue Marrow* (its *âniskwâpitamâcimowin*) by embedding the ancestors' stories in the collective memory and sacred history of their people. Grounding the ancestors' stories in Cree sacred history anchors

---

30 For a telling of this story, see "Wesakaychak and the Tomtits" in Edward Ahenakew, "Cree Trickster Tales," *Journal of American Folklore* 42 (1929): 347–49.

the chorus of ancestral voices and thus also contributes, if indirectly, to the poem's narrative grid. All these intertextual references to Cree *âtayôh-kêwina* are, in other words, relational word bundles.

As noted above, the passages spoken by the narrator are marked with the formulaic tag âcimowinis, "small story." This clearly "stories" the narrator: she is the keeper of the stories gathered in *Blue Marrow*, but she also carries her own story. Some of the narrator's story is revealed in the conversations with her father and mother toward the closing of the poem. Prior to these conversations, however, her contributions to the poem are primarily of a meta-fictional nature. In fact, *Blue Marrow* is a self-reflective poem whose very composition is witnessed by readers as they listen to the narrator's account of textualizing Cree oral history—which is but one of the effects of the poem's meta-fictional tendencies. More importantly, the meta-fictional moments in *Blue Marrow* establish links between the narrator and her ancestors, whose stories she is in the process of writing down for future generations. These meta-fictional moments involve either the foremothers speaking directly to the narrator—

> All Women. Grandmothers and
> the Eternal Grandmothers beseech
> êy êy êy nôsisim [my grandchild]
> *here this needle*
> *thread its eye*
> *oh these* âcimowinisa (63)

—or the narrator describing her transcription of the voices' messages:

> *We will guide your feather*
> *dipped in ink* (27)

> They sing me to *kîwêtinohk.*
> North. They bundle me home (60)

The foremothers and forefathers address the narrator by using kinship terms (*nitânis, nôsisim*), thus emphasizing their close relationship. *Blue Marrow* connects current and future generations of Cree with their ancestors, strengthening kinship bonds through *âniskwâpitamâcimowin*. Where intertextuality aims at grounding the ancestors' stories in Cree sacred history, meta-fiction emphasizes the nature and relevance of these stories and this history for the continuity of the Cree people. Out of her embodied understanding grows the narrator's *poetic dreaming*, which performs kinship and, with that, peoplehood. As do intertextual references to Cree sacred history, these meta-fictional moments function as relational word bundles. They perform a significant narrative function by helping constitute the poem's intertextual connecting, thus contributing to the poem's narrative grid, and they do so carrying a large bundle of meaning, by pointing to the process of composition underlying the poem.

There is still more to be said about the use of meta-fiction in Halfe's *Blue Marrow*, for it is the poem's self-reflective tendencies that provide readers with an understanding of how the narrator has gained the ancestral knowledge that she is passing on to the next generations. Every time the narrator or the ancestors mention or allude to the narrator's task, they evoke an event that is retold in the poem's opening and closing frame. In other words, the narrative function of the meta-fictional relational word bundles in *Blue Marrow* also lies in establishing narrative relations between this frame and the ancestors' stories in the main part of the poem. And it is in this frame that the narrator's role as a poetic dreamer tapping into the Great Mystery is established. As with any other narrative frame, the opening and closing frame in Halfe's poem must be constructed somehow. As in the works discussed in previous chapters (see particularly chapter 5), this is done by way of relational word bundles.

The ancestors' stories in *Blue Marrow* are framed by a prayer and song that fully anchor them into *mamâhtâwisiwin*, the process of tapping into the Great Mystery. The poem begins with the following lines:

> Voice Dancer *pawâkan*, the Guardian of Dreams and Visions, prayer, brings to you this gift.

> *Glory be to* okâwîmâwaskiy
> *To the* nôhkom âtayôhkan
> *To* pawâkan
> *As it was in the Beginning,*
> *Is now,*
> *And ever shall be,*
> *World without end.*
> *Amen. Amen.* (1)

With the lines "*Glory be to* okâwîmâwaskiy / *To the* nôhkom âtayôhkan / *To* pawâkan," the narrator invokes Mother Earth (okâwîmâwaskiy), the Grandmother Keeper of the Sacred Legends (nôhkom âtayôhkan), and the Guardian of Dreams and Visions (pawâkan)—all of whom are important figures in Cree spirituality. Substituting these figures for the Holy Trinity, the poem's opening lines contain a subversive rewriting of the *Gloria Patri*.

Given the description of pawâkan as "Voice Dancer *pawâkan*, the Guardian of Dreams and Visions," the stories between this opening prayer and the invocation of the fore- and grandmothers at the end of the opening seem to serve as a retelling of the narrator's "vision." In the course of this vision, the narrator awakes to "the brilliant ribbon of Northern Lights melt[ing] into a sunrise" (2). The northern lights are the spirits of her ancestors dancing in the night sky, telling their stories of colonization. They will become Halfe's very poem, as her narrator receives these stories via nôhkom, who, we may assume, is the nôhkom âtayôhkan invoked in the opening prayer (2). *Nôhkom*'s song is that of the ancestors, whose very bones guide the narrator as she gathers their stories: "The prairie is full of bones. The bones stand and sing and I feel the weight of them as they guide my fingers on this page. See the blood" (2–3). Hidden beneath okâwîmâwaskiy lies the collective memory of the narrator's people, access to which the narrator is granted through the powers bestowed on her by pawâkan. But the responsibility to remember requires that the narrator share her knowledge, thereby honouring her relations, or practicing what McLeod calls a "poetics of empathy" (see above). "I began the walk for them" (3), she declares, and she shouts out the names of numerous women—four pages of names interspersed with subversive, Cree-infused parodies of the Hail Mary, the *Gloria Patri*, and the Lord's Prayer—and the women's stories she now "feeds" to future generations: "Grandmothers hold me. / I must pass all that I possess, / every morsel to my children. / These small gifts" (7).

As the narrator accepts her intermediate position between the past generations and those still to come, it becomes clear that the initial description of *pawâkan* was anything but accidental. "Voice Dancer *pawâkan*, the Guardian of Dreams and Visions" circumscribes the meaning and function of pawâkan; however, by evoking both the northern lights ("voice dancer") and their role as "guardian" of the narrator's dreams and vision, this phrase also connects two crucial elements from the opening with the poem. It is with this link—between the messages of the ancestors and the narrator's dreams and vision—that the poem is born. "Voice Dancer *pawâkan*, the Guardian of Dreams and Visions," then, tells in one phrase the story of the narrator gaining vision, hence explaining the poem's origin and its grounding in Cree ancestral knowledge. The roles of those who will accompany the narrator on her walk to vision—Mother Earth, the eternal grandmother and keeper of legends, and the Guardian of Dreams and Visions—are anticipated in the lines "*Glory be to* okâwîmâwaskiy / *To the* nôhkom âtayôhkan / *To* pawâkan," but this phrase is also a metonymic invocation of the metaphor that the narrator uses after her vision: "The prairie is full of bones. The bones stand and sing and I feel the weight of them as they guide my fingers on this page. See the blood." It is with the help of *okâwîmâwaskiy, nôhkom âtayôhkan,* and *pawâkan,* who guide the narrator to vision, that she is able to hear her ancestors' stories. The phrase "I began the walk for them" becomes a metaphor of her decision to speak for the ancestors who surround her so fully (their bones in Mother Earth and their spirits in the sky, dancing as the northern lights), to become their intermediary, and thus to translate their stories into the poem that she offers to her children as if it were food: "every morsel to my children. / These small gifts." The metaphor that ends the poem's opening points to the importance of stories and of poetic dreaming: they ensure the people's continued survival.

The phrases discussed above—all of them relational word bundles—are important figures of speech that constitute the structural foundation on which the opening of *Blue Marrow* rests: they evoke both the narrator's vision and her acceptance of the poetics of empathy. Her vision makes the narrator a poetic dreamer tapping into the Great Mystery; she connects with ancestral knowledge and, realizing her responsibility to both past and future generations, she shares the knowledge and insights she gains on her path. Thus, the opening offers to readers of *Blue Marrow* the poem's interpretative and spiritual contexts. What they are reading is the result of *mamâhtâwisiwin,* the attempt to make sense of contemporary issues facing Cree people by connecting with ancestral knowledge. In that sense, the opening also constitutes part of the narrative grid that holds the poem together.

Another important narrative element of the poem's structure is provided by its closing, which perfects its narrative frame; the closing, too, is constructed with the help of relational word bundles, all of which take the form of backshadowing to the narrator's vision told in the opening. References are first made to the narrator's retelling of her vision in the opening in her dialogue with her parents. Subtle at first, these references grow particularly obvious in the "Ram Woman Poem," in which the narrator relives and retells her vision. This time, however, she directly addresses *nôhkom* (*âtayôhkan*) as Ram Woman and refers to their meeting as "a Vision" (97). When the narrator describes Ram Woman as "stone-aged wrinkled," this description underlines her age and further supports a reading of her as the *nôhkom* (*âtayôhkan*) of the opening. Like *nôhkom* (*âtayôhkan*), Ram Woman stares with one "large eye" and sings to the narrator (96, 97; see also 2). As in the opening, the narrator stands "naked beneath the falls," exposed and vulnerable (96; see also 1). The "Ram Woman poem" also contains a reference to the northern lights that "Ribboned the Sky" in the opening, whereas "Raw-boned / they left their blood" refers to the bones populating the prairie whose stories the narrator is collecting. Thus, the "Ram Woman Poem" in the closing fills in all of those blanks left open in the opening. In addition to these intratextual connections to the story of the narrator's vision, the poem's closing points yet again to the importance of *okâwîmâwaskiy* and *nôhkom âtayôhkan*. The latter are evoked by way of an intertextual reference to *wîsahkêcâhk* and the narrator's version of the Cree earth diver story (quoted above). Having recounted part of the Cree story of Creation, the narrator joins "Grandmother danc[ing] at Midnight," eventually closing her narrative with the words "A pagan. Again. / All my relations. *ahâw*" (90).

In that it moves from vision to prayer, the closing of *Blue Marrow* is its opening told backward, hence establishing a cyclical structure within the frame. Still, there is a significant difference between the opening of Halfe's poem and its closing: whereas in the former the narrator parodies Christian prayers to have them reflect Cree spiritual concepts, she does not use parody in her closing prayer. She does acknowledge that telling her foremothers' stories has turned her into "A pagan. Again." These words are ironic, however. It is through embracing the colonizer's evaluation of her as non-Christian that the narrator expresses her own self-discovery and self-affirmation as an Indigenous woman with strong ties to her people. As if to further highlight the political statement implied in "A pagan. Again," the narrator's last words in English are "All my relations." King explains the significance of this phrase in this way:

"All my relations" is at first a reminder of who we are and of our relationship with both our family and our relatives. It also reminds us of the extended relationship we share with all human beings. But the relationships that Native people see go further, the web of kinship extending to the animals, to the birds, to the fish, to the plants, to all the animate and inanimate forms that can be seen or imagined.

More than that, "all my relations" is an encouragement for us to accept the responsibilities we have within this universal family by living our lives in a harmonious and moral manner.[31]

"All my relations," then, is a very appropriate phrase with which to end
the narrator's prayer/song in *Blue Marrow*. Evoking the central role of
okâwîmâwaskiy (Mother Earth) and *nôhkom âtayôhkan* (Grandmother
Keeper of Sacred Legends) for both the poem and her people, the narrator
is finally prepared to say *ahâw*, a formulaic discourse marker used to end
a conversation in Cree. Her task has been fulfilled; she has walked for her
foremothers and imparted their knowledge to the next generation. Dreaming her people's history through connecting with her ancestors in story,
and framing the process as a prayer, the narrator continues in the footsteps
of the ancient poetic dreamers who used their embodied understandings
to interpret and read the world around them. The narrative frame is more
than mere decoration; it makes *âniskwâpitamâcimowin*, the connecting
through storytelling, relevant for contemporary Cree by showing them
the history of colonization that still informs their lives today, and it clearly
contextualizes *Blue Marrow* in the tradition of *mamâhtâwisiwin*, the process of tapping into the Great Mystery.

So what can we take from the above discussion of Halfe's *Blue Marrow*?
Above all, it shows that her poetic dreaming in her poem is a performance of peoplehood. Halfe's engagement with the history of the fur trade
evokes *wîsahkêcâhk*, the first Cree ceremonialist and poetic dreamer; indeed, through poetic dreaming, Halfe's narrator follows in the footsteps of
the Cree elder brother. Employing a Cree-infused use of the English language that relies on holophrastic traces and relational word bundles, Halfe
further connects with the sacred history of her people, as suggested in the
intertextual references to *âtayohkewina* and in the central role of *nôhkom
âtayôhkan* in *Blue Marrow*. By giving this engagement the form of a prayer,
Halfe points to her people's *ceremonial cycle*, which expresses their unique
relationship with the *land*, which in turn is the source of the narrator's connecting through story in *Blue Marrow*—a contemporary Cree text composed in English that, in its practicing of *mamâhtâwisiwin*, marks a holistic
expression of Cree peoplehood as it dreams a future for the people.

---

31   Thomas King, "Introduction," in *All My Relations: An Anthology of Contemporary Canadian Native Fiction*, ed. Thomas King (Toronto: McClelland and Stewart,
1990), ix.

LOUISE BERNICE HALFE'S *THE CROOKED GOOD*

Blue Marrow evokes *nôhkom âtayôhkan* (Grandmother Keeper of Sacred Legends) and makes brief intertextual references to Cree *âtayôhkêwin* tradition, thus embedding in Cree sacred history and collective memory the oral history of the fur trade recovered by the poem's narrator. In *The Crooked Good*, Halfe engages directly with Cree mythical past through an elaborate retelling and interpretation of the story of *cihcipiscikwân* (Rolling Head). As *âtayôhkêwin* (sacred narrative), this story forms part of the *wîsahkêcâhk* cycle, the Cree story of Creation. In fact, as is eventually revealed in the cycle, *cihcipiscikwân* and her husband are the parents of the Cree elder brother. The retelling of cihcipiscikwân's story in *The Crooked Good* is framed as a storytelling performance: the collection's first-person narrator, *ê-kwêskît* (Turn-Around Woman), recalls her mother telling her children the story of Rolling Head one winter night (19–29). *The Crooked Good* is therefore clearly marked as embodied understanding—doubly so, in fact, because the narrator's remembering of her mother's storytelling performance also frames her own interpretation of the narrative of *cihcipiscikwân* in the light of her own life story, "this story" she tells to the readers (3). *The Crooked Good*, then, is *âcimisowin*, a "story about oneself" or autobiographical story. However, since Cree notions of identity are always communal, the life story *ê-kwêskît* shares in the poem is also the story of her family, particularly that of her mother and sisters. Their shared narrative is one of sexual and racial abuse that is so representative of the stories of many Cree and other Aboriginal women across North America. Framed as an interpretation of the story of Rolling Head—that is, as *âniskwâpitamâcimowin*—*The Crooked Good* is an elaborate and beautifully crafted example of *mamâhtâwisiwin*: the process of poetic dreaming that involves the retelling and interpreting of ancient stories in the light of new experiences—in this case, colonialism and its ravaging effects on Aboriginal women. In fact, *ê-kwêskît* names the ancient story keepers (*âtayôhkanak*) directly—"*These gifted mysterious people of long ago,* / kayâs kî-mamâhtâwisiwak iyiniwak"—when she points to them as the "origin of stories and the source of poetic insight."[32]

> In Rib Woman
> stories are born.
> The Old Man called it psychology. Me,
> I just dream it.

---

32 McLeod, "Cree Poetic Discourse," 112–13.

These gifted mysterious people of long ago,
kayâs kî-mamâhtâwisiwak iyiniwak[33]

my mother, Gone-For-Good, would say.

They never died. They are scattered here, there,
everywhere, somewhere. They know the language,
the sleep, the dream, the laws, these singers, these healers,
âtayôhkanak, *these ancient story keepers*

I, Turn-Around Woman, am not one of them. (3)

Particularly noteworthy in this passage is *ê-kwêskît*'s use of the verb *mamâhtâwisi*, "to tap into the Great Mystery," which is repeated twice in the collection (22, 26) and, according to McLeod, denotes the process of *mamâhtâwisiwin. Ê-kwêskît* may not be an ancient story keeper, but she is a contemporary poetic dreamer ("I just dream it") who engages directly with the ancient story keepers when she reinterprets the Rolling Head narrative. She is practicing kinship through her connecting in stories.

Because *ê-kwêskît*'s life story is so fully embedded into an interpretation of the story of Rolling Head, it is apt to begin this discussion of *The Crooked Good* by briefly summarizing this *âtayôhkêwin*. In this story, a legendary woman becomes Rolling Head when her husband beheads her upon learning that she has been having an affair with a snake. The husband ascends to heaven, becoming the morning star, as does his wife's torso, which turns into the evening star, forever chasing after the husband in the sky. The woman's head, on the other hand, rolls over the land in search of her two fleeing sons who, fearful of their mother and equipped with four powerful gifts from their father, eventually manage to escape to safety. Rolling Head eventually drowns, her head sinking to the bottom of a deep lake and becoming a sturgeon.[34]

---

33 Using McLeod's translation of *mamâhtâwisi*, the line "kayâs kî-mamâhtâwisiwak iyiniwak" translates as "a long time ago, the people tapped into the Great Mystery." In the glossary to *The Crooked Good*, the line is given as "a long time ago people were filled with the gift of Mystery—spiritual gifts that materialize in gifted people" (Halfe, *The Crooked Good*, 129).

34 Halfe, "Keynote Address," 66–68. Other tellings of *cihcipiscikwân-âtayôhkêwin* are found in Ahenakew, "Cree Trickster Tales," 309–13; Bloomfield, *Sacred Stories*, 8–20; James R. Stevens, *Sacred Legends of the Sandy Lake Cree* (Toronto: McClelland and Stewart, 1971), 48–52.

Given the central role of snakes in the narrative—Rolling Head has an affair with a snake, resulting in snake offspring, all of whom are killed by her jealous husband—it may be tempting to read the narrative of *cihcipiscikwân* in the context of the biblical Fall of Man. As McLeod has demonstrated, however, the snakes in *cihcipiscikwân-âtayôhkêwin* are clearly a pre-Christian element. Moreover, McLeod reads Halfe's treatment of the story as grounded in a poetics of empathy that allows "non-Christian interpretations" of the figure of the snake in *cihcipiscikwân-âtayôhkêwin*, and in Cree narrative tradition more generally, where snakes are seen less as evil creatures than as helpers of the Cree people.[35] Similarly, in her keynote address delivered at the 2004 "For the Love of Words: Aboriginal Writers of Canada" conference, Halfe points to the power that snakes were traditionally thought to have held among Crees:

> [Rolling Head's] husband provided well, but apparently was unavailable otherwise. If you leave things or people to themselves they go elsewhere for nourishment. Hence the snakes reciprocated her affection and took pity upon her. Perhaps they rewarded her with medicines to heal her people, for snakes are closest to the earth. They feel the vibrations of the earth, hear her heartbeat, know her touch, know her sounds, and know her scents and medicines.[36]

In fact, Halfe's own grandmother was a medicine woman who used the skins of snakes as medicine, though this work garnered her "more fear than respect in spite of the healing that occurred."[37] Halfe does not say so herself, but this reaction from her grandmother's own people may already have been a result of internalized colonialism. When, in *The Crooked Good*, Halfe explores *cihcipiscikwân*'s story from her perspective rather than that of the betrayed husband, she does so to create understanding for contemporary Cree women, by challenging not just colonialism as such but particularly its gendered violence against women, their families, and their communities. Halfe constructs this exploration of *cihcipiscikwân*'s perspective through the voice of *ê-kwêskît*, whose story closely resembles that of *cihcipiscikwân*.

The analogies between their stories occur early in the poem. In its opening pages, *ê-kwêskît* admits that

---

35 McLeod, "Cree Poetic Discourse," 116.
36 Halfe, "Keynote Address," 69.
37 Ibid., 70.

I am not a saint. I am a crooked good.
My cousins said I was easy, therefore
I've never been a maiden.
I am seventy, but still
I carry my sins. Brothers-in-law
I meet for the first time wipe their hands
as if I am still among the maggots. I didn't
know their women wept when their men
slept in my bed. I am not a saint. (4)

The oxymoron of the poem's title, "crooked good," suggests a more nuanced notion of good and evil than the essentialist binary suggested in the Bible. In fact, crooked and good are oxymoronic only in the context of Christian notions of good and evil; in Cree thought, by contrast, good and evil "exist in all possibilities, all moments, and all beings."[38] This balanced notion of good and evil allows a more nuanced and empathetic reading of snakes and, by implication, of *cihcipiscikwân*'s story as well as that of *ê-kwêskît* and her family.[39]

The Crooked Good, then, offers a reading of Cree sacred history and contemporary issues that is decidedly *not* grounded in Christian beliefs of purity and chastity. Indeed, these Christian values are deliberately ironized by the narrator through "making their presence in her text peripheral and revealing their logic to be simplistic and ultimately faulty."[40] *The Crooked Good* weaves into its narrative three excerpts from *The Jesuit Relations (1632–1673)*, the annual accounts of Jesuit missions in Nouvelle France that document, among other things, the attempts by priests to convert Aboriginal people to Christianity. Though left unaltered, these intertexts are transformed through the words placed around them. In the first Jesuit quotation, Father Francis du Person's comment on the inability of "[my] savages" to distinguish between good and evil is juxtaposed with the narrator's intent to listen to and share the story of *cihcipiscikwân*, which in turn is followed by "First Sound," a poem that celebrates the orgasmic creation of new life in which the poet and her siblings revel (8–9). The second Jesuit quotation is inserted into the narrator's description of her first few years with her white husband and includes a priest's request,

---

38 McLeod, "Cree Poetic Discourse," 117.
39 Ibid., 116.
40 Jennifer Andrews, *In the Belly of a Laughing God: Humour and Irony in Native Women's Poetry* (Toronto: University of Toronto Press, 2011), 67.

made to a young, apparently Aboriginal woman, to honour him and her father by living a good life. This request is contrasted with another, by *ê-kwêskît*'s grandmother, who urges *ê-kwêskît* to "Never forget you're Cree" (62–63). Finally, the third quotation from *The Jesuit Relations* is incorporated as ironic commentary on her husband's sexual hungers: when he demands sexual intercourse from her one day, she makes sure, afterwards, to show him the passages a Jesuit priest had written about an Aboriginal woman who had sinned through bodily acts, as if saying "Look! Sex is a sin. Doesn't that make you a sinner, too?" (105–106). These reworkings of Euro-Western texts place Halfe's engagement with Cree sacred history into the larger context of the history of colonialism without, however, compromising Cree stories or traditions. *The Crooked Good* ironizes the colonizer's positions by fully embracing the very stories that are savage and sinful in the colonizer's eyes: "We all had loves. Secret loves. Snake-tongued lovers" (7). But these same stories of "romantic fever run[ning] in [the] family" are also framed by stories about the ravaging effects on Aboriginal women of all those government policies targeted at assimilation, most notably the residential school system. Transformed into Cree ancient poetic pathways, then, Euro-Western texts never usurp Halfe's poetic dreaming in *The Crooked Good*; instead, Halfe uses these texts in her struggle towards decolonization, which she pursues through the process of *mamâhtâwisiwin*, the deliberate rooting in *cihcipiscikwân-âtayôhkêwin* of the women's stories shared in *The Crooked Good*.

How does this process work in this particular poem? In brief, it works through the analogies drawn between Rolling Head and *ê-kwêskît* mentioned above. The most explicit analogy between the two is found in the closing poem of the collection, which gives in separate columns the voice of *ê-kwêskît* (left column, titled "Gave My Name") and that of Rolling Head (right column, titled "*âtayôhkan*"). As each of the two women provides a brief account of her life, as if to summarize the stories gathered in the collection, the similarities between their stories become all the more obvious. More specifically, *ê-kwêskît* calls herself "the sturgeon of the depths," thereby evoking the ending of Rolling Head's story, when her head sinks to the depths of a lake, becoming a sturgeon. The poem thus "links a contemporary understanding to a past understanding."[41] This intimate connection between past and present is expressed in the very first lines of the poem and runs throughout the narrative, thus providing the poem's narrative grid. In order to understand this connection, we need to

---

41   McLeod, "Cree Poetic Discourse," 117.

analyze the relationship between Rolling Head and Rib Woman, a third central figure in *The Crooked Good* (besides *cihcipiscikwân* and *ê-kwêskît*). It may be tempting for non-Aboriginal readers to read Rib Woman as an adaptation of the biblical Eve,[42] but as we shall soon see, such a reading ultimately ignores that Rib Woman is essentially another version of Rolling Head.

In "Braids," the prologue poem to *cihcipiscikwân-âtayôhkêwin*,

> *âtayôhkân* says when she drowned
> she became a sturgeon. I don't know this.
> I witness only what my ears held.
>
> * *
>
> Over brooks, ponds, rivers, lakes and seas,
> her winds caused great floods. She cleared
> her throat, swelled, tore dirt, shot arrow-spiked rains.
> She'd glide over mountains, unbuckle her soul,
> colour the sky with her laughter, her howl.
> She slept so long. Rocks are her spine, rivers
> bury her seeds. No one knows her age. *In the spring*
> *Rolling Head awakens, becomes Rib Woman.*
> The lodge, her hair.
> Willow people form her flesh, a basket woven
> Over weeping dreamers. The spring berry is her heart.
> I told you this.
> This dreamer. A ghost-faced woman with short blunt
> black hair. Snakes dance on her shoulders, hips, belly
> and thighs. (20; emphasis mine)

And then, a few lines later, we learn that

> The swan's breast
> is filled with adulterous tales,
> still
> the obsessed continue
> long after they first notice her. (21)

---

42   See, for example, the interpretation in Andrews, *In the Belly of a Laughing God*, 68.

What may we gather from these excerpts? One, Rolling Head is not dead; she lives on, not in the form of a sturgeon but as Rib Woman, who surfaces every spring, that time of the year when everything and everyone awakens, including their dreams, desires, and yearnings. And two, when Rolling Head resurfaces as Rib Woman, it is as if she enlightens a romantic fever, producing new tales of adultery. "In Rib Woman / stories are born" (3)—literally. There is first the story of Rolling Head's adultery, that first story which also serves as the beginning of the Cree story of Creation, thus linking the theme of adultery with that of creation and *wâhkôhtowin*, kinship—the epitome of the crooked good. And finally, there are all those other "adulterous tales," which continue to take place not just because Rolling Head awakens every spring but also because "the obsessed continue / long after they first notice her." Rib Woman is the story of Rolling Head's adultery, or rather, *ê-kwêskît*'s reading of that adultery. We may say that Rib Woman is a version of Rolling Head, as this story affects contemporary Crees, including those women whose stories of "romantic fever" *ê-kwêskît* has gathered together in *The Crooked Good*. With Rib Woman, Halfe has thus introduced an organic notion of story into her poem, of story as living entity.

Rib Woman figures repeatedly in Halfe's poem, and one may argue that this is no coincidence. *The Crooked Good* is, if you will, a collection of adulterous tales, some ancient, others contemporary. The ways in which the figure of Rib Woman is woven into *ê-kwêskît*'s narrative turns Rib Woman into a symbol: of adultery, of an adulterous life, and of adulterous women more generally. As *ê-kwêskît* admits in the poem "*ê-kwêskît*—Turn-Around Woman,"

> I married Abel, a wide green-eyed man. Fifty years now.
> Inside Rib Woman I shook hands with promise.
> Promise never forgot, trailed me year after year.
> His Big Heavens a morning lake
> drowns me in my lair.
> I learned how to build Rib Woman
> one willow at a time, one skin at a time. (4)

When first mentioning her husband, *ê-kwêskît* connects promise to a life not with him but with Rib Woman. The lair in which *ê-kwêskît* drowns evokes how "*cihcipiscikwân* knows how yearning / crawls underground, blind hands / feeling in the lair. Desire flicks its tongue" (21). A few lines later in the same poem we learn that the narrator "learned how to build Rib Woman / one willow at a time, one skin at a time." *Ê-kwêskît*'s adultery, in other words, has been a long process.

Rib Woman is more than a symbol, however; she also functions as an important structural device: "I build this story like my lair. One willow, / a rib at a time. Bent it into my hip, grounded into earth" (6). These lines are an almost verbatim repetition of lines from the poem "*ê-kwêskît*—Turn-Around Woman" (quoted above): "I learned how to build Rib Woman / one willow at a time, one skin at a time," substituting "this story" and "a rib at a time" for "Rib Woman" and "one skin at a time." Thus, just as *ê-kwêskît* learns how to carefully build Rib Woman—her life of secret loves—she crafts her life story carefully, with Rib Woman's help. Rib Woman provides the original story, the template *ê-kwêskît* uses to read her own life. Rib Woman is the origin of *âniskwâpitamâcimowin* that Halfe practices in *The Crooked Good*. Every mention of Rib Woman in the poem helps weave the stories shared in *The Crooked Good* into a coherent whole. Every mention of Rib Woman is a symbolic rib building the poem's torso. As symbol, Rib Woman is a figure of speech that, through its frequent repetition, holds together the poem's multitude of stories; in fact, as a version of Rolling Head, Rib Woman also provides a summary of the poem, thus producing its narrative grid. All of this is to say that Rib Woman—in her various textual variations—functions as the central relational word bundle in *The Crooked Good*.

Of course, relational word bundles in *The Crooked Good* are not restricted to Rib Woman alone, though this is arguably the most pertinent relational word bundle in the poem. Much like Rib Woman, intertextual references to Rolling Head also serve important functions in rooting *ê-kwêskît*'s story in the tradition of *mamâhtâsiwin*, as do the few meta-fictional asides found throughout the poem. These highlight the very process of *mamâhtâwisiwin*, such as the notion of building the poem like a lair as well as the following excerpt from the poem "Dear Magpie," appearing toward the end of *The Crooked Good*:

> These days, ancient legends work their way
> into how I've tasted, ate and swallowed my life.
> *I reframe them*, hope they will live another way.
> The wise live in the lake, sway in the tall grass,
> light up the universe in the prairie storm.
> I listen,
> and eventually

the voices penetrate my thick skull
where my heart attempts
to understand. (121–22; emphasis mine)

This passage describes no less than *ê-kwêskît*'s attempt to tap into the Great Mystery; her poem, which readers are just in the process of reading, is the result of these very efforts. Last but not least, there is the narrator's declaration that ends her poem: "*When* ê-kwêskît *sinks,* / *head on pillow* / *I surface* / with camera, telephone, television / and a big screen" (124; emphasis mine). These lines allude to the poetic dreaming involved in *mamâhtâsiwin*; at the end of the poem, this dreaming is no longer documented using just one's voice.

Just like *Blue Marrow*, then, Halfe's third collection of poetry is a powerful celebration of Cree peoplehood. Again, Halfe evokes *wîsahkêcâhk*, the first Cree ceremonialist and poetic dreamer, and she does so through both her own poetic dreaming in the voice of *ê-kwêskît* and her very reinterpretation of *cihcipiscikwân-âtayôhkêwin* from a decidedly anti-Christian, Cree feminist point of view. Halfe engages with *Cree sacred history* in order to empower Cree *iskwêwak* and their families and communities, and she does so once again by building her poem with a Cree-infused use of the English language based on relational word bundles. The *land* and the people's *ceremonial cycle* figure less overtly in *The Crooked Good* than in Halfe's previous collection, *Blue Marrow*, although the land is referred to directly in at least one passage of the poem. In fact, Rib Woman is associated with, even tied to, *nêhiyânâhk* (Cree country), the home of *ê-kwêskît* to which she refers as *tawinikêwin*—"spacious beautiful, abundance of land; a cleared space; spacious creation" (69, 130). When *ê-kwêskît* and her husband live in Toronto for some years, "Bones, pottery and polished silver fought. / Hockey, theatre, ballet strutted while *Rib Woman* / *waited*" as did aspin, the narrator's mother (62). Hence, the kinship performed in *The Crooked Good* also includes connections to the land, as expressed in the people's ceremonial cycle. Continuing the tradition of *mamâhtâwisiwin*, *The Crooked Good* marks an expression of Cree peoplehood that builds a future for *nêhiyawak* by empowering *iskwêwak* and, through them, all members of the community.

What can we take from these readings of Halfe's poetry? First, by reading her narrative poems as part of the tradition of *mamâhtâwisiwin*, it is possible to engage with the ways in which these poems are embedded in the complex matrix that defines Cree peoplehood. Second, nationalist readings of *Blue Marrow* and *The Crooked Good* may be facilitated by holophrastic reading, among other strategies. Holophrastic reading, in a Cree-specific version focused on *mamâhtâwisiwin*, allows readers to access the deeper meanings of Halfe's poetry. Reading is something like navigating a foreign territory using a map. It is easy to recognize the multiplicity of voices in *Blue Marrow*; it is an entirely different matter to make out the links between these voices and the relevance of these connections, both within the poem and outside the text—among the stories of the ancestors, between their stories and Cree sacred history, and between this accumulated ancestral knowledge and the poem's first-person narrator. Similarly, the connections between Rolling Head and Rib Woman, on the one hand, and between Rib Woman and *ê-kwêskît*, on the other, are important ones to make for readers of *The Crooked Good* who want to gain a more nuanced understanding of the poem—one grounded in Cree rather than Western traditions of thought, the latter of which tend to assume Rib Woman is an adaptation of the biblical Eve.

The process of tapping into the Great Mystery is a process that is always grounded in language. *Mamâhtâwsiwin* doesn't merely exist; rather, it needs to be performed as much as peoplehood has to be performed in language. That holophrastic traces and relational word bundles are such salient structures has everything to do with the fact that they draw attention to the rhetorical processes that allow *âniskwâpitamâcimowin* and, by implication, *mamâhtâwisiwin* to occur on the printed page. In other words, if *mamâhtâwsiwin* is the main principle underlying Halfe's poetry, then holophrastic reading may be used as a reading strategy to make sense of this process of tapping into the Great Mystery that Halfe performs in her work. For McLeod, *mamâhtâwsiwin*, or Cree poetics, refers primarily to the art of *making* discourse, whether through storytelling or writing. Poetic dreamers such as Halfe reconnect with ancient knowledge and narrative to dream a future for their people. What emerges in this process are the stories and poems that the readers end up reading. Reading and writing (or storytelling) are two distinct actions that are nevertheless analogous, which is why contemporary notions of poetics are focused not just on the making of discourse but also on the *reading of discourse*. There is another side to Cree poetics, then, one that concerns the reading of Cree literature rather than its composition. Grounded in the dominant language structure of the Cree language, holophrastic reading contributes to this art of reading Cree literature, by allowing readers to trace and make sense of the practice of *mamâhtâwsiwin* by Cree storytellers and writers.

FURTHER READING

Tom Holm, Ben Chavis, and J. Diane Pearson discuss their notion of the peoplehood matrix in "Peoplehood: A Model for the Extension of Sovereignty in American Indian Studies" (*Wicazo Sa Review* 18.1 [2003]). For a discussion of the relevance and challenges of Indigenous literary sovereignty, particularly in Canadian contexts, see the essay "Canadian Indian Literary Nationalism?: Critical Approaches in Canadian Indigenous Contexts" (*Canadian Journal of Native Studies* 29.1–2 [2009]), co-authored by Kristina Fagan, Daniel Heath Justice, Keavy Martin, Sam McKegney, Deanna Reder, and Niigaanwewidam James Sinclair. Neal McLeod offers an excellent discussion of Cree literature and poetics in *Cree Narrative Memory* (Saskatoon: Purich, 2007) and "Cree Poetic Discourse" (in *Across Cultures, Across Borders: Canadian Aboriginal and Native American Literatures*, ed. DePasquale, Eigenbrod, and LaRocque, Toronto: Broadview, 20).

CHAPTER 8

(RADICAL) DEPARTURES OF INDIGENOUS LITERATURES

ationalist approaches to Indigenous writing privilege the specific national/tribal contexts out of which this writing grows. They seek to empower Indigenous people in their own traditions by deliberately facing inward. Like any other form of nationalism, however, Indigenous literary nationalism also entails a range of challenges. One of these challenges is the question of how to adequately approach those Indigenous texts that, for one reason or another, do not fit into the nationalist paradigm. Indigenous literary nationalism implies a direct commitment to the issues and concerns of specific Native communities. As Womack writes in *Red on Red*, "The attempt . . . is to break down oppositions between the world of literature and the very real struggles of American Indian communities, arguing for both an intrinsic and extrinsic relationship between the two."[1] However important this relationship, not all Indigenous texts engage directly with a specific Native community; indeed, there are even Native texts that refrain altogether from engaging with Native concerns and issues. According to McKegney, "ethical critical work" implies a commitment both to Indigenous communities and "to the autonomy of Indigenous literary production."[2] McKegney therefore

---

1 Womack, *Red on Red*, 11.
2 Sam McKegney in Fagan et al., "Canadian Indian Literary Nationalism?," 31.

warns against excluding certain Indigenous texts from the discussion because they do not fit into the nationalist models developed by Womack, Warrior, Weaver, and other nationalist critics (see chapter 7). The work of Cherokee scholar and writer Thomas King comes to mind here. King grew up estranged from his Cherokee roots. He borrows freely from various Indigenous (rather than just Cherokee) traditions and engages heavily with Euro-Western texts. Although his third novel, *Truth and Bright Water* (1999), has been read by Daniel Heath Justice (Cherokee) as reflecting a Cherokee experience—if one that is "made particularly difficult as a result of the demographic scattering of so many Cherokees by the policies of removal"[3]—King's work remains largely pan-Indigenous. But there exist also other kinds of "disparate Indigenous texts," as Kristina Fagan (Labrador Métis) and Sam McKegney call those works that do not fit into the literary nationalist paradigm, such as multi-national writing (e.g., the work of Afro-Creek poet Melvin Tolson) or urban writing.[4] In their discussion, Fagan and McKegney refer to Haisla/Heiltsuk novelist Eden Robinson's second novel, *Blood Sports* (2006), as a particularly extreme case of "disparity": not only is this novel an example of urban literature, but it also refuses "to engage explicitly, or even thematically, with Native communities," thus challenging the very notion of Indigenous literatures as put forward by literary nationalists.[5]

With Thomas King's *Green Grass, Running Water* (1993) and Anishnaabe/Métis writer Cherie Dimaline's *Red Rooms* (2007), this chapter focuses on two texts whose very contribution to Indigenous literatures and communities is that they do not fit into narrow, nationalist definitions of Indigenous writing. At the same time, the two works differ considerably from each other, and not just in their "disparity" from nationalist models. One of the most-taught Native texts in Canadian literature classrooms, *Green Grass, Running Water* is a critically acclaimed novel whose story centres on the lives of a small group of Blackfoot people from a reserve in southern Alberta. Despite this relatively local focus, however, *Green*

---

3   Justice, *Our Fire Survives*, 170.

4   Kristina Fagan and Sam McKegney, "Circling the Question of Nationalism in Native Canadian Literature and Its Study," *Review: Literature and Arts of the Americas* 41.1 (2008): 38.

5   Ibid., 37. Set in Vancouver's Downtown Eastside, Eden Robinson's *Blood Sports* tells the story of Tom Bauer, a young husband and father caught up in the sinister, violent world of his dealer/pimp cousin Jeremy; although this neighbourhood has a large Aboriginal population, both Tom and Jeremy are Caucasian, and so are all the other characters in the novel.

Grass is ultimately pan-Indigenous in outlook, borrowing freely from various different Indigenous traditions. Unlike King's seminal novel, Dimaline's *Red Rooms* was published as debates about literary nationalism were well underway. Along with other young authors such as Richard Van Camp and Eden Robinson, Dimaline belongs to "a new generation of Native writers in Canada . . . increasingly willing to diverge from nationalist expectations."[6] Indeed, *Red Rooms* is set not on a reserve but in a big, though never explicitly identified, Canadian city. That the book has hitherto received hardly any critical attention, even though it is now in its second printing, may be due in part to its genre (story cycles tend to be less popular than novels, even with critics). Equally significant, if not more, is that Dimaline ventures into territory not often associated with Aboriginal people: the city as setting for Aboriginal writing.

The point of this chapter will not be to consider *Green Grass, Running Water* and *Red Rooms* in terms of their "nationhood and peoplehood specificities"—something that remains to be done for "urban, pan-Native, or multitribal literary traditions and writers" more generally.[7] Rather, by tracing the use of holophrastic traces and relational word bundles in *Green Grass, Running Water* and *Red Rooms*, respectively, I aim to show how texts that avoid direct engagement with a specific Indigenous nation and that nation's particular history, politics, and intellectual traditions may yet be approached in ways that empower Indigenous people—although, in this case, the *focus inward* is decidedly *rhetorical*. Derived from the holophrase, a dominant Indigenous language structure, holophrastic reading allows readers to refocus their readings of Indigenous texts on questions of Indigenous poetics, for the benefit of the works they are studying and ultimately also the communities in which these works originate.

THOMAS KING'S *GREEN GRASS, RUNNING WATER*

Thomas King's second novel—replete with intertexts from both Indigenous and Euro-Western traditions and with meta-fictional self-references; built on magic realism, discontinuous narration, and a multiplicity of discourses—shares many characteristics generally associated with post-modernism. A few critics have therefore identified *Green Grass, Running Water* as a postmodern text,[8] while others have offered readings of the

---

6   Fagan and McKegney, "Circling the Question," 36.

7   Daniel Heath Justice in Fagan et al., "Canadian Indian Literary Nationalism?," 26.

8   See, for example, Linda Lamont-Stewart, "Androgyny as Resistance to Authoritarianism in Two Postmodern Canadian Novels," *Mosaic* 30.3 (1997): 115–30; Dieter

novel that posit it as being more generically complex than is suggested on its surface.[9] I ultimately side with the latter of these two approaches to the novel. The way I read it, *Green Grass, Running Water* makes use of meta-fictionality in an attempt to create the performative situation of oral storytelling; it employs a multiplicity of discourse that turns out to be one coherent discourse, telling a single story; and it uses multiple narrators, while the novel is literally tricked into being by one of its characters. King appears to have written a novel that tricks readers into approaching it from postmodern and, by implication, Euro-Western perspectives when, in fact, *Green Grass, Running Water* is highly indebted to Native traditions of storytelling. What I mean by this observation can best be demonstrated in a holophrastic reading of *Green Grass, Running Water* because such as reading allows us to approach King's novel from the point of view of the very traditions from which it derives. Such a reading forces readers to consider Euro-Western genres written in English by thinking outside of Euro-Western traditions.

From a strictly formal point of view, the embeddedness of King's novel in Indigenous linguistic and discursive traditions is less obvious than, for example, that of the writings of Louise Bernice Halfe (Cree), Maria Campbell (Métis), or Richard Wagamese (Anishnaabe), discussed in previous chapters. *Green Grass, Running Water* does not feature a whole lot of Indigenous words, let alone holophrases, and yet the few instances where Cherokee is used in the novel underscore King's sensibility regarding Cherokee traditions. The heading of each of the novel's four volumes is composed of words written in the Cherokee syllabary, giving a direction and a colour (East/red, South/white, West/black, and North/blue[10]), which, taken as a whole, suggest (narrative) continuity through the metaphor of the sun's daily journey across the sky, thus evoking Indigenous concepts of time as

Petzold, "Thomas King's *Green Grass, Running Water*: A Postmodern Postcolonial Puzzle; or, Coyote Conquers the Campus," in *Lineages of the Novel: Essays in Honour of Raimund Borgmeier*, ed. Bernhard Reitz and Eckart Voigts-Virchow (Trier, Germany: Wissenschaftlicher, 2000), 243–54.

9   Arnold E. Davidson, Priscilla L. Walton, and Jennifer Andrews, for example, argue that *Green Grass, Running Water* "displays a distrust of the postmodern delight in de-centring and transgressing borders, and in doing so, offers a meta-critique of its own formulaic strategy" (*Border Crossings: Thomas King's Cultural Inversions* [Toronto: University of Toronto Press, 2003], 70).

10   Thomas King, "Peter Gzowski Interviews Thomas King on *Green Grass, Running Water*," by Peter Gzowski, *Canadian Literature* 161–62 (1999): 72–73; Jane Flick, "Reading Notes for Thomas King's *Green Grass, Running Water*," *Canadian Literature* 161–62 (1999): 143.

cyclical rather than linear. The only other section in *Green Grass, Running Water* that features the Cherokee language is the opening of the story of First Woman, one of four creation stories that together form the novel's mythological narrative strand. The Lone Ranger, who is telling this story, uses a number of Euro-Western formulae before finding "a proper start with the mention of First Woman in Cherokee, *Higayv:ligé:i*" (8–12), followed by "the ceremonial opening of storytelling [used] in a Cherokee divining ceremony," the "Going to the Water" ceremony.[11] The opening of First Woman's story thus offers a beginning deeply rooted in Cherokee spirituality—a beginning to the novel's first creation story and, arguably, to the novel itself. Though rare, code switching in *Green Grass, Running Water* is used very effectively; turning to an ancestral language rather than English, King is able to define the spiritual context for the novel on its own terms.

The novel's use of holophrastic traces is similarly effective. While it does not rely on a specific Indigenous English code, the novel incorporates some direct and indirect holophrastic traces. Though subtle, these traces work toward contextualizing the story of the novel within Indigenous (as opposed to Euro-Western) traditions of discourse. And interestingly enough, these holophrastic traces are found throughout all three narrative strands:

- the realistic narrative, which tells the story of a group of Blackfoots in Alberta;
- the mythological narrative, which tells the stories of First Woman, Changing Woman, Thought Woman, and Old Woman, all of which are modelled on Aboriginal creation stories; and
- the frame narrative formed by the interspersed conversations between the first-person narrator and Coyote, which frame the stories told in the other two narrative strands.

The frame narrative essentially consists of nothing but direct discourse and therefore relies heavily on the use of quotatives to enable readers to differentiate between the speech acts of the master narrator and those of Coyote. Moreover, King generally uses the same *verbum dicendi* ("verb of speaking") but inverts subject and verb depending on the person talking.

---

11   Flick, "Reading Notes," 147; Helen Hoy quoted in ibid., 144; Alan Kilpatrick, *The Night Has a Naked Soul: Witchcraft and Sorcery among the Western Cherokee* (Syracuse, NY: Syracuse University Press, 1997), 99.

"What's bestiality?" *says Coyote.*
"Sleeping with animals," *I says.*
"What's wrong with that?" *says Coyote.*
"It's against the rules," *I says.*
"But he doesn't mean Coyotes," *says Coyote.* (146; emphases mine)

The rhythm thus created is simple but astonishingly regular, amounting to an almost musical effect. More importantly, King's reliance on quotatives in the frame narrative evokes the abundant presence of evidentials in much Indigenous-language discourse. Although the prominent use of quotatives in *Green Grass, Running Water* is found primarily in its frame narrative, which is the shortest of the three narrative strands, this use is notable, nonetheless, because the frame narrative frequently interrupts the telling of the story in the other narrative strands. The indirect holophrastic trace of evidentiality hence provides King's novel with a very effective structural marker.

Another important formal marker, though of a different type, are the various kinds of direct holophrastic traces found in the mythological narrative strand. Complex compounding in *Green Grass, Running Water* is restricted primarily, though not exclusively, to personal names that recreate Indigenous traditions of name giving and imitate the word-formation processes of holophrastic languages, thus creating the illusion of English loan translation. Some of these personal names are used only in the realistic narrative strand—for example, Eli Stands Alone (quotation compound), Charlie Looking Bear (idiom-like lexical phrase), Will Horse Capture (synthetic compound); however, they are used primarily in shortened form, that is, using only the first name (e.g., Eli). In the mythological narrative strand, on the other hand, personal names that qualify as direct holophrastic traces are always repeated in full, such as "Changing Woman" (deverbal adjective-noun compound) and "Young Man Walking On Water" (idiom-like lexical phrase). The mythological narrative strand also contains several noun-epithet formulae that personify animals, plants, or inanimate objects, thus reflecting Indigenous notions of humans and non-humans as being equal. For example, the river that Thought Woman runs into one day is not merely a river but "one cold River" and "a tricky River" (231); similarly, Coyote's dream becomes a "silly Dream" and a "noisy Dream," and its eyes turn into "Dream Eyes" (1). These noun-epithet formulae mirror the figurative uses of language often encountered in Indigenous languages, which in turn are invited by holophrasis. That direct holophrastic traces personifying non-humans or suggesting Indigenous personal names figure mainly in the mythological narrative strand is note-worthy but ultimately not surprising, given the fact that, in its retellings of Aboriginal creation stories, the mythological strand explicitly evokes and contemporizes Indigenous oral traditions.

Particularly dominant in *Green Grass, Running Water* is the use of indirect holophrastic traces, that is, features of language use that don't so much recreate the structure of actual holophrases as they recreate discourse features that can be associated with holophrastic discourse. I have already mentioned the frequent use of evidentials in the novel's frame narrative. What we find in the realistic narrative strand—the narrative strand that appears to be the most contemporary of the three—is an abundance of echoes of Indigenous verb complexity in the form of pronoun copying and subject dropping. Both types of echoes emphasize verbs, the central component of Indigenous languages. Subject dropping highlights the verb, since the absence of a subject allows the verb to move to the beginning of the sentence or clause, whereas pronoun copying imitates the seemingly repetitive structures (repetitive, that is, from the point of view of Indo-European languages) that result from the holistic nature of holophrastic verbs. The pervasiveness with which these echoes of Indigenous verb complexity are encountered in the realistic narrative strand of *Green Grass, Running Water* makes them strong textual markers of Indigenous linguistic traditions, even if they are unable to suggest *specific* ancestral language influences, as the Cherokee code switching in the novel does.

With the exception of code switching, all of the above language features can be found in some Euro-Western writing. In other words, neither pronoun copying and subject dropping nor noun epithets, compounds, and quotatives are discourse elements exclusive to Indigenous writing. What makes these features of language use significant in *Green Grass, Running Water* is the fact that, by reading them as holophrastic traces, we are able to approach King's novel from within the discourse traditions from which it derives (as generic as these may be). This observation carries all the more weight when discussing an Indigenous text that engages so fully—or, at least, seems to do so—with one of the most "beloved" of contemporary Euro-Western theories, postmodernism. Holophrastic traces are, however, but one part of holophrastic reading. So let us end this discussion of King's *Green Grass, Running Water* by examining its use of relational word bundles, which are just as crucial as holophrastic traces in acknowledging the novel's groundedness in Indigenous linguistic and discursive traditions.

Green Grass, Running Water fictionalizes its own creation by way of framing its main story within a conversation between the narrator and his student, Coyote, whose actions bring the novel into being. King's Coyote is a rather generic version of culture heroes featured in the sacred histories of specific Indigenous nations. To use King's own words, his particular rendering of Coyote in *Green Grass, Running Water* serves to introduce a "sacred clown" into the novel "as a part of the chorus, if you will, and in some ways, as a creator."[12] When, on the very last page of the novel, the master narrator ends his narration on the exact note with which he started it, he does not seem to be aware of the impact of Coyote's actions on his storytelling. Without Coyote's constant interferring, in particular, *Green Grass, Running Water* would lack the circle established in the realistic and mythological narrative strands as well as, more importantly, the circle formed by the novel proper. "By dividing himself" into two, Coyote "both *tells* the story and *is* 'in' the story."[13] Coyote does indeed assume the role of *creator* by bringing into being a novel whose structure mimics the generic conventions of Indigenous oratures and emphasizes the value of Indigenous worldviews. Creation in Indigenous traditions is usually a shared responsibility. Although Coyote may be responsible for giving the novel its particular shape, there would be no novel if it weren't for the master narrator's willingness to share a story; then again, he wouldn't be telling the story if Coyote hadn't agreed to be his student. What is more, the novel's very form is a representation of Indigenous (as opposed to Judeo-Christian) notions of the world: it does not present a "master narrative" with a beginning, middle, and end, but rather a narrative that is cyclical. The narrative structure of *Green Grass, Running Water* hence provides the key to a much more nuanced reading of King's novel—one that sees beyond King's ironic engagement with Euro-Western criticism. The novel's narrative structure doesn't simply appear out of nowhere, however; it is shaped in language, and readers may study its structure by reading the text for relational word bundles.

The first step toward uncovering the narrative structure of *Green Grass, Running Water* is to study the relationships between its component parts.

---

12 Quoted in Jeffrey Canton, "Coyote Lives: Thomas King," in *The Power to Bend Spoons: Interviews with Canadian Novelists*, ed. Beverley Daurio (Toronto: Mercury, 1998), 96.

13 Anne Doueihi, "Inhabiting the Space between Discourse and Story in Trickster Narratives," in *Mythical Trickster Figures: Contours, Contexts, and Criticisms*, ed. William J. Hynes and William G. Doty (Tuscaloosa: University of Alabama Press, 1993), 200; emphasis mine.

The novel consists of a realistic and a mythological narrative strand, which are framed by the discussions between a teacher—the narrative "I"—and his student, Coyote. By listening to the story told by "I" in the other narrative strands, Coyote is expected to learn the art of storytelling so that he will eventually be able to tell the story himself. But does the narrator really tell *one* story? The existence of both a realistic and a mythological narrative strand seems to suggest not; as it turns out, however, the realistic and mythological narrative strands are actually different components of the same story, which unfolds by means of flashbacks that contain further flashbacks and cross narrative boundaries.

The master narrator's story begins with the introduction of a group of Blackfoots from the southern Alberta town of Blossom and the nearby reserve. The central characters are Lionel Red Dog; his cousin, Charlie Looking Bear; their mutual lover, Alberta Frank; Lionel's and Charlie's uncle, Eli Stands Alone; and Lionel's sister, Latisha. As each character is on his or her way to the reserve for the annual Sun Dance, where they all eventually meet at the end of the novel, their life stories are untangled in a series of flashbacks. The Sun Dance marks both the key event in the novel and its ending: an earthquake on the morning of the second day of the Sun Dance changes the characters' lives considerably. Eli drowns in the flood that destroys both his mother's cabin and the dam he has been blocking. Alberta finally conceives the desired baby (through an immaculate conception), Charlie loses his job, and Lionel considers going back to university. Despite these life-changing events, however, the surviving characters are all quite hopeful about their future and decide to build a cabin where Eli's used to stand.

There is more to the plot in the realistic narrative strand, however. As Lionel, Charlie, Alberta, Eli, and Latisha travel to the annual Sun Dance, they meet four mysterious old Indians who have escaped from a psychiatric hospital in Florida and are now travelling through Canada, "trying to fix up the world" (133). More specifically, the four old Indians attempt to fix Lionel's life by helping him to protect his Blackfoot tradition in front of Alberta, the woman he loves. Despite the central role of the four old Indians in the novel, however, their identities remain unclear through most of the text. According to their hospital records, they are "Mr. Red, Mr. White, Mr. Black, and Mr. Blue," but they refer to themselves as the Lone Ranger, Ishmael, Robinson Crusoe, and Hawkeye; to make matters even more complicated, the hospital's janitor, Babo Jones, insists that they are, in fact, "women, not men" (54–55). Why the four old Indians were locked up in the security wing of the hospital Dr. J. Hovaugh, the doctor in charge of them, cannot really explain; likewise, their escape also remains "a mystery" to him (81). In fact, the mystery surrounding the escape of the Lone Ranger, Ishmael, Robinson Crusoe, and Hawkeye and their eventual return to the hospital by the end of the novel is explained not in the realistic but in the mythological narrative strand.

The creation stories in the mythological narrative strand are told as the four old Indians travel through Canada and meet the characters in the realistic narrative strand. These creation stories thus form a subnarrative of their own, contained within the overall story of the novel in the form of a flashback to the realistic narrative strand. Each of the four creation stories follows the same pattern and introduces its respective narrator, thus revealing that the four old Indians are really the women and Indigenous culture heroes featured in the corresponding creation stories. Moreover, the stories of Changing Woman (volume 2), Thought Woman (volume 3), and Old Woman (volume 4) are arranged as flashbacks to the story of First Woman (volume 1), which serves to introduce the Lone Ranger's (First Woman's) friends with whom First Woman escapes from Fort Marion at the end of her story (106). But what happens after this escape is not revealed until—at the end of Old Woman's story in volume 4 (457)—the narration at last resumes where First Woman's story ended in volume 1. Of course, the escape of the four old Indians from the fort in the mythological narrative strand is not identical to their escape from the hospital in the realistic narrative strand, but there is "a pattern" (49): ever since they were first arrested, the four women have left their prison every once in a while to go on a mission to fix up the world; once their mission is complete, they return to prison. The story of the four Indigenous women's first of many escapes forms a bridge between the realistic and mythological narrative strands in *Green Grass, Running Water*, thus connecting the past with the present. By having two seemingly different narrative strands float into each other to form one story, the novel's structure embodies Indigenous notions of the interrelatedness of past and present, of contemporary reality and sacred history.

Having established that *Green Grass, Running Water* does indeed tell one coherent story, we can now examine its structure in more detail. The realistic narrative strand ends with a flood of water—"Below, in the valley, the water rolled on as it had for eternity" (455)—which is what the mythological narrative strand had started with: "So. In the beginning, there was nothing. Just the water" (1). After the earthquake, the breaking of the Grand Baleen Dam, and Eli's death, Lionel, his aunt Norma, Alberta, Latisha, and Charlie gather near the place where Eli's cabin had once stood. As they examine what is left of it, Norma decides to have it rebuilt: "Norma stuck her stick in the earth. 'We'll start here,' she said. 'So we can see the sun in the morning'" (464). Her observation is as much an allusion to the new beginning each character faces after the earthquake as a reference to the story itself, for the notion of the sun rising in the morning recalls the title of volume 1: "East/red." The new beginning evoked at the end of the novel thus marks a new beginning also for the readers outside the story. Norma's remark qualifies as a relational word bundle: it is a rhetorical figure (allusion; figure of recovery/recollection) that, by pointing back to volume 1 (backshadowing), helps to create the cyclical shape of the story and thus forms part of the novel's narrative grid. What is more, in taking the form of a circle, the story narrated in *Green Grass, Running Water* essentially forms a story cycle. This cycle is made up of various layers of cyclical structures that are intertwined with one another and established by the novel's other central relational word bundles, many of which take the form of formulae, as we shall see next.

The escape of the four old Indians and their subsequent return to the hospital in Florida mark the beginning and the end of the realistic narrative strand.[14] Moreover, the section narrating their return is a more or less exact repetition of their escape (465–66; 12–14). When, upon their return to the hospital, the four old Indians meditate about whose life they will fix the "next time" they go on a journey, proposing to help Dr. Hovaugh (466–67), it becomes obvious that the realistic narrative strand does not end at this point but will begin anew; that is, it has come full circle. In other words, the realistic narrative strand is framed by a formulaic opening (the first Dr. Hovaugh scene) and a formulaic closing (the last Dr. Hovaugh scene), both of which function as *large clusters of relational word bundles*. These formulaic clusters are intratextual references (back- or foreshadowing) and hence take the form of a figure (of recovery/recollection or of anticipation); they also lend the realistic narrative its cyclical shape and thus help constitute the novel's overall narrative grid.

---

14 Strictly speaking, the first episode in the realistic narrative strand tells of Lionel and Norma driving back to the reserve (7–8) and is followed by a conversation among the four old Indians—discussing the correct beginning of their story—in the mythological narrative strand (8–12). Only then does the narration shift to Dr. Hovaugh contemplating his garden. Hence, the realistic narrative strand does not actually *begin* with the first Dr. Hovaugh garden scene, and yet the first episode in the realistic narrative strand contains an allusion to the escape of the four old Indians; after all, the reason for their escape is their mission to fix up Lionel's life. Of course, this connection becomes obvious to readers only after Lionel picks up the four old Indians, towards the end of volume 1, to give them a ride to Blossom.

. The cyclical form of the mythological narrative strand is also established by way of formulaic clusters of relational word bundles. When Old Woman arrives at the fort in Florida (in volume 4), the last paragraph of the story of First Woman (from volume 1) is repeated almost verbatim. This repetition connects the four creation stories into one larger narrative that culminates at the end of volume 4, but not before turning back on itself as it echoes the ending of the story of First Woman (see table 8.1).

TABLE 8.1 THE CYCLICAL STRUCTURE OF THE FOUR CREATION STORIES IN *GREEN GRASS, RUNNING WATER*

END OF FIRST WOMAN'S STORY IN VOLUME 1	END OF OLD WOMAN'S STORY IN VOLUME 4

It's the Lone Ranger, the guards shout. It's the Lone Ranger, they shout again, and they open the gate. So the Lone Ranger walks out of the prison, and the Lone Ranger and Ishmael and Robinson Crusoe and Hawkeye head west.
 	
    Have a nice day, the soldiers say. Say hello to Tonto for us. And all the soldiers wave.
(106)
	It's the Lone Ranger, the guards shout. It's the Lone Ranger, they shout again. And they open the gate. So the Lone Ranger walks out of the prison, and the Lone Ranger and Ishmael and Hawkeye and Robinson Crusoe head west.
	
	    Have a nice day, the soldiers say. Say hello to Tonto for us. And all the soldiers wave.
	(457)

The repetition of this crucial scene produces this strand's cyclical form, hence forming part of the novel's narrative grid. The cycle established in the mythological narrative strand is also mirrored in the names assigned to the four (wo)men (see fig. 8.1). Symbolizing the four cardinal directions, the four seasons, the course of the sun, as well as the four stages of life, the four (wo)men in the mythological and realistic narrative strands represent the epitome of the sacred circle in many Indigenous spiritual traditions. What is more, the four colours in the volume headings reappear in the official names of the four (wo)men, according to Dr. Hovaugh's files in the realistic narrative strand, whereas the four cardinal directions in the volume headings and the course of the sun are evoked in the very order (tracing the four stages of life) and form (circular) in which the four (wo)men tell their stories in the mythological narrative strand. Evidently, the four (wo)men are the key to bridging the "gap" between the realistic and mythological narrative strands: their travelling from one strand of the story to the other is the "place" where the two circles embodied by the realistic and the mythological narrative strands touch. In other words, these two circles are actually part of an even larger cyclical structure, namely, the story itself.

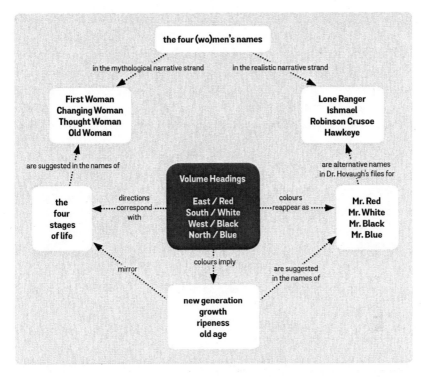

FIG. 8.1 THE NARRATIVE FUNCTION OF THE FOUR (WO)MEN IN *GREEN GRASS, RUNNING WATER*[15]

Through their very symbolism, the four women's names—First Woman, Changing Woman, Thought Woman, and Old Woman—provide a structural framework for the novel that evokes Indigenous generic conventions. As figures of speech (symbol) that perform a significant narrative function and contribute to the novel's narrative grid, the women's names act as relational word bundles in the text.

This being said, the cyclical structure formed by the realistic and mythological narrative strands is part of an even larger cycle, formed by the novel's narrative frame. Marlene Goldman has compared the master narrator in *Green Grass, Running Water* with the announcer at the Sun Dance, who oversees the ceremony and ensures that a certain "standard of

---

15   The meaning of the directions and the colours as displayed here is based on the Northern Cheyenne interpretation of the Medicine Lodge; see Peter J. Powell, *Sweet Medicine: The Continuing Role of the Sacred Arrows, the Sun Dance, and the Sacred Buffalo Hat in Northern Cheyenne History* (Norman: University of Oklahoma Press, 1969), 2:852n14.

traditional behaviour" is met.[16] Ironically, however, the master narrator's authority is challenged by the involvement of different culture heroes in the novel, in particular Coyote, for the *circle formed by the novel proper* is due to none other than the master narrator's student. As becomes evident in the course of *Green Grass, Running Water*, Coyote cares less about the story itself as he does about the playground provided for him by the story: he constantly interrupts the master narrator's narration, often doesn't pay attention to the story, and even jumps into it, thereby changing its outcome, most notably by causing the earthquake. In fact, when Coyote is finally given a chance to retell the story he has just been given, he screws up its beginning and the master narrator has to begin anew, using the same kind of formulaic expressions he used in the novel's opening—formulaic expressions that also happen to be repeated at other points in the narrative, either verbatim or in variation, namely,

- "So. In the beginning, there was nothing. Just the water." (1; see also 100, 103, 107, 112, 469).
- "Where did all that water come from?" (3; see also 37, 97, 104, 469)
- "But there is water everywhere." (3; see also 469)
- "And here's how it happened." (3; see also 114, 158, 387, 469)

The colloquial "so" marks the performative situation of the narrative and calls for the readers' attention: the novel is about to start. What follows immediately after this utterance is not the beginning of the story performed by the master narrator, however, but an introductory scene, the purpose of which is to lead the reader closer to the story told in the novel. In this scene, Coyote is dreaming, and one of his dreams gets loose and thinks that it is in charge of the world. The dream wakes Coyote and complains about wanting to be a "big god." Sick of the dream's constant shouting, Coyote finally gives in.

> "Now you've done it," I says.
> "Everything's under control," says Coyote. "Don't panic."
> *Where did all that water come from?* shouts that G O D.
> "Take it easy," says Coyote. "Sit down. Relax. Watch some television."
> *But there is water everywhere,* says that G O D.

---

16 Marlene Goldman, "Mapping and Dreaming: Native Resistance in *Green Grass, Running Water,*" *Canadian Literature* 161–62 (1999): 35–36.

> "Hmmmm," says Coyote. "So there is."
> "That's true," I says. "*And here's how it happened.*" (3; emphases mine)

The formulaic "And here's how it happened" indicates that the actual story can now begin. The opening of *Green Grass, Running Water,* then, consists of three stages. The narrative "I" opens the novel with a formulaic expression to indicate the beginning of a story; he then moves on to relate an introductory scene, followed by the use of another formula that connotes what lies at the core of the novel: a story and its performance. Although this opening is not actually part of the story performed, its key phrases are nonetheless repeated in the novel's closing when it is Coyote's turn to tell the story:

> "Okay, okay," says Coyote. "I got it!"
> "Well, it's about time," I says.
> "Okay, okay, here goes," says Coyote. "*In the beginning, there was nothing.*"
> "Nothing?"
> "That's right," says Coyote. "Nothing."
> "No," I says. "*In the beginning, there was just the water.*"
> "Water?" says Coyote.
> "Yes," I says. "Water."
> "Hmmmm," says Coyote. "Are you sure?"
> "Yes," I says, "I'm sure."
> "Okay," says Coyote, "*if you say so. But where did all the water come from?*"
> "*Sit down,*" I says to Coyote.
> "*But there is water everywhere,*" says Coyote.
> "That's true," I says. "*And here's how it happened.*" (469; emphases mine)

With the help of the overarching narrative frame, readers are thus gradually guided into, as well as out of, the *novel proper,* which, too, has a cyclical shape. As in the case of the cyclical structures of the realistic and mythological narrative strands, the opening and closing frame in *Green Grass, Running Water* is established by way of relational word bundles: the formulae constituting the opening and the closing take the form of back- and foreshadowing (thus qualifying as rhetorical figures) and perform the significant narrative function of providing the novel's overarching circle—a central part of the novel's overall narrative grid.

We can, therefore, read King's *Green Grass, Running Water* as a highly intricate story cycle, a coherent but complex story consisting of a series of entangled circles that could stand alone as separate narratives but create an even more elaborate story in their interdependence. The story cycle is a very prominent form in many Indigenous literary traditions; in particular, Indigenous stories of creation are often constructed as complex cycles (see, for example, the Cree *wîsahkêcâhk* cycle referred to in the previous chapter). King himself has noted—in an interview with Constance Rooke about his first novel, *Medicine River*—that this particular traditional Indigenous genre has influenced his own writing.[17] In fact, *Green Grass, Running Water* is in many ways a fictionalized version of King's doctoral dissertation, which discusses contemporary Indigenous writing in relation to Indigenous creation stories.[18] King describes the plot in Indigenous creation stories as "considerably flatter" than that of the story in Genesis because they lack the ideas of a main character, conflict, and climax—elements that define Euro-Western discourse, including the biblical creation story. Instead, King argues, Indigenous creation stories are "structured like a chain, where one creation leads to another, one understanding to the next," with none of these elements being "any more important or dramatic than the last or the next."[19] Through the addition of the mythological narrative strand, *Green Grass, Running Water* gains "a more Native sense of the creation of the world."[20] In addition to the formal differences King identifies between Indigenous and Euro-Western creation stories, he ultimately also incorporates into his novel a unique, if admittedly generalized, Indigenous narrative form: that of a story cycle using a flat narrative line. The latter element is so prominent in contemporary Indigenous writing that King has described it as characteristic of what he calls "associational literature," a type of writing that is centred on an Indigenous community and Indigenous realities and that arranges "the elements of plot along a rather flat narrative line that ignores the ubiquitous climaxes and resolutions that are so valued in non-Native literature."[21]

---

17 Thomas King, "Interview with Tom King," by Constance Rooke, *World Literature Written in English* 30.2 (1990): 64.

18 Thomas King, "Inventing the Indian: White Images, Native Oral Literature, and Contemporary Native Writers" (PhD diss., University of Utah, 1986).

19 Ibid., 122.

20 King, "Peter Gzowski Interviews Thomas King," 71.

21 Thomas King, "Godzilla vs. Post-Colonial," *World Literature Written in English* 30.2 (1990): 14.

For a first-time reader of *Green Grass, Running Water*, it is difficult not to notice the exceptionally open and fluid nature of the novel: there are multiple narrative strands, plus the novel boasts multiple narrators and is full of intertextual references to both Native and Euro-Western literary traditions, particularly the Bible and Anglo-American literary traditions. What may not be so obvious, however, is the function performed by the frame narrative in establishing an intricate cyclical narrative structure in which past, present, and future melt into one single, coherent story. As noted above, *Green Grass, Running Water* would lack the cycle established in the realistic and mythological narrative strands, as well as the cycle formed by the novel proper, if it weren't for Coyote's refusal to carefully listen to the story he is being taught by the narrator. In order for readers to realize that the novel's seemingly complex narrative structure is actually quite straightforward, they must look beyond the surface of the text. In fact, others before me have done so and have noted that what may otherwise appear to be postmodern narrative chaos is indeed a coherent whole—a text that, despite its author's lack of any strong connections to any specific Native community, is carefully embedded in Indigenous discourse traditions and worldviews. The novel's use of generic conventions of Indigenous oratures is nothing new, then.[22] What this discussion of *Green Grass, Running Water* offers instead is a reading of King's novel as grounded in Indigenous language and discourse traditions—the result of approaching the novel *from within those very traditions* rather than relying on Euro-Western critical theories to do so. The pronoun copying and subject dropping, the evidentials, and noun epithets and Indigenous personal names are not just markers of orality; they are, above all, Indigenous language influences, or, to be more specific, formal traces in English of a dominant Indigenous language structure, the holophrase. Similarly, the decidedly cyclical structure of King's novel is one that is achieved not by way of just any structure, but by way of structures equivalent in function to the holophrase. A holophrastic reading of *Green Grass, Running Water* allows us to approach this text's use of English by thinking outside that very language, by making its relation to Indigenous language and discourse traditions, however generalized these may be, the focus of our reading. In other words, a holophrastic reading of *Green Grass, Running Water* allows us to focus inward, by emphasizing and privileging Indigenous generic and other traditions in our reading—and

---

22 See, for example, Davidson, Walton, and Andrews, *Border Crossings*, and Blanca Schorcht, *Storied Voices in Native American Texts: Harry Robinson, Thomas King, James Welch, and Leslie Marmon Silko* (New York: Routledge, 2003).

to do so despite the fact that this novel avoids any engagement with a specific Indigenous nation.

CHERIE DIMALINE'S *RED ROOMS*

Despite the pan-Indigenous tendencies of *Green Grass, Running Water*, which uses intertexts from several different Indigenous literary traditions, the novel's plot centres on a specific Blackfoot community in southern Alberta. And while some of the novel's characters lead, or have led, more or less succesful lives in the city (Calgary, Edmonton, Toronto)—Eli is a retired professor, Alberta teaches history, and Charlie works as a lawyer—the novel's main action is set in the small town of Blossom and on the nearby reserve. In fact, the novel traces Alberta's and Charlie's movements as they travel to the reserve for the annual Sun Dance. In other words, while urban spaces do figure in *Green Grass, Running Water*, the novel's main focus ultimately is the reserve community. Cherie Dimaline's debut work, *Red Rooms*, on the other hand, follows the lives of several Aboriginal people, each from a different nation, who live in one of Canada's largest cities. Dimaline's choice of setting is noteworthy because it runs counter to general assumptions about both Indigenous writing and contemporary Indigenous experiences.

Classic Indigenous novels, such as N. Scott Momaday's *House Made of Dawn* (1969), James Welch's *Winter in the Blood* (1974), and Leslie Marmon Silko's *Ceremony* (1977) feature what critic William Bevis has called "homing in." In these novels, Bevis argues, "coming home, staying put, contracting, even what we call 'regressing' to a place, a post where one has been before, is not only the primary story, it is a primary mode of knowledge and a primary good."[23] Lindsey Claire Smith correctly notes that this observation is problematic as it creates the impression that "espousing authentic Native identity necessitates living in a predominantly Indigenous community, usually on a reservation, and rejecting urbanization, which is often equated with assimilation." Drawing such a conclusion is necessarily "incomplete" given Indigenous realities in North America today.[24] Similarly, in her discussion of Spokane/Coeur d'Alene writer Sherman Alexie's story collection *Ten Little Indians* (2003), critic Jennifer Ladino

---

23   William Bevis, "Native American Novels: Homing In," in *Recovering the Word: Essays on Native American Literature*, ed. Brian Swann and Arnold Krupat (Berkeley: University of California Press, 1987), 582.

24   Lindsey Claire Smith, "'With These Magic Weapons, Make a New World': Indigenous Centered Urbanism in Tomson Highway's *Kiss of the Fur Queen*," *Canadian Journal of Native Studies* 29.1–2 (2009): 145.

has stressed the need to highlight Indigenous texts "that reflect the multifaceted dimensions of urban Indian life," in order "to begin combating lingering stereotypes and complicating notions of contemporary Indian identity in productive ways."[25] What Ladino alludes to here is that, despite the fact that the majority of Indigenous people in Canada and the United States live in urban areas,[26] stereotypes of Native people as "wear[ing] headdresses, liv[ing] in tipis, paddl[ing] canoes, and liv[ing] in perfect harmony with plants and animals in a prehistoric pastoral world" still prevail among the non-Native population in both countries.[27] Given this discrepancy between Indigenous realities and mainstream myths about contemporary Indigenous experiences, it may seem ironic that scholars have paid relatively little attention to urban Indigenous writing. As Smith explains, urban Indigenous realities "have been associated in literature (and also in 'real life') with cultural ambivalence, usually accompanied by 'hybrid' or mixed-blood identities," which tend to be associated with "Indigenous alienation."[28] A shift to more positive portrayals of urban Indigenous experiences is only relatively recent.[29] Smith points particularly to the work of Greg Sarris (Pomo/Miwok), Susan Power (Standing Rock Sioux), Sherman Alexie, and Tomson Highway (Cree) as moving away

25 Jennifer K. Ladino, "'A Limited Range of Motion?': Multiculturalism, 'Human Questions,' and Urban Indian Identity in Sherman Alexie's *Ten Little Indians*," *Studies in American Indian Literatures* 21.3 (2009): 36–37.

26 According to Donald L. Fixico, "more than two-thirds of the total American Indian population of 2.1 million lives in urban areas" ("Foreword," in *American Indians and the Urban Experience*, ed. Susan Lobo and Kurt Peters [New York: Altamira, 2001], ix), compared with 54 per cent of Canada's total Aboriginal population of 1.2 million (Statistics Canada, "2006 Census: Aboriginal Peoples in Canada in 2006," last modified September 22, 2009, http://www12.statcan.gc.ca/census-recensement/2006/as-sa/97-558/p3-eng.cfm).

27 Ladino, "'A Limited Range of Motion?,'" 36–37.

28 Smith, "'With These Magic Weapons,'" 144, 146.

29 For more contemporary examples of Bevis's homing-in model, see, for example, Thomas King's *Green Grass, Running Water* (1993), in which one of the many main characters, the retired university professor Eli, leaves Toronto to move into his mother's cabin, thus preventing the completion of the Grand Baleen Dam. Richard Wagamese's *Keeper'n Me* (1994) fits even more clearly into Bevis's model: Garnet Raven returns for good to his home reserve after being caught and sentenced for dealing drugs in Toronto. See also work by Isabel Schneider, who traces the development of portrayals of Indigenous experiences and identities in Indigenous writing since the 1970s ("Survivors: New Models of Culture and Identity in Contemporary North American Indigenous Fiction," in *Colonies, Missions, Cultures in the English Speaking World: General and Comparative Studies*, ed. Gerhard Stilz [Tübingen, Germany: Stauffenburg, 2001], 287–98).

from the notion of urban Indigenous identities as necessarily implying alienation that, in turn, triggers the eventual return to reserve communities.[30] Dimaline's work could easily be added to Smith's list; her collection *Red Rooms* perfectly illustrates the notion that urban Indigenous fiction need not be just any kind of urban fiction but, rather, one that is deeply informed by Aboriginal values, worldviews, and realities.

In *Red Rooms*, readers are introduced to an urban Aboriginal space that is linked in different ways to various Aboriginal homeland communities across the country and that imagines the possibility of what Smith calls an "Indigenous-centered urbanism," an alternative construction of Indigenous identity that is based neither on hybridity nor on diaspora.[31] I am deliberately using the word "possibility" because the portrayal of such an alternative urban Aboriginal space is less explicit in Dimaline's book than in, for example, Tomson Highway's *Kiss of the Fur Queen* (1998). Smith has analyzed Highway's novel as constructing a cityspace in which the novel's two protagonists succeed in claiming their "Cree identity within an urban, transnational landscape" by embracing Cree language and cosmology.[32] Not only does Dimaline's *Red Rooms* feature Native characters from different nations; her text also omits any elaborate scenes depicting and tracing the building of an Indigenous-centered space in which characters embrace and transform their traditions in the city. There are, however, scattered among the collection's five stories, moments of cultural affirmation (e.g., the occasional references to the city's annual Native festival, the jingle dress dancing of one of the characters, the Native youth project another character organizes, the Métis sash yet another character has himself buried in) that suggest the existence or the possibility of such an Indigenous-centered urban space. Such moments are important, especially given the limits of the genre in terms of developing elaborate plotlines. *Red Rooms* is less a novel than a patchwork of stories. In fact, the text's very structure is actually the best expression—or, rather, embodiment—of the "Indigenous-centered urbanism" for which, I believe, *Red Rooms* argues.

Red Rooms tells the stories of five contemporary Aboriginal men and women, all of them guests at a modern three-star chain hotel in an unnamed Canadian metropolis. There is the young Anishnaabe prostitute whose client falls asleep, so she spends the night wandering the city, chased by visions, only to come back to find her client has died a mysterious death; the

---

30 Smith, "'With These Magic Weapons,'" 146–47.
31 Ibid., 147.
32 Ibid., 160.

Métis cosmetic designer and collector of couture purses who gives himself an overdose to avoid the painful death from bone cancer that awaits him; the Cree photographer who travels the world in search of what defines a community's identity, only to find the answers at his very doorstep; the curatorial expert on Native artefacts and historical documents who, partly to drown the pain of her failed marriage, jumps into an obsessive affair with a Native lawyer; and the Anishnaabe businesswoman who spends the night reading the diary of an Anishnaabe jingle dress dancer that she finds in her room's dresser. Each of these stories is a story in its own right, fully fleshed and able to function as an individual text. Taken together, Dimaline's stories become even more powerful. For one thing, by focusing each story on a different Aboriginal character, *Red Rooms* is able to capture the scope of contemporary Aboriginal urban lives—not just of the poor but also of the upper middle class and everything in between. Moreover, what makes *Red Rooms* special, as Lee Maracle (Stó:lō) aptly notes on its back cover, "is Dimaline's sometimes cryptic, sometimes comedic, always compassionate and visionary housekeeper who offers hindsight, insight and foresight to the reader in the representation of [the other characters'] lives." The stories of love, obsession, death, and community presented in *Red Rooms* are all the product of housekeeper Naomi's imagination. Playing "the urban anthropologist, discerning lives and interpreting trends through trash can contents and receipts left on bedside tables" (1), she weaves what eventually becomes *Red Rooms*. Naomi is, then, not only the main narrator (of both the stories and the first-person prologues opening each story); above all, she turns the individual stories into a story cycle that is more than the sum of its pieces. However, it is not Naomi's mere presence in the text that produces the cycle's narrative structure; rather, it is the way in which she weaves together the individual stories that creates the web of narrative relations in *Red Rooms*—a web that functions as a symbol for community. The "hindsight, insight and foresight" Lee Maracle mentions is also mirrored on a textual level, namely, in the form of relational word bundles that use back- and foreshadowing to create narrative links between individual stories, particularly between the closing story and the remainder of the collection. As noted in the discussion of *Green Grass, Running Water*, the story cycle is a prominent genre in many Indigenous literary traditions. The one in Dimaline's *Red Rooms* is less complex than the one in King's novel; it also has a very different setting, replacing the reserve with the city. By inventing a storyteller who invents a series of interconnected stories, Dimaline highlights the act of storytelling, the weaving together of stories, rather than simply the stories themselves. Compared with *Green,*

Grass, Running Water, however, the connections between individual narratives in *Red Rooms* are more subtle.

The best place to start looking at the subtle relationships among different parts of *Red Rooms* is in the last story in the cycle. Natalie, a moderately successful Anishnaabe businesswoman, checks into the hotel planning to attend an important business meeting the next morning. In her room's dresser, she comes across a book—not the usual hotel-room Bible, but the diary of a previous guest who, Natalie discovers, was a young Anishnaabe jingle dress dancer. Natalie ends up reading the diary until dawn the next day. In many ways, this last story serves as an epitome of the collection. A character in the story spies on another character by reading her diary much as Naomi, and by implication the readers, spy on the hotel guests. What is more, this last story evokes all previous stories in the collection and also links back to its very opening:

- Natalie's thoughts of "her only boyfriend . . . lying in her top drawer nestled comfortably beside the underwear" (125) and the prospect to spend her free night "watch[ing] soft-porn by herself" (126) evoke the profession of "the girl" in **story 1** who, in turn, takes on the guise of "a great fucking businesswoman" before she re-enters the room where her client is sleeping (33).
- Natalie's expensive designer briefcase (referred to simply as "her $2400 bag" [153]) and her obsession to buy "things she would never use" (125) evoke Marcel's "monumental handbag obsession" (55) in **story 2**.
- Natalie's "unformed sense of homesickness but, oddly, for a place she doesn't really know. It was like a blood memory" parallels the photographer's search in **story 3** for what constitutes "a community's distinct identity" (72)—a search he eventually completes with an exhibit entitled "Finding Home" (86–87).
- The jingle dress dancer's affair with a man "who was still with the mother of his sons" (139) evokes the main conflict in **story 4**, in which Constance has an obsessive affair with a married man and then feels just as relieved as T. (the jingle dress dancer) did when she finally ends her affair. The connection between these two characters is further strengthened by T.'s ambition to become "a forensic archaeologist to specialize in early Native American civilizations" (142), paralleling Constance's own work as "curatorial expert on Native artifacts and historical documents" (96).

I have listed these parallels in such detail here for two reasons: one, to point out the relational word bundles that establish the narrative links between story 5 and the stories preceding it. They all take the form of back- and foreshadowing, which are based on the figures of anticipation and recovery/recollection, respectively, and are part of the "hindsight, insight and foresight" (Maracle, quoted above) that help create the spiderweb-like structure of the story cycle. And two, I want to illustrate that certain parts of stories 1 to 4 reappear in story 5—and not just any parts, but some of their character's more prominent actions, behaviours, and/or characteristics. A little bit of the nameless prostitute, of Marcel, of the photographer, and of Constance can be found in Natalie's and T.'s story that ends the story cycle.

It is true that the links among the stories in *Red Rooms* are subtle—as are the hints, or tracks, that Naomi picks up to invent her stories—and they are vague enough so as not to undermine the integrity of the individual stories. A reading for relational word bundles is able to reveal these links quite easily, however, and it also reveals the collection's intricate structure. Each of the five stories exists in and of itself and yet evokes still other stories, just as the characters in these stories exist and live their lives in and of themselves, yet there is a connectedness between them that neither Naomi nor the readers may quite be able to put their finger on, but that exists nonetheless. As Natalie puts it at the end of the cycle, "She hoped they [she and the jingle dress dancer] could talk, but, if not, it would be enough to put a face to the biography. And somewhere in the crowds, she was hoping to find that warm comfort that skated across the journal pages" (153). Like the individual members of the photographer's home community in story 3, the stories shared in *Red Rooms* "are not pieces of a separate whole, they are each in and of themselves perfect, and they are all connected and inside of one another like a set of cedar Babushka dolls" (87). What Dimaline's debut work points to here, and what I believe is also reflected in the text's narrative structure, are Indigenous notions of community as synecdochic, that is, as taking the form of part-to-whole rather than part-to-part.[33] Similarly, the stories in *Red Rooms* achieve their potential most fully when seen in terms of "story in collection" rather than "story and collection." In other words, the very structure of *Red Rooms* is testament to the photographer's epiphany in story 3 about the value and nature of home and community, as understood by Aboriginal communities across the continent.

---

33 Weaver, *That the People Might Live*, 39.

Story 3 therefore acts very much as a turning point in the cycle, which begins with two deaths and closes with the hope for new beginnings. The photographer's story holds the key to the main theme of the story cycle: the connection between identity, community, and home. What is more, the story has the photographer "swing[ing] down to the pow wow" (87). This relational word bundle refers back to "*the annual Native festival* [that] *rolls into town*" that Naomi mentions in her opening prologue (4); further, it also foreshadows Natalie's own exit to the stadium where the pow wow takes place, which has her feeling "like fancy dancers were twisting their way through her ribcage" (153). In other words, some of the cycle's stories, most notably its closing story, link directly to the cycle's opening, in which the creator and performer of these stories, housekeeper Naomi, provides readers with some context as to how she stumbled upon the stories she is sharing.

Red Rooms, then, takes on a decidedly web-like structure. The text is a concatenation of threads that originate in one story but run into other stories, often criss-crossing one another. These threads do not concern the closing story alone but also establish narrative relations between yet other parts in the cycle. It is these relations that I will analyze further before ending this chapter on a discussion of the theme of community in *Red Rooms*. Marcel's suggestion in story 2, that Naomi get him "a Portuguese boy with long hair and a vodka martini" (41), parallels the situation at the beginning of story 1, in which the prostitute is getting ready to sell her body to a client, but in many ways Marcel's scene is a repetition with a major difference: he is making a joke, knowing all too well that in his position (he is dying of cancer) he is not likely capable of having sexual intercourse. The same playful, humorous treatment of sex is also suggested in story 5 by "the collection of butt plugs" that one of Naomi's co-workers once found "in a briefcase under the bed" (122) and once again in story 3, when the photographer realizes that with his new job "he didn't really have any problems getting women to go into the laundry room with him" (81).

One story that picks up the more sombre mood of the first story is story 4. There is a moment of power that Constance cherishes when she is with her lover, a moment when "she felt like God," which came when "she waited just a minute, without touching him" (95). This depiction of a shifting power hierarchy in Constance's relationship is reminiscent of when the nameless prostitute in story 1, becoming hawk-like, "crosse[s] the space between the bathroom and the bed smirking to show her superiority and demonstrate her control over this moment and every other moment that would come" (9). Both scenes feature a sense of lingering doubt: Constance admits that "she could not always wait out this excruciating minute" (95), while the prostitute's observation that "This was, after all, her office, regardless of who leased out the space" (9) reads much like a feeble attempt at persuading herself that she is indeed in control. Sex is the main theme in only two of the five stories (1 and 4), but it can also be found lurking in the other stories of *Red Rooms*, thus revealing the double meaning of the book's title: red refers both to the Native hotel guests and to sex—and arguably to something else, for red is also the colour of love and belonging. It takes all of these—sex and love and belonging—to create and ensure community.

The question of home and identity figures prominently in the stories of *Red Rooms*. This question is made the main theme of the story, as in the case of the photographer (story 3), or it affects the stories in yet other ways: away from her home community and a family that watches out for her, the prostitute and drug addict of story 1 is lost in the jungle of the big city; Marcel spent his life entirely indifferent to his Métis ancestry, but decides to have himself buried with a Métis sash in order to reflect his true identity; Constance lets go of an obsessive relationship the moment she realizes she has become a captive and ghost; and Natalie and T. are both looking for a focus in their lives, which, judging by the story's ending, seems to lie in community and family for both. Aside from these more general resemblances, the text also features relational word bundles that connect the individual stories by highlighting the theme of community. Variations of the "plastic-topped table back home," used by the prostitute's aunties to hold council (6), and "her auntie's old couch," on which the prostitute "sle[pt] fitfully" as a child (23) reappear in the old Baule woman's house in Africa: the plastic table becomes "a solid wooden table surrounded by benches" and the couch is "hideously flowered" (76). Yet, in both cases, the table and couch are symbols of community and family, of storytelling and gossip. It is not surprising that the value of community and home is highlighted in both stories through the voice of grandmothers, given their role as carriers of knowledge. When Kokum shares a story from her childhood with the photographer in story 3, she speaks of a night when she and her siblings "went up to the top of the hill," afraid "the old lady woke up" (85). They were going to toboggan down the hill in the dark, even though their mother had forbidden them to go outside that day. Similarly, in story 1, the hill is associated with evil if only for the "old lady up the hill" who lives there (7). That same woman is eventually revealed to be the prostitute's grandmother in story 1; she appears to her grandchild in the form of "butterfly woman" (31): "almost everything about this woman reminded her of a butterfly. She looked so fragile in her age, yet ready to travel many miles before settling to rest" (11). Interestingly, the same bittersweet mood is expressed through another butterfly image, in story 2, when Marcel's friend loses his battle against AIDS: "Jack died on a Wednesday.... Leaves that had just begun to change into colourful paper butterflies blew off ema-ciated branches and stuck to the windows, making stained glass for their own amusement" (59). In Marcel's case, however, the butterflies even-tually become powerless, while the butterfly woman in story 1 manages to save her grandchild's life by appearing to her in a vision, in which the prostitute overhears her grandmother tell her own daughter that the child needs her mother for guidance (29–30). The story ends with the prostitute "running towards [the star-filled sky] as fast as she could," as if she wanted to embrace her relations dancing in the night sky. Whether the prostitute's mother does indeed come to help her daughter, the story doesn't say, but it seems to suggest the prostitute's willingness for community, an eventual rebuilding of those ties she cut when she moved to the city, never returning home, not even to visit.

Through back- and foreshadowing, relational word bundles establish important links between the individual stories of *Red Rooms* as much as they point to the central question raised in Dimaline's story cycle—that of how to make an urban Aboriginal community that is built on Aboriginal values. The table and couch as well as the butterfly are important symbols, of family and community as well as of the value and delicacy of ancestral knowledge; each requires care and nurturing and each is a prerequisite to leading a good life. This, I think, is what is suggested in the reference to "the Native Rosetta Stone" Natalie encounters in the closing story, the Na-tive Rosetta Stone being T.'s diary: "It was as if she were figuring out which shape fit into which hole in her own life. It was as if this simple book full of mundane domestic details and barbed and luscious insights were the very key to her life. She felt as though she had stumbled upon the Native Rosetta Stone" (142). The notion is quite common: readers identify with characters, with stories, partly because they see themselves, or parts of their own lives, reflected in those characters and their stories. In the case of Natalie, however, there is more. There is a sense of connection and fam-iliarity she feels for T. that goes beyond simple sympathy and identifica-tion. The book's ending refers, then, as much to the opening—to the world that Naomi has created in that nameless hotel—as to the outside world in the big city, the real world. When Natalie, the successful Anishnaabe businesswoman, runs out of the hotel intent on tracking down and meet-ing the rightful owner of the diary she spent the night reading, rather than attending her important morning meeting, the final story in *Red Rooms* takes the stories shared by Naomi beyond the world of the collection, in search of further connections. Natalie's search for focus, for meaning in her life, ultimately becomes a search for community. She longs for both her home community and an Aboriginal community in the city, and this longing is strong enough to make her miss an important business meeting; it is stronger than the appeal of the city as *homo economicus*, the site of capitalism and Euro-Western hegemony. Thus, Dimaline ends her story cycle on the notion that Aboriginal values persist, regardless of the omnipresence of Euro-Western values in urban spaces.

In terms of setting, plot, and characters, *Red Rooms* reflects more clearly than so-called canonical works (Eden Robinson's first novel, *Monkey Beach*, comes to mind, as well as Thomas King's *Green Grass, Running Water*) the realities of contemporary Indigenous people in North America, the majority of whom leave their home communities to make a life for themselves in towns and often the bigger cities. When Dimaline has T. email her friend Nathaniel that "the city isn't really a bad place for kids. . . . In Chinese, the word for crisis is the same as the word for opportunity" (144), these lines read much like the moral of *Red Rooms*. Some form of "crisis" may lead many Aboriginal people to leave their home communities (such as the search for proper housing, health care, education, and other social services), but in such a move also lies a chance for renewal—provided (the closing story of *Red Rooms* seems to caution) they help build a vibrant urban Aboriginal space, creating "communities that are away from but connected to traditional homelands."[34] Paiute activist Laverne Roberts calls these spaces, which may be either geographical or virtual, Native *hubs*. Renya K. Ramirez (Winnebago) defines a hub as "a mechanism to support Native notions of culture, community, identity, and belonging away from tribal land bases."[35] Expanding on Roberts's notion, Ramirez notes that "like a hub on a wheel . . . urban Indians occupy the center, connected to tribal communities by social networks represented by the wheel's spokes."[36] Ramirez has studied Native urban hubs in Silicon Valley, observing that "many urban Native Americans maintain connections to tribal communities or assert their tribal identities while living away from a land base."[37] Similarly, *Red Rooms* stresses that urban Aboriginal communities exist always with and in relation to the people's home communities. Leaving the reserve to live

---

34 Smith, "'With These Magic Weapons,'" 149.

35 Renya K. Ramirez, *Native Hubs: Culture, Community, and Belonging in Silicon Valley and Beyond* (Durham: Duke University Press, 2007), 1.

36 Ibid., 2.

37 Ibid., 3.

in the city does not imply that one severs all ties to one's home community. The nameless prostitute arguably suffers the consequences of having done just that, while the photographer's life in the city begins to thrive the moment he realizes the importance of his relationship to his folks back home. *Red Rooms* is, then, a manifesto for an Indigenous-centered urbanism, one that has urban Indigenous people "reinscrib[e] the hegemonic landscape" of urban capitalism by establishing and maintaining relationships (between urban areas and reserves and amongst urban Native people).[38] Yet, while *Red Rooms* argues for an Indigenous-centered urbanism, it is not a detailed portrayal of such an urbanism in practice. The different characters in *Red Rooms* never meet in the space outlined by the text, but their stories intersect, and so do their desires for home, community, and belonging. This interrelatedness is suggested most notably in the Native festival that some of the characters are drawn to and presumably also attend. As a symbol of a modern urban, multi-tribal Aboriginal community, the Native festival achieves its fullest "presence" in the collection's closing scene, in which Natalie creates a space grounded in Aboriginal notions of belonging when she misses her business meeting in order to find T. Not only is community dynamic and prone to change, *Red Rooms* proposes, but it requires above all *a willingness for community*, what Daniel Justice calls the "willingness to perform the necessary rituals—spiritual, physical, emotional, intellectual, and familial—to keep the kinship network in balance with itself and the rest of creation."[39] Dimaline's *Red Rooms* embodies this very willingness for community: its structure is as synecdochic and web-like as Indigenous notions of kinship and community. Dimaline's strongest argument for an Indigenous-centred urbanism, then, exists in the very ways she builds the narrative in *Red Rooms*.

The intricate structure of *Red Rooms* may be subtle, but it is difficult not to notice it, and the remarkable rhetorical achievement it represents, when reading Dimaline's story cycle for its use of relational word bundles. Holophrastic reading is certainly not the only means by which to uncover the subtleties and nuances of Dimaline's writing, but it is a coherent reading method that allows readers to approach her work from within the discourse traditions to which it belongs, thereby showing respect to the very argument Dimaline is making in *Red Rooms*.

---

38 Ibid., 96–97.

39 Daniel Heath Justice, "'Go Away, Water!': Kinship Criticism and the Decolonization Imperative," in *Reasoning Together: The Native Critics Collective*, ed. Craig S. Womack, Daniel Heath Justice, and Christopher B. Teuton (Oklahoma: University of Oklahoma Press, 2008), 152.

What can we take from these readings of King's *Green Grass, Running Water* and Dimaline's *Red Rooms*? First and foremost, they show that reading Indigenous writing as *text* actually helps bring back into focus those works that seem to fall outside of critical paradigms designed to empower Indigenous communities by focusing inward, such as Indigenous literary nationalism. *Green Grass, Running Water* and *Red Rooms* speak particularly to pan-Indigenous and urban Indigenous communities across North America. Despite their refusal to engage with the history and politics of a specific Native community, these two works are nonetheless embedded in Indigenous worldviews. Creation—whether the creation of the world, the inventing and telling of a story, or the rebuilding of a cabin—is to be both balanced and cooperative, King argues; further, an individual's identity takes shape only in relation to that individual's home community, Dimaline emphasizes. Documenting the broad spectrum of Aboriginal experiences in contemporary North America, *Green Grass, Running Water* and *Red Rooms* contribute to the development and vibrancy of Indigenous literatures and communities through their very divergence from narrow, nationalist definitions of Indigenous writing. It would be a mistake, however, to read this divergence as an embrace of Euro-Western traditions, whether intellectual or literary. For what may look like Aboriginal attempts at Euro-Western mimicry (postmodern writing in the case of *Green Grass, Running Water*; mainstream urban literature in the case of *Red Rooms*) has its roots in Aboriginal intellectual and narrative traditions. Reading *Green Grass, Running Water* and *Red Rooms* for holophrastic manifestations in English highlights the significance of Indigenous values; it also demonstrates that these so-called disparate Indigenous texts may yet be approached from within Indigenous discourse traditions, however generalized these traditions may be. While holophrastic reading is not the only meaningful approach to pan-Indigenous and urban Indigenous writing, it offers a great deal of value to readers of Indigenous literatures.

In my introductory remarks to this chapter, I mentioned Eden Robinson's expression of authorial freedom in *Blood Sports*, a novel that, in refusing all forms of engagement with Native communities, is a much more radical departure than King's *Green Grass, Running Water* or Dimaline's *Red Rooms*. In their discussion of *Blood Sports*, Kristina Fagan and Sam McKegney argue that if Indigenous "literary nationalism is to succeed in rendering literary criticism relevant to Native communities and individuals, it needs to find ways of engaging with disparate Indigenous texts on their own terms."[40] On their own terms also means *in their own texts*. To value the contributions of "radical departures in Native literature" and to "recognize their ongoing significance to Native people and Native communities"[41] therefore implies that as readers of Indigenous literatures we must deliberately refocus our attention onto the more formal aspects of reading literature, not for the sake of form per se, but for the sake of the texts, their authors, and the communities to which they speak. Seen from this perspective, it is the (radical) departures of Indigenous literatures that may yet make the strongest contribution to Indigenous poetics. Disparate Indigenous works challenge us to shift our focus to the *texts* in front of us, and the rhetorical events these texts perform, in order to give them the critical attention they deserve. Ideally, this critical attention will arise from within the texts themselves, including the very language and discourse traditions from which they emerge.

FURTHER READING

Kristina Fagan and Sam McKegney's essay "Circling the Question of Nationalism in Native Canadian Literature and Its Study" (*Review: Literature and Arts of the Americas* 41.1 [2008]), which inspired the title of this chapter, examines the question of how to adequately approach those Indigenous texts that do not fit into nationalist models of reading Indigenous literatures. For a discussion of the relevance and contributions of Indigenous urban literature, see Jennifer K. Ladino's essay "'A Limited Range of Motion?'" (*Studies in American Indian Literatures* 21.3 [2009]) and Lindsey Claire Smith's article "'With These Magic Weapons, Make a New World'" (*Canadian Journal of Native Studies* 29.1–2 [2009]). Arnold E. Davidson, Priscilla L. Walton, and Jennifer Andrews have offered a comprehensive study of Thomas King's work, in *Border Crossings: Thomas King's Cultural Inversions* (Toronto: University of Toronto Press, 2003). Daniel Heath Justice analyzes Thomas King's Cherokee sensibility in chapter 4 of his book *Our Fire Survives the Storm* (Minneapolis: University of Minnesota Press, 2006).

---

40 Fagan and McKegney, "Circling the Question," 38.
41 Ibid., 42.

PERMISSIONS ACKNOWLEDGEMENTS

Grateful acknowledgement is made to the following for permission to reprint previously published material:

Excerpts from Maria Campbell's *Stories of the Road Allowance People: The Revised Edition* (Saskatoon: Gabriel Dumont Institute, 2010). Print. Reprinted by permission of the publisher.

Excerpts from *Write It on Your Heart,* © 1989, 2004 Harry Robinson and Wendy Wickwire (Talonbooks, Vancouver, 2004). Reprinted by permission of the publisher.

Excerpts from Louise Halfe's *The Crooked Good* (Regina, Coteau, 2007) and *Blue Marrow* (Regina: Coteau, 2004). Used by permission of the publisher.

The Decolonizing Poetics of Indigenous Literatures is the culmination of ten years of research, bits and pieces of which I first presented in other publications. Sections of chapters 1 and 2 first appeared in the introduction to *"That's Raven Talk": Holophrastic Readings of Contemporary Indigenous Literatures* (Regina: CPRC Press, 2011); "What's in a Frame?: The Significance of Relational Word Bundles in Louise Bernice Halfe's *Blue Marrow*," in *Listening Up, Writing Down, and Looking Beyond: Interfaces of the Oral, Written, and Visual,* ed. Susan Gingell and Wendy Roy, pp. 221-37 (Waterloo: Wilfrid Laurier University Press, 2012), reprinted with permission; "'Holo What?' or, the Exceptional Business of Naming: A Dialogue," *ESC:*

English Studies in Canada 37.1 (2012): 63–84; and "Indigenous Rhetorics and Kinship: Towards a Rhetoric of Relational Word Bundles," *Canadian Journal of Native Studies* 33.1 (2013): 125–45, reprinted with permission. My reading of Paul Seesequasis's "The Republic of Tricksterism" was first presented in "Indigenous Rhetorics and Kinship." Parts of chapter 3 first appeared as "The Rhetoric of Harry Robinson's 'Cat with the Boots On,'" in *Mosaic* 44.2 (2011): 35–51, reprinted with permission; and "The Marriage of Mother and Father: Michif Influences as Expressions of Métis Intellectual Sovereignty in *Stories of the Road Allowance People*," in *Studies in American Indian Literatures* 22.1 (2010): 20–48. Sections on Louise Bernice Halfe's *The Crooked Good* previously appeared in "Reading the Prairies Relationally: Louise Bernice Halfe and 'Spacious Creation,'" in *Canadian Literature* 215 (Winter 2012): 86–102, as well as in "'What's in a Frame?" Sections on Alootook Ipellie's *Arctic Dreams and Nightmares*, on Louise Bernice Halfe's *Blue Marrow*, on Thomas King's *Green Grass, Running Water*, and on Richard Van Camp's *The Lesser Blessed* first appeared in *"That's Raven Talk."*

WORKS CITED

Ahenakew, Edward. "Cree Trickster Tales." *Journal of American Folklore* 42 (1929): 309–53.

Alexie, Robert Arthur. *Porcupines and China Dolls*. Toronto: Stoddart, 2002.

Alexie, Sherman. *Ten Little Indians: Stories*. New York: Grove, 2003.

Alfred, Taiaiake. "Restitution is the Real Pathway to Justice for Indigenous Peoples." In *Response, Responsibility, and Renewal: Canada's Truth and Reconciliation Journey*, edited by Gregory Younging, Jonathan Dewar, and Mike DeGagné, 179–87. Ottawa: Aboriginal Healing Foundation, 2009.

Allen, Paula Gunn. *The Sacred Hoop: Recovering the Feminine in American Indian Traditions*. 1986. Reprint, Boston: Beacon, 1992.

Andrews, Jennifer. *In the Belly of a Laughing God: Humour and Irony in Native Women's Poetry*. Toronto: University of Toronto Press, 2011.

Attla, Catherine. *K'etetaalkkaanee, the One Who Paddles among the People and Animals: The Story of an Ancient Traveller*. Translated by Eliza Jones. Fairbanks: Alaska Native Language Center, 1990.

Aupilaarjuk, Mariano, Tulimaq *Aupilaarjuk*, Lucassie Nutaraakuk, Rose Iqallijuq, Johanasi Ujarak, Isidore Ijituuq, and Michel Kupaaq. *Cosmology and Shamanism*. Vol. 4 of *Interviewing Inuit Elders*, edited by Bernard Saladin d'Anglure. Iqaluit: Nunavut Arctic College, 2001.

Baker, Mark C. *The Atoms of Language: The Mind's Hidden Rules of Grammar.* New York: Basic, 2001.

Bakker, Peter. *A Language of Our Own: The Genesis of Michif, the Mixed Cree-French Language of the Canadian Métis.* Rev. ed. New York: Oxford University Press, 1997.

Balzer, Geraldine. "'Bring[ing] Them Back from the Inside Out': Coming Home through Story in Richard Wagemese's *Keeper'n Me.*" In "Textualizing Orature and Orality," edited by Susan Gingell. Special issue, *Essays on Canadian Writing* 83 (2005): 222–39.

Bartelt, Guillermo. "American Indian English in Momaday's *House Made of Dawn.*" *Language and Literature* 19 (1994): 37–53.

———. *Socio- and Stylolinguistic Perspectives on American Indian English Texts.* Lewiston, NY: Edwin Mellen, 2001.

Barthes, Roland. *Elements of Semiology,* translated by Annette Lavers and Colin Smith. London: Jonathan Cape, 1967.

———. "An Introduction to the Structural Analysis of Narrative." *New Literary History* 6.2 (1975): 237–72.

Bauman, Richard. *Verbal Art as Performance.* Prospect Heights, IL: Waveland, 1984.

Bear, Glecia. *Wanisinwak iskwêsisak: awâsisasinahikanis / Two Little Girls Lost in the Bush: A Cree Story for Children,* edited and translated by Freda Ahenakew and H. Christoph Wolfart. Saskatoon: Fifth House, 1991.

Bear Nicholas, Andrea. "The Assault on Aboriginal Oral Traditions: Past and Present." In *Aboriginal Oral Traditions: Theory, Practice, Ethics,* edited by Renée Hulan and Renate Eigenbrod, 13–43. Halifax: Fernwood, 2008.

Bevis, William. "Native American Novels: Homing In." In *Recovering the Word: Essays on Native American Literature,* edited by Brian Swann and Arnold Krupat, 580–620. Berkeley: University of California Press, 1987.

Bird, Gloria, and Joy Harjo. "Introduction." In *Reinventing the Enemy's Language: Contemporary Native Women's Writings of North America,* edited by Gloria Bird and Joy Harjo, 19–31. New York: W.W. Norton, 1997.

Bloomfield, Leonard. *Sacred Stories of the Sweet Grass Cree.* 1930. Reprint, Saskatoon: Fifth House, 1993.

Brooks, Lisa, Michael Elliott (chair), Arnold Krupat, Elvira Pulitano, and Craig Womack. "Cosmopolitanism and Nationalism in Native American Literature: A Panel Discussion." Roundtable conducted at Emory University, April 22, 2011. In *Southern Spaces,* June 21, 2011. http://southernspaces.org/2011/cosmopolitanism-and-national-ism-native-american-literature-panel-discussion.

Campbell, Maria. "Maria Campbell." Interview by Hartmut Lutz and Konrad Gross. In *Contemporary Challenges: Conversations with Canadian Native Authors,* compiled by Hartmut Lutz, 41–65. Saskatoon: Fifth House, 1991.

Campbell, Maria. "'One Small Medicine': An Interview with Maria Campbell." By Susan Gingell. In "Textualizing Orature and Orality," edited by Susan Gingell. Special issue of *Essays on Canadian Writing* 83 (2004): 188–205.

——, trans. *Stories of the Road Allowance People.* Rev. ed. Saskatoon: Gabriel Dumont Institute, 2010.

Canada. *House of Commons Debates.* June 11, 2008 (Right Hon. Stephen Harper, Prime Minister, CPC) http://www.parl.gc.ca/HousePublications/Publication.aspx?DocId=3568890&Language=E&Mode=1&Parl=39&Ses=2.

Canton, Jeffrey. "Coyote Lives: Thomas King." In *The Power to Bend Spoons: Interviews with Canadian Novelists,* edited by Beverley Daurio, 90–97. Toronto: Mercury, 1998.

Cariou, Warren. "Dances with Rigoureau." In *Troubling Tricksters: Revisioning Critical Conversations,* edited by Deanna Reder and Linda M. Morra, 157–67. Waterloo: Wilfrid Laurier University Press, 2010.

Chafe, Wallace L. "Discourse Effects on Polysynthesis." In *Discourse across Languages and Cultures,* edited by Carol Lynn Moder and Aida Martinovic-Zic, 37–52. Amsterdam: John Benjamins, 2004.

Chandonnet, Ann. Preface to *The Epic of Qayaq: The Longest Story Ever Told by My People,* by Lela Kiana Oman, vii–xii. Edited by Priscilla Tyler and Maree Brooks. Ottawa: Carleton University Press, 1995.

Comrie, Bernard. *Language Universals and Linguistic Typology: Syntax and Morphology.* Oxford: Basil Blackwell, 1981.

Cook, Méira. "Bone Memory: Transcribing Voice in Louise Bernice Halfe's *Blue Marrow." Canadian Literature* 166 (2000): 85–110.

Darnell, Regna. "The Primacy of Writing and the Persistence of the Primitive." In *Papers of the Thirty-First Algonquian Conference,* edited by John D. Nichols, 54–67. Winnipeg: University of Manitoba, 2000.

Davidson, Arnold E., Priscilla L. Walton, and Jennifer Andrews. *Border Crossings: Thomas King's Cultural Inversions.* Toronto: University of Toronto Press, 2003.

Doueihi, Anne. "Inhabiting the Space between Discourse and Story in Trickster Narratives." In *Mythical Trickster Figures: Contours, Contexts, and Criticisms*, edited by William J. Hynes and William G. Doty, 193–201. Tuscaloosa: University of Alabama Press, 1993.

Du Ponceau, Peter Stephen. "Report of the Corresponding Secretary to the Committee, of his Progress in the Investigation Committed to him of the General Character and Forms of the Languages of the American Indians." In *Transactions of the Historical & Literary Committee of the American Philosophical Society, held at Philadelphia, for promoting Useful Knowledge*, vol. 1, xvii–xlvi. Philadelphia: American Philosophical Society, 1819.

Dyck, E. F. "Symbol as Figure." *Semiotic Inquiry* 14.3 (1994): 47–57.

——. "Topos in Rhetorical Argumentation: From Enthymeme to Figure." In *Proceedings of the Fifth International Conference of the International Society for the Study of Argumentation*, edited by Frans H. van Eemeren, Rob Grootendorst, J. Anthony Blair, and Charles A. Willard, 261–64. Amsterdam: SIC SAT, 2003.

Eigenbrod, Renate. *Travelling Knowledges: Positioning the Im/Migrant Reader of Aboriginal Literatures in Canada*. Winnipeg: University of Manitoba Press, 2005.

Éjchenbaum, Boris M. "The Illusion of *Skaz*." *Russian Literature Triquarterly* 12 (1975): 233–36.

Episkenew, Jo-Ann. "Afterword." In "Reconciling Canada," edited by Jennifer Henderson and Pauline Wakeham. Special issue, *ESC: English Studies in Canada* 35.1 (2009): 193–200.

——. *Taking Back Our Spirits: Indigenous Literature, Public Policy, and Healing*. Winnipeg: University of Manitoba Press, 2009.

Evans, Nicholas, and Hans-Jürgen Sasse. "Introduction: Problems of Polysynthesis." In *Problems of Polysynthesis*, edited by Nicholas Evans and Hans-Jürgen Sasse, 1–13. Berlin: Akademie, 2002.

Fagan, Kristina, Daniel Heath Justice, Keavy Martin, Sam McKegney, Deanna Reder, and Niigaanwewidam James Sinclair. "Canadian Indian Literary Nationalism?: Critical Approaches in Canadian Indigenous Contexts—A Collaborative Interlogue." *Canadian Journal of Native Studies* 29.1–2 (2009): 19–44.

Fagan, Kristina, and Sam McKegney. "Circling the Question of Nationalism in Native Canadian Literature and Its Study." *Review: Literature and Arts of the Americas* 41.1 (2008): 31–42.

Fixico, Donald L. "Foreword." In *American Indians and the Urban Experience*, edited by Susan Lobo and Kurt Peters, ix–x. New York: Altamira, 2001.

Flick, Jane. "Reading Notes for Thomas King's *Green Grass, Running Water*." *Canadian Literature* 161–62 (1999): 140–72.

Flynn, Darin. "Decline of Aboriginal Languages." University of Calgary website. Accessed January 27, 2013, http://www.ucalgary.ca/dflynn/ aboriginal/aboriginal-languages-of-canada/decline-of-aboriginal-languages.

Fraser, Minnie. "His First Moose." In *Kôhkominawak otâcimowiniwâwa / Our Grandmothers' Lives, as Told in Their Own Words*, edited and translated by Freda Ahenakew and H. Christoph Wolfart, 103–121. 1992. Reprint, Regina: Canadian Plains Research Center, University of Regina, 1998.

French, David H., and Kathrine S. French. "Personal Names." In *Languages*, edited by Ives Goddard, 200–221. Vol. 17 of *Handbook of North American Indians*, edited by William C. Sturtevant. Washington, DC: Smithsonian Institution Press, 1996.

Fulford, George. "What Cree Children's Drawings Reveal about Words and Imagery in the Cree Language." In *Papers of the Twenty-Eighth Algonquian Conference*, edited by David H. Pentland, 162–80. Winnipeg: University of Manitoba, 1997.

Gingell, Susan. "Lips' Inking: Cree and Cree-Metis Authors' Writings of the Oral and What They Might Tell Educators." *Canadian Journal of Native Education* 32 (2010): 35–61.

Goetsch, Paul. "Fingierte Mündlichkeit in der Erzählkunst entwickelter Schriftkulturen." *Poetica* 17.3–4 (1985): 202–218.

Goldman, Marlene. "Mapping and Dreaming: Native Resistance in *Green Grass, Running Water*." *Canadian Literature* 161–62 (1999): 18–41.

Grainger, James. Review of *Porcupine and China Dolls*, by Robert Alexie. *Quill & Quire* (May 2002): 25. http://www.quillandquire.com/review/porcupines-and-china-dolls/.

Halfe, Louise Bernice. *Bear Bones and Feathers*. Regina: Coteau, 1994.

——. *Blue Marrow*. Regina: Coteau, 2004.

——. *The Crooked Good*. Regina: Coteau, 2007.

——. "Keynote Address: The Rolling Head's 'Grave' Yard." *Studies in Canadian Literature* 31.1 (2006): 65–74.

Henderson, Jennifer, and Pauline Wakeham. "Colonial Reckoning, National Reconciliation?: Aboriginal Peoples and the Culture of Redress in Canada." In "Reconciling Canada," edited by Jennifer

Henderson and Pauline Wakeham. Special issue, *ESC: English Studies in Canada* 35.1 (2009): 1–26.

Highway, Tomson. *Dry Lips Oughta Move to Kapuskasing.* Saskatoon: Fifth House, 1989.

———. *Kiss of the Fur Queen.* Toronto: Doubleday Canada, 1998.

Hinton, Leanne. "Language Revitalization." *Annual Review of Applied Linguistics* 23 (2003): 44–57.

Hobson, Geary. Review of *The Lesser Blessed*, by Richard Van Camp. *Studies in American Indian Literatures*, 10.4 (1998): 77–79.

Holm, Tom, J. Diane Pearson, and Ben Chavis. "Peoplehood: A Model for the Extension of Sovereignty in American Indian Studies." *Wicazo Sa Review* 18.1 (2003): 7–24.

Hutcheon, Linda. *A Theory of Parody: The Teachings of Twentieth-Century Art Forms.* New York: Methuen, 1985.

"Indian Residential Schools Settlement Agreement." Official court notice. May 8, 2006. http://www.residentialschoolsettlement.ca/IRS%20Settlement%20Agreement-%20ENGLISH.pdf.

Inuktitut: A Multi-Dialectal Outline Dictionary (with an Aivilingmiutaq Base). Compiled by Alex Spalding. Iqaluit: Nunavut Arctic College, 1998.

Ipellie, Alootook. *Arctic Dreams and Nightmares.* Penticton, BC: Theytus, 1993.

Iser, Wolfgang. *Der Akt des Lesens: Theorie asthetischer Wirkung.* Munich: Wilhelm Fink, 1976.

Jacobs, Madelaine. "Hell Will Not Prevail." Review of *Jacob's Prayer*, by Lorne Dufour, and *Porcupines and China Dolls*, by Robert Arthur Alexie. *Canadian Literature* 206 (2010): 110–11. http://canlit.ca/reviews/hell_will_not_prevail.

Justice, Daniel Heath. "'Go Away, Water!': Kinship Criticism and the Decolonization Imperative." In *Reasoning Together: The Native Critics Collective*, edited by Craig S. Womack, Daniel Heath Justice, and Christopher B. Teuton, 147–68. Oklahoma: University of Oklahoma Press, 2008.

———. "The Necessity of Nationhood: Affirming the Sovereignty of Indigenous National Literatures." In *Moveable Margins: The Shifting Spaces of Canadian Literature*, edited by Chelva Kanaganayakam, 143–59. Toronto: TSAR, 2005.

———. *Our Fire Survives the Storm: A Cherokee Literary History.* Minneapolis: University of Minnesota Press, 2006.

Kayman, Martin A. "The State of English as a Global Language: Communicating Culture." *Textual Practice* 18.1 (2004): 1–22.

Kellogg, Robert. "Oral Narrative, Written Books." *Genre* 10 (1977): 655–65.

Kendall, Martha B. "Exegesis and Translation: Northern Yuman Names as Texts." *Journal of Anthropological Research* 36.3 (1980): 261–73.

King, Thomas. "Godzilla vs. Post-Colonial." *World Literature Written in English* 30.2 (1990): 10–16.

——. *Green Grass, Running Water*. 1993. Reprint, Toronto: HarperPerennial Canada, 1999.

——. "Interview with Tom King." By Constance Rooke. *World Literature Written in English* 30.2 (1990): 62–76.

——. "Introduction." In *All My Relations: An Anthology of Contemporary Canadian Native Fiction*, edited by Thomas King, ix–xvi. Toronto: McClelland and Stewart, 1990.

——. "Inventing the Indian: White Images, Native Oral Literature, and Contemporary Native Writers." PhD diss., University of Utah, 1986.

——. *Medicine River*. Markham, ON: Viking Canada, 1989.

——. "Peter Gzowski Interviews Thomas King on *Green Grass, Running Water*." By Peter Gzowski. *Canadian Literature* 161–62 (1999): 65–76.

——. *The Truth about Stories: A Native Narrative*. Toronto: Anansi, 2003.

Kilpatrick, Alan. *The Night Has a Naked Soul: Witchcraft and Sorcery among the Western Cherokee*. Syracuse, NY: Syracuse University Press, 1997.

Kinkade, M. Dale, and Anthony Mattina. "Discourse." In *Languages*, edited by Ives Goddard, 244–74. Vol. 17 of *Handbook of North American Indians*, edited by William C. Sturtevant. Washington, DC: Smithsonian Institution Press, 1996.

Kirman, Paula E. "Cultural Selves: An Interview with Richard Wagamese." *Paragraph: The Canadian Fiction Review* 20.1 (Summer 1998): 2–5.

Kleist, Makka. "Pre-Christian Inuit Sexuality." In *Me Sexy: An Exploration of Native Sex and Sexuality*, edited by Drew Hayden Taylor, 15–19. Vancouver: Douglas and McIntyre, 2008.

Kleivan, Inge, and Birgitte Sonne. *Eskimos: Greenland and Canada*. Leiden, The Netherlands: E.J. Brill, 1985.

Koch, Peter, and Wulf Oesterreicher. "Sprache der Nahe—Sprache der Distanz: Mündlichkeit und Schriftlichkeit im Spannungsfeld von Sprachtheorie und Sprachgeschichte." *Romanistisches Jahrbuch* 36 (1985): 15–43.

Ladino, Jennifer K. "'A Limited Range of Motion?': Multiculturalism, 'Human Questions,' and Urban Indian Identity in Sherman Alexie's

Ten Little Indians." *Studies in American Indian Literatures* 21.3 (2009): 36–57.

Lamont-Stewart, Linda. "Androgyny as Resistance to Authoritarianism in Two Postmodern Canadian Novels." *Mosaic* 30.3 (1997): 115–30.

Leap, William L. *American Indian English.* Salt Lake City: University of Utah Press, 1993.

Lee, A. Robert. "Introduction." In *Loosening the Seams: Interpretations of Gerald Vizenor,* edited by A. Robert Lee, 1–19. Bowling Green, OH: Bowling Green State University Popular Press, 2000.

Lengelle, Reinekke, and Frans Meijers. "Mystery to Mastery: An Exploration of What Happens in the Black Box of Writing and Healing." *Journal of Poetry Therapy* 22.2 (2009): 57–75.

Lincoln, Kenneth. *Native American Renaissance.* Berkeley: University of California Press, 1983.

Lyons, Scott Richard. "Rhetorical Sovereignty: What Do American Indians Want from Writing?" *College Composition and Communication* 51.3 (2000): 447–68.

Martin, Keavy. "Truth, Reconciliation, and Amnesia: *Porcupines and China Dolls* and the Canadian Conscience." In "Reconciling Canada," edited by Jennifer Henderson and Pauline Wakeham. Special issue, *ESC: English Studies in Canada* 35.1 (2009): 47–65.

Mattina, Anthony, and Clara Jack. "Okanagan Communication and Language." In *Okanagan Sources,* edited by Jean Webber and En'owkin Centre, 143–65. Penticton, BC: Theytus, 1990.

McGrath, Robin. *Canadian Inuit Literature: The Development of a Tradition.* Ottawa: National Museums of Canada, 1984.

McKegney, Sam. *Magic Weapons: Aboriginal Writers Remaking Community after Residential School.* Winnipeg: University of Manitoba Press, 2007.

———. "Writer-Reader Reciprocity and the Pursuit of Alliance through Indigenous Poetry." In *Indigenous Poetics in Canada,* edited by Neal McLeod, 43–60. Waterloo: Wilfrid Laurier University Press, 2014.

McLeod, Neal. "Coming Home through Stories." In *(Ad)dressing Our Words: Aboriginal Perspectives on Aboriginal Literatures,* edited by Armand Garnet Ruffo, 17–36. Penticton, BC: Theytus, 2001.

———. *Cree Narrative Memory: From Treaties to Contemporary Times.* Saskatoon: Purich, 2007.

———. "Cree Poetic Discourse." In *Across Cultures, Across Borders: Canadian Aboriginal and Native American Literatures,* edited by Paul

DePasquale, Renate Eigenbrod, and Emma LaRocque, 109–121. Toronto: Broadview, 2010.

——, ed. *Indigenous Poetics in Canada*. Waterloo: Wilfrid Laurier University Press, 2014.

Mithun, Marianne. *The Languages of Native North America*. Cambridge: Cambridge University Press, 1999.

Momaday, N. Scott. *House Made of Dawn*. New York: Harper and Row, 1968.

Nelson, Robert M. *Leslie Marmon Silko's* Ceremony: *The Recovery of Tradition*. New York: Peter Lang, 2008.

Neuhaus, Mareike. "'Holo What?' or, The Exceptional Business of Naming: A Dialogue." *ESC: English Studies in Canada* 37.1 (2012): 63–84.

——. "Indigenous Rhetorics and Kinship: Towards a Rhetoric of Relational Word Bundles." *Canadian Journal of Native Studies* 33.1 (2013): 125–45.

——. "Reading the Prairies Relationally: Louise Bernice Halfe and 'Spacious Creation.'" *Canadian Literature* 215 (Winter 2012): 86–102.

——. *"That's Raven Talk": Holophrastic Readings of Contemporary Indigenous Literatures*. Regina: Canadian Plains Research Center Press, 2011.

——. "The Marriage of Mother and Father: Michif Influences as Expressions of Métis Intellectual Sovereignty in *Stories of the Road Allowance People*." *Studies in American Indian Literatures* 22.1 (2010): 20–48.

——. "The Rhetoric of Harry Robinson's 'Cat with the Boots On.'" *Mosaic* 44.2 (2011): 35–51.

——. "What's in a Frame?: The Significance of Relational Word Bundles in Louise Bernice Halfe's *Blue Marrow*." In *Listening Up, Writing Down, and Looking Beyond: Interfaces of the Oral, Written, and Visual*, edited by Susan Gingell and Wendy Roy, 221–37. Waterloo: Wilfrid Laurier University Press, 2012.

The New Princeton Encyclopedia of Poetry and Poetics, edited by Alex Preminger and T. V. F. Brogan. Princeton: Princeton University Press, 1993.

Nida, Eugene A., and Charles A. Taber. *The Theory and Practice of Translation*. Leiden, The Netherlands: E.J. Brill, 1969.

Nungak, Zebedee, and Eugene Arima. "A Review of Central Eskimo Mythology." In *Unikkaatuat sanaugarngnik atyingualiit Puvirngniturngmit/Eskimo Stories from Povungnituk, Quebec, Illustrated in*

Soapstone Carvings, edited by Zebedee Nungak and Eugene Arima, 111–37. Ottawa: National Museums of Canada, 1969.

Oman, Lela Kiana. *The Epic of Qayaq: The Longest Story Ever Told by My People*, edited by Priscilla Tyler and Maree Brooks. Ottawa: Carleton University Press, 1995.

Ortiz, Simon J. "Towards a National Indian Literature: Cultural Authenticity in Nationalism." *MELUS* 8.2 (1981): 7–12.

Park, Jeff. *Writing at the Edge: Narrative and Writing Process Theory*. New York: Peter Lang, 2005.

Perreault, Jeanne, and Sylvia Vance, comps. and eds. *Writing the Circle: Native Women of Western Canada: An Anthology*. Edmonton: NeWest, 1990.

Petzold, Dieter. "Thomas King's *Green Grass, Running Water*: A Postmodern Postcolonial Puzzle; or, Coyote Conquers the Campus." In *Lineages of the Novel: Essays in Honour of Raimund Borgmeier*, edited by Bernhard Reitz and Eckart Voigts-Virchow, 243–54. Trier, Germany: Wissenschaftlicher, 2000.

Powell, Malea D. "Sarah Winnemucca Hopkins: Her Wrongs and Claims." In *American Indian Rhetorics of Survivance: Word Medicine, Word Magic*, edited by Ernest Stromberg, 69–94. Pittsburgh: University of Pittsburgh Press, 2006.

Powell, Peter J. *Sweet Medicine: The Continuing Role of the Sacred Arrows, the Sun Dance, and the Sacred Buffalo Hat in Northern Cheyenne History*. 2 vols. Norman: University of Oklahoma Press, 1969.

Ramirez, Renya K. *Native Hubs: Culture, Community, and Belonging in Silicon Valley and Beyond*. Durham: Duke University Press, 2007.

Rayburn, Alan. "The Real Story of How Toronto Got Its Name." *Canadian Geographic* 114.5 (1994): 68–70.

Rice, Sally. "'Our Language Is Very Literal': Figurative Expression in Dene Sųłiné." In *Endangered Metaphors*, edited by Anna Idström and Elisabeth Piirainen, 21–76. Amsterdam: John Benjamins, 2012.

——. "Posture and Existence Predicates in Dene Sųłiné (Chipewyan): Lexical and Semantic Density as a Function of the 'Stand'/'Sit'/'Lie' Continuum." In *The Linguistics of Sitting, Standing, and Lying*, edited by John Newman, 61–78. Amsterdam: John Benjamins, 2002.

Robinson, Eden. *Blood Sports*. Toronto: McClelland and Stewart, 2006.

——. *Monkey Beach*. Toronto: A. Knopf Canada, 2000.

Robinson, Harry. *Living by Stories: A Journey of Landscape and Memory*, compiled and edited by Wendy Wickwire. Vancouver: Talonbooks, 2005.

———. *Nature Power: In the Spirit of an Okanagan Storyteller*, compiled and edited by Wendy Wickwire. 2nd ed. Vancouver: Talonbooks, 2004.

———. *Write It on Your Heart: The Epic World of an Okanagan Storyteller*, compiled and edited by Wendy Wickwire. Vancouver: Talonbooks, 1989.

Rodden, John. "How Do Stories Convince Us?: Notes towards a Rhetoric of Narrative." *College Literature* 35.1 (2008): 148–73.

Ruppert, James. "Fiction: 1968–Present." In *The Cambridge Companion to Native American Literature*, edited by Kenneth M. Roemer and Joy Porter, 173–88. Cambridge: Cambridge University Press, 2005.

Saladin d'Anglure, Bernard. "An Ethnographic Commentary: The Legend of Atanarjuat, Inuit, and Shamanism." In *Atanarjuat, the Fast Runner: Inspired by a Traditional Inuit Legend of Igloolik*, by Paul Apak Angilirq, 196–227. Toronto: Coach House/Isuma, 2002.

———. "Nanook, Super-Male: The Polar Bear in the Imaginary Space and Social Time of the Inuit of the Canadian Arctic." In *Signifying Animals: Human Meaning in the Natural World*, edited by Roy Willis, 178–95. London: Unwin Hyman, 1990.

———. "The 'Third Gender' of the Inuit." *Diogenes* 52.4 (2005): 134–44.

Saussure, Ferdinand de. *Course in General Linguistics*. Translated by Wade Baskin. Edited by Charles Bally and Albert Sechehaye. London: Peter Owen, 1960.

Schneider, Isabel. "Survivors: New Models of Culture and Identity in Contemporary North American Indigenous Fiction." In *Colonies, Missions, Cultures in the English Speaking World: General and Comparative Studies*, edited by Gerhard Stilz, 287–98. Tübingen, Germany: Stauffenburg, 2001.

Schorcht, Blanca. *Storied Voices in Native American Texts: Harry Robinson, Thomas King, James Welch, and Leslie Marmon Silko*. New York: Routledge, 2003.

Scott, Jill. "Conditions of Possibility for Apology: Toward an Indigenous Framework of Redress." Paper presented at the annual conference of the Canadian Association for Commonwealth Literature and Language Studies, University of New Brunswick, Fredericton, May 28, 2011.

Seesequasis, Paul. "The Republic of Tricksterism." In *An Anthology of Canadian Native Literature in English*, edited by Daniel David Moses and Terry Goldie, 468–74. 3rd ed. Toronto: Oxford University Press, 2005.

Silko, Leslie Marmon. *Ceremony*. 1977. Reprint, New York: Penguin, 1986.

——. "Language and Literature from a Pueblo Indian Perspective." In *English Literature: Opening up the Canon*, edited by Leslie A. Fiedler and Houston A. Baker Jr., 54–72. Baltimore: Johns Hopkins University Press, 1981.

——. *Storyteller*. New York: Arcade, 1981.

Sing, Pamela V. "Intersections of Memory, Ancestral Language, and Imagination; or, the Textual Production of Michif Voices as Cultural Weaponry." In "For the Love of Words: Aboriginal Writers of Canada," edited by Renate Eigenbrod and Jennifer Andrews. Special Issue of *Studies in Canadian Literature* 31.1 (2006). https://journals.lib.unb.ca/index.php/scl/article/view/10202/10552.

Smith, Lindsey Claire. "'With These Magic Weapons, Make a New World': Indigenous Centered Urbanism in Tomson Highway's *Kiss of the Fur Queen*." *Canadian Journal of Native Studies* 29.1–2 (2009): 143–64.

Stevens, James R. *Sacred Legends of the Sandy Lake Cree*. Toronto: McClelland and Stewart, 1971.

Stratton, Billy J., and Frances Washburn. "The Peoplehood Matrix: A New Theory for American Indian Literature." *Wicazo Sa Review* 23.1 (2008): 51–72.

Sutherland, Xavier. "Cahkâpêš nêsta mâka mistâpêskwêwak / Chahkabesh and the Giant Women." In *âtolôhkâna nêsta tipâcimôwina / Cree Legends and Narratives from the West Coast of James Bay*, edited and translated by C. Douglas Ellis, 104–109. Winnipeg: University of Manitoba Press, 1995.

Taylor, Christopher. "North America as Contact Zone: Native American Literary Nationalism and the Cross-Cultural Dilemma." *Studies in American Indian Literatures* 22.3 (2010): 26–44.

Ticasuk [Emily Ivanoff Brown]. *The Longest Story Ever Told: Qayaq, the Magical Man*. 2nd ed. Fairbanks: University of Alaska Press, 2008.

Twain, Mark. *A Tramp Abroad*. Hartford, CT: American Publishing Company; London: Chatto and Windus, 1880.

Van Camp, Richard. *The Lesser Blessed*. 1996. Reprint, Vancouver: Douglas and McIntyre, 2004.

——. "Review of *Porcupines and China Dolls*." Hanksville website. Accessed June 3, 2015. http://www.hanksville.org/storytellers/VanCamp/writing/Porcupines.html.

Wagamese, Richard. *Keeper'n Me*. Toronto: Doubleday Canada, 1994.

Warrior, Robert Allen. *Tribal Secrets: Recovering American Indian Intellectual Traditions*. Minneapolis: University of Minnesota Press, 1994.

Weaver, Jace. *That the People Might Live: Native American Literatures and Native American Community.* New York: Oxford University Press, 1997.

Weaver, Jace, Craig S. Womack, and Robert Warrior. *American Indian Literary Nationalism.* Albuquerque: University of New Mexico Press, 2006.

Welch, James. *Winter in the Blood.* New York: Harper and Row, 1974.

White, Frederick H. "Language Reflection and Lamentation in Native American Literature." *Studies in American Indian Literatures* 18.1 (2006): 83–98.

Wickwire, Wendy. Introduction to *Write It on Your Heart: The Epic World of an Okanagan Storyteller,* compiled and edited by Wendy Wickwire, 9–28. Vancouver: Talonbooks, 1989.

——. "Stories from the Margins: Toward a More Inclusive British Columbia Historiography." *Journal of American Folklore* 118.470 (2005): 453–74.

Willett, Thomas. "A Cross-Linguistic Survey of the Grammaticization of Evidentiality." *Studies in Language* 12.1 (1988): 51–97.

Willinsky, John. "The Paradox of Text in the Culture of Literacy." In *After Literacy: Essays,* 59–82. New York: Peter Lang, 2001.

Wolfart, H. Christoph. "Cree Literature." In *Encyclopedia of Literature in Canada,* edited by W. H. New, 243–47. Toronto: University of Toronto Press, 2002.

Wolfart, H. Christoph, and Janet F. Carroll. *Meet Cree: A Guide to the Cree Language.* 2nd. ed. Edmonton: University of Alberta Press, 1981.

Wolfe, Alexander. "Introduction." In *Earth Elder Stories: The Pinayzitt Path,* xi–xxii. Saskatoon: Fifth House, 1989.

Womack, Craig S. *Red on Red: Native American Literary Separatism.* Minneapolis: University of Minnesota Press, 1999.

Wray, Alison. "Holistic Utterances in Protolanguage: The Link from Primates to Humans." In *The Evolutionary Emergence of Language: Social Function and the Origins of Linguistic Form,* edited by Chris Knight, Michael Studdert-Kennedy, and James R. Hurford, 285–302. Cambridge: Cambridge University Press, 2000.

INDEX